Leo Strauss's Defense
of the Philosophic Life

Leo Strauss's Defense of the Philosophic Life

Reading "What Is Political Philosophy?"

EDITED BY RAFAEL MAJOR

THE UNIVERSITY OF CHICAGO PRESS   CHICAGO AND LONDON

RAFAEL MAJOR is the director of faculty development at the Jack Miller Center for Teaching America's Founding Principles and History and teaches at Ursinus College.

The University of Chicago Press, Chicago 60637
The University of Chicago Press, Ltd., London
© 2013 by The University of Chicago
All rights reserved. Published 2013.
Printed in the United States of America
22 21 20 19 18 17 16 15 14 13   1 2 3 4 5

ISBN-13: 978-0-226-92420-5 (cloth)
ISBN-13: 978-0-226-92421-2 (paper)
ISBN-13: 978-0-226-92423-6 (e-book)
ISBN-10: 0-226-92420-3 (cloth)
ISBN-10: 0-226-92421-1 (paper)
ISBN-10: 0-226-92423-8 (e-book)

Elements of the introduction and chapters 1, 3–4, and 6–8 in this volume appeared in *Perspectives on Political Science* 39, no. 2 (April–June 2010), published by Taylor and Francis Group.

Library of Congress Cataloging-in-Publication Data
Leo Strauss's defense of the philosophic life : reading "What is political philosophy?" / edited by Rafael Major.
    pages ; cm
  Includes bibliographical references and index.
  ISBN-13: 978-0-226-92420-5 (cloth : alkaline paper)
  ISBN-10: 0-226-92420-3 (cloth : alkaline paper)
  ISBN-13: 978-0-226-92421-2 (paperback : alkaline paper)
  ISBN-10: 0-226-92421-1 (paperback : alkaline paper)
  [etc.]
    1. Strauss, Leo. What is political philosophy? 2. Political science—Philosophy.
I. Major, Rafael.
  JC251.S8L456 2013
  320.01—dc23   2012020623

♾ This paper meets the requirements of ANSI/NISO Z39.48-1992 (Permanence of Paper).

Contents

Thinking Through Strauss's Legacy

Rafael Major

sine ira et studio — Tacitus, *The History* 1.1

The year 2009 marked the fiftieth anniversary of the publication of *What Is Political Philosophy? and Other Studies*. The book is a collection of previously published essays and selected book reviews composed in the 1940s and 1950s by an American political scientist, and its continued publication would defy explanation for most readers, if not for the reputation and influence of its author: Leo Strauss. The teaching and thought of Strauss have been the subject of speculation and controversy since even before his death in 1973.[1] But why would there be widespread controversy surrounding a scholar who focused mainly on interpretations of classical and medieval political philosophy? The continuing interest in Strauss is sustained in part by the large number of active academics who were his contemporaries—if only as graduate students in the 1960s and early 1970s—but this does not explain why Strauss in particular is singled out from this period for so much praise and blame. His persistent notoriety among contemporary political scientists is puzzling. Before the enigmatic reputation of Leo Strauss can be addressed, however, readers must begin by attempting to understand his writings. The volume to follow is the first systematic textual study that seeks to understand a single work of Strauss on its own terms.

What Is Political Philosophy? is perhaps the best introduction to the thought of Leo Strauss because it contains extended reflections on all the major themes of his life's work. As the title indicates, the book as a whole is a bold attempt to describe a distinctive approach to the study of politics. For Strauss, the term "philosophy" in the expression "political philosophy" indicates the "manner of treatment" of political phenomena (Strauss 1959, 10).[2] The attempt to gain philosophical clarity about the "subject matter" of politics is not unique to our time, however, and this forces us to devote at least our initial attention to understanding the recorded history of political philosophy. Readers approaching Strauss for the first time will be struck by his repetitive concern for the literary character of philosophic texts. His focus on "the art of writing," or an author's "manner" or "mode of expression," is sometimes so pronounced that it seems to be more important than a particular author's explicit teaching (e.g., 206, 265, 274, 285, 303). This attention to "how" an author expresses an argument, alongside the usual concern for "what" is being argued, can be peculiar. Considerations of this type are made every day by concerned citizens discussing the discrepancy between the speeches and actions of living politicians, for example, but it is unusual to speak this way about written texts. Strauss's procedure is made even more unusual when it leads to novel conclusions about works whose meaning has been authoritatively established and anthologized through centuries of respected scholarship. This is exactly how Strauss does proceed, however, and he frequently writes with confidence on the difference between an author's teaching or his purpose versus the "roots" of his thought (290).[3] In order to justify this approach, he addresses the historical and philosophical obstacles that have prevented others from appreciating the decisively literary character of older texts (chaps. 1–2). He goes to great lengths to reinterpret the ancient history of political thought (chaps. 3–4) and purports to demonstrate how that thought was deliberately adapted (chaps. 5–6) or abandoned (chaps. 7–8) in a series of self-conscious and epoch-making choices of later writers (e.g., 272, 288). All of this is complicated by the claim that political philosophers in very different epochs share a common and urgent concern with perennial human longings and demands.[4] This combination of unconventional considerations is what gives his analysis of the history of political philosophy its unique flavor and the label "Straussian."

The introductory character of *What Is Political Philosophy?* is not the entire story, however, as several passages appear to go beyond historical analysis. Just beneath the surface, so to speak, there is a kind of "Socratic method" that is outwardly preoccupied with sharpening issues and honing questions but that is simultaneously teaching. This didactic character of the book must also be addressed, because close attention to the collected commentaries draws readers to ponder Strauss's personal view. His historical efforts to recover the thought of the past appear to be riddled with subtle assertion. These commentaries—and book reviews—draw readers to attempt the obvious: to read Strauss in the meticulous way he read others. After introducing several issues surrounding the philosophical treatment of political life, for example, he approaches the same issues from a different angle:

> From this point of view the adjective "political" in the expression "political philosophy" designates not so much a subject matter as a manner of treatment; from this point of view, I say, "political philosophy" means primarily not the philosophic treatment of politics, but the political, or popular, treatment of philosophy, or the political introduction to philosophy. (93–94)

If we take him at his word, the introductory question "what is political philosophy?" is also an introduction to the life of philosophy. The initial attempt to recover the history of political philosophy is somehow transformed into the question of the possibility of philosophy tout court. While attempting to define "political philosophy" it becomes more and more urgent to assess what we mean—and what we hope to gain—by combining the two terms. From this "point of view," the book *What Is Political Philosophy?* is nothing less than an articulation and defense of Strauss's overall philosophic approach.[5] Precisely because the book has this foundational or argumentative character, the attempt to understand it requires a careful reading of each of its chapters on its own terms. All of the scholars in this volume were chosen, not for any particular view of Strauss's achievement and influence, but because of their expertise in the subject matter of their assigned section. Each contributor interprets Strauss's contribution to a specific aspect of the history of political philosophy, but the combined attempt to deal with *What Is Political Philosophy?* as a whole will also offer an assessment of Leo Strauss as a thinker in his own right. Understanding his effort to recover the history of political philosophy requires that we consider whether he was a philosophic thinker himself.

The foregoing would be a sufficient introduction to this volume, but approaching *What Is Political Philosophy?* on its own terms is complicated by the character of Strauss's reputation. The persistent scholarly interest in his writings is shadowed and partly fueled by a swirl of controversy surrounding the man himself. New readers almost always approach his works with premade conclusions. This is as true for those who have been led to believe that Strauss has a great deal to teach them as for those who have been warned of his unorthodox scholarship and zealous following.

Prominent scholars are often singled out for focused critiques by fellow academics and those who aspire to prominence themselves, but Strauss's critical or scholarly reception in the four decades following the publication of *What Is Political Philosophy?* is unique in that it is almost always mixed with extrascholarly considerations. For example, Strauss has been characterized as the "master-mind" of a particularly "demonic strain" of scholarship (Skinner 1969); or as an intellectual "guru" whose sole demand is that would-be followers "surrender their critical intellect" (Burnyeat 1985). Accusations such as these run so deep that those who are influenced by him—"Straussians"—are likewise accused of being Manichaean fanatics (Schaar and Wolin 1963) or dismissed as epigone, mynah birds, automatons, and mindless "disciples" (e.g., Rothman 1962).

These charges must be taken seriously, but for those readers with an earnest interest in discovering if they are true, or those "Straussians" with a passionate interest in defending themselves, or perhaps some historian in the future trying to make sense of the multifaceted debate, the primary and essential task is to read Strauss himself. For those coming to Strauss's works for the first time, this direct confrontation may be easier than it was even a decade ago. The recent publication of the *Cambridge Companion to Leo Strauss* (Smith 2009) marks a kind of watershed for Strauss's legacy because it is an indication that his thought is more than a residual fashion of mid-twentieth-century American political science. Indeed, given the severe criticism alluded to above, it is all the more remarkable that Strauss's interpretive approach has not withered but seems to be gaining in scholarly popularity.[6]

The Original Critical Reception of *What Is Political Philosophy?*

Revisiting the initial reaction to the publication of *What Is Political Philosophy?* in 1959 can be illuminating because the intense conjecture and suspicion surrounding Strauss himself had not yet become dominant.[7] By returning to the historical reception of *What Is Political Philosophy?* we may gain some historical perspective that could aid us in distinguishing between Strauss's own arguments and the muddle of praise and blame that continues to swirl around his name. The initial reception of Strauss's works was little different from that accorded the works of a number of other refugee scholars who made an impact in the United States in the years following the Second World War. Scholars like Hannah Arendt, Herbert Marcuse, and Eric Voegelin quickly distinguished themselves in the American academy for their apparently novel approaches to interpreting texts, as well as their philosophic probity (e.g., Gunnell 1986). During this same period, however, the academic discipline of political science in the United States was undergoing a revolution in scope and in methods.[8] The tools of the natural sciences, such as statistical analysis, were being applied to questions of politics and human behavior in an unprecedented manner. Traditional political science was being consciously transformed by a new "behavioral mood" (Dahl 1961). In the midst of this intellectual upheaval, the émigré scholars found themselves included within a "resistance movement" composed of multiple factions within the political science discipline (Germino 1963). The resistance to the new behavioral political science, however, was not unified by any underlying agreement. For a diversity of reasons, some scholars sought to preserve the status quo, but there were others who sought to change the traditional study of political science by redirecting it on a different nonbehavioral course.[9] Leo Strauss was not alone in opposing the new positivist approach in political science, yet it was the unique character of his critique that would eventually isolate him and his students from the rest of academic political science.

The crucial event that gave rise to Strauss's effective reputation in the latter half of the twentieth century was the appearance of a single book chapter, his "Epilogue," in the edited volume *Essays on the Scientific Study of Politics* (Storing 1962, esp. 301–27). The chapter was a self-consciously polemical attempt to attack the new behavioral political science on its own terms. Indeed the book as a whole was considered polemical enough that the editor of the *American Political Science Review*, Harvey C. Mansfield Sr., solicited a very lengthy response that set off an incendiary debate within the pages of the discipline's most prestigious journal.[10] From this point forward, the *controversy* surrounding Strauss's status in the discipline of political science eclipsed attempts to deal with his writings on scholarly terms. Strauss and his students had received preferential attention from the editor of the *American Political Science Review* in the years leading up to 1962, but after the spirited responses to the "Epilogue," the "Straussians" were relegated to an isolated fringe of the profession.[11] Since then, interpreters have had to approach Strauss's difficult writings while avoiding the temptation to judge them on the "impressions" of others (cf. 74, 76–77). In contrast to his reputation today, the striking feature of the initial critical reaction to *What Is Political Philosophy?*, then, is the relative absence of controversy.[12] Even the most negative reviewers approach

Strauss as a scholar—albeit one with debatable positions—and the elements of ad hominem reasoning evident in later criticisms are missing.

This critical attitude toward Strauss before he became mired in controversy is instructive. It gives those already familiar with his writings an unexpected view of his initial reception, but more important, the reviews taken together contain the nascent dividing lines of future controversy. The reviews are clearly unified in the conclusion that Strauss desires a return to the *practical* teaching of classical philosophers like Plato and Aristotle. Strauss, we are told repeatedly, is intent upon reinvigorating such concepts as meaningful moral principles (Rees 1962), standards of transcendence (Niemeyer 1961; Wasserman 1960), absolute knowledge (Gale 1961), the ideal of virtue (McRae 1960), universally valid truths (Muller 1960), and even the reinstitution of aristocracy (Barnes 1960; Deane 1961). Further, both negative and positive reviewers stand in agreement that Strauss fails to prove his thesis as they understand it.[13] The book appears to them as unsystematic in its approach, because it fails to deliver what it apparently advocates. This charge is more serious than it may appear because a majority of the reviews focus on the opening chapter alone. It is not the wide range of thinkers in *What Is Political Philosophy?* as a whole but something about Strauss's "manner of writing" that evokes this response. On the one hand, there appears to be a strong degree of certainty on Strauss's part, but then a lingering sense on the other—for many readers—that his bold prose amounts to so much assertion. This is the conclusion, willy-nilly, of both positive and negative reviews. There are those who agree and those who disagree with Strauss's thesis (as presented by them), but then near-unanimous agreement that the book fails in its aim to prove the same thesis.

We can look at two representative reviews to get a sense for how Strauss was both praised and criticized on the same grounds. First, the negative reviewer, K. D. McRae, points to the benighted character of Strauss's arguments by declaring, "Western man is too conscious of his past to recapture the sense of immediacy and timelessness that made possible for Greek civilization a belief in unchanging values" (1960, 499; also see *WIPP* 95–96). On the other hand, the positive reviewer, D. D. Raphael, says of Strauss's contentions: "I myself am disposed to accept them. But Professor Strauss's recommendation of them is not as clear as it might be." He continues, "It is a pity that [he] . . . should not have taken the opportunity to elaborate his position more systematically" (1961, 86). According to both men, Strauss fails to make a sufficient case for the reinvigoration of "timeless values," but it is precisely here that we should wonder whether either reviewer grasps the intention of the volume.[14] Both McRae and Raphael sense that Strauss is arguing for a moral and political order based on the teachings of classical political thought, but do Strauss's arguments in *What Is Political Philosophy?* confirm their judgment?

Strauss does mention "timeless values," but contrary to what we have been led to expect, he speaks of them in a decisively pejorative way as an underlying notion of "decayed Platonism" or a reactionary and insufficient response to historicism (26).[15] Even if we blithely assume that he preferred classical political thought to all competitors, it is puzzling that Strauss's initial discussion of the subject culminates in the conclusion that classical political science "did not consist in the simple subsumption [of political choice] under a simple, universal, an unalterable rule" (33) and did not offer a "single true account of the whole" (228). If Socrates viewed man in light of "unchangeable ideas," we must understand those ideas as "fundamental and permanent problems" rather than as a commitment to a "specific cosmology" (38–39, 116). Strauss does speak approvingly of the decisive difference between the classical approach and the modern ones as lying in the search for the best political order, but the emphasis in these passages is on the "search for" or "question of" the best regime (34, 79, 87).[16] There are passages in Strauss's writing that lend themselves to the assumption that they have a prescriptive character, but it is vitally important to see that there can be a chasmic difference between discussing "timeless values," "unchangeable ideas," and "best regime(s)" and claiming to know or proselytizing for them.[17]

If we return to the historical context of the upheaval within the academic discipline of political science around the publication of *What Is Political Philosophy?*, one of the now forgotten aspects of the intellectual controversy is the seeming boundless hope in the new behavioral approach. It is difficult for us in the twenty-first century to imagine the excitement generated by the new science. A generation of rebellious scholars—the "young turks"—recovering from the memories of war, looked to the new scientific study of politics with an optimism that would appear zealous today:

No one can deny that the idea is fascinating—the idea of subduing the phenomena of politics to the laws of causation, of penetrating to the mystery of its transformations, of symbolizing the trajectory of its future; in a word, of grasping destiny by the forelock and bringing it prostrate to earth. The very idea is itself

worthy of the immortal gods. . . . If nothing ever comes of it, its very existence
will fertilize thought and enrich imagination (Easton 1966, epigraph).

This optimism regarding the eventual results of the new political science
was accompanied with genuine hope for future generations of mankind.
After the recent horrors of fascism and totalitarianism in Europe, the new
political science seemed to provide the best defense against, if not the permanent extinction of, threats from political actors intent on manipulating
populations through both recognized and previously unrecognized sources
of power. The methodological advances of the new political science—in
certain areas of study—were vast improvements over now outdated methods (Dahl 1961). But more decisive for the increasing popularity of empirical methods were the hopes for their practical application. It was thought
that the obstacles to human flourishing could eventually be overcome by
the empirical knowledge of human behavior. Science, it seemed, could
provide valid and knowable standards for guiding political life.[18] In such
an environment, critics of the new political science were often viewed with
suspicion as being simpleminded traditionalists, reactionary promoters of
the status quo, or perhaps something even worse.

In June of 1962, on the eve of the reaction to the publication of Strauss's
polemical critique of political science in the "Epilogue," Stanley Rothman
published a foundational critique of Strauss's criticism of "social science
positivism" in the pages of the *American Political Science Review*. Relying
in large part on the authority of the mathematician and philosopher of
science Ernest Nagel, Rothman attempted to show that Strauss's criticism
of positivism was plagued by a fundamental confusion regarding the principles of the modern scientific method.[19] According to Rothman, Strauss
constructs a "straw man" of modern social science by seizing on well-
known difficulties associated with describing social phenomena in scien-
tifically neutral or descriptive language. The observation that "positivists
claim to eschew value judgments, but they constantly bring these through
the back door" was one that competent social scientists were acutely aware
of (Rothman 1962, 342).[20] By seizing on an obvious difficulty and reducing social science to giving an account of itself on this single issue, Strauss
creates a red herring. Even if Strauss could prove "the tendency of many
social scientists to confuse personal commitments with empirical propositions," it only proves the obvious; many social scientists are "mediocre"
(Rothman 1962, 344–45). Our awareness of this type of error is exactly
what distinguishes the enterprise of modern social science from earlier

methods of political analysis. Approaching the precarious distinction between facts and values in full awareness of its importance is what makes
social science possible. By characterizing modern social science from a
reductionist point of view, Strauss fails to confront the new methods on
their own terms.[21]

This dispute over the appropriateness of scientific methodology for
the study of political life is very typical of the period. The more foundational and still resilient aspect of Rothman's critique of Strauss, however,
is of a different character. After demonstrating Strauss's confusion over
the modern social scientific enterprise, he is forced to give an account of
the puzzling phenomenon of the growing influence of the "Straussians."
According to Rothman, Strauss's entire corpus is a sophisticated subter-
fuge in which Strauss pretends that he shares the basic premises of his
readers, while simultaneously manipulating their better judgment. All of
Strauss's writings are invidiously "accompanied by the rejection of the
values underlying the American experience" and are designed specifically
for the purpose of the eventual coronation of Leo Strauss himself as the
King of America along with his retinue of guardian disciples (Rothman
1962, 352).[22] Strauss takes advantage of those who follow him, according
to Rothman, by appealing to their simplistic passion for certainty—exac-
erbated by the failure of "liberal clichés"—in the face of the specter and
uncertainty of thermonuclear war. Because of the cowardly refusal of a
large number of human beings to seize control of the potentially destructive power of science like "real men," Strauss's benighted appeal to an
antiquated longing for a "closed society" is the real source of his attraction. According to Rothman, this is a fundamental betrayal of the essence
of man, whose dignity depends upon the model of Prometheus—with the
strength of will and creativity to stand against the gods "and bend the universe" (Rothman 1962, 352).

We could dismiss Rothman's hyperbolic accusations against Strauss
out of hand except that his charges became the epicenter for wave after
wave of similar claims.[23] Nor would it be sufficient to counter Rothman
in the same way he defended the social scientific enterprise: the possible
existence of "Straussians" who are interested in a simplistic desire for
certainty or who longed for a closed society would prove only that there
are many "mediocre" Straussians. Rothman's arguments must be faced
squarely, because his underlying analysis of Strauss's ultimate purposes reveals itself to be virtually identical to the initial reviews of *What Is Political
Philosophy?* we examined above. Rothman's conclusions derive not from

a dispute over social science methodology but rather from his sense or suspicion that Strauss opposes the new behavioral mood from a position of political or moralistic certainty. He thinks that the "Straussians" claim to possess a "natural standard" or an "objective moral basis" (Rothman 1962, 341, 345) that lies at the heart of their critique of social science. Simply put, he believes that Strauss's criticism of social science is not theoretical but rather a product of indignation over society's failure to recognize a transcendent norm or an authoritative "good" (Rothman 1962, 345, 346).

Rothman's critique of Strauss presents itself as a close-quarter response on the issues of the new social science, but much of the rhetorical force is generated by the conclusion that Strauss has a hidden moralistic motive and hence a political agenda. Rothman's defense of the possibility of a new science of man is shadowed by the insinuation that Strauss's ultimate philosophical positions pose a great threat to modern society. Like the original positive and negative reviews of *What Is Political Philosophy?*, Rothman assumes that Strauss's criticism of modern social science, combined with his apparent appeal to the superiority of classical thought, amounts to a claim to know some transcendent good. Again, we are confronted with the assertion that Strauss seeks to articulate grounds for a prescriptive return to classical political life. Just as in the case of the original reviews, however, it is imperative to confirm whether this is an accurate assessment of either Strauss's theoretical position or his practical goal. Unlike the original reviews, Rothman's article is long enough to provide more substantial scholarly evidence for his judgment. It is surprising that such a demonstration is not attempted. After charging Strauss with the duplicitous manipulation of modern readers in an effort to reconstitute society on the basis of an authoritative "good" or transcendent norm, Rothman makes the puzzling claim that these "Straussian" lessons are Leo Strauss's "esoteric" teaching (Rothman 1962, 351–52). Given that Rothman's critique relies so heavily on his explicit judgment of Strauss's moral and political aspirations (Rothman 1962, 341, 342, 345, 346), there is a troubling lack of any explicit evidence for his most incendiary claims. Rather than marshal traditional scholarly evidence, Rothman resorts to a mere parody of Strauss's mode of reading and writing.[24] While Rothman's defense of social science positivism is now largely forgotten, the speculative character of his condemnation of Strauss remains.

Given the unanimity among the original reviewers regarding Strauss's political intentions, it would appear unfair to fault these critics for patent misunderstanding. Strauss himself, or the way he chooses to present his interpretations and arguments, surely bears a great deal of the responsibility. To repeat, the points of agreement among the reviews seem overwhelming, but it is difficult to establish evidence from Strauss's text to support their conclusions. If *What Is Political Philosophy?*—or Strauss's other writings—advocates the practical reinstatement of a society governed by an "authoritative good" or "transcendent norm," there should be abundant evidence of the charge. The persistence of the accusation, however, requires that we address Strauss's puzzling manner of writing.

Strauss's "Manner of Writing"

In order to understand the literary character of Strauss's writing, it is vital to appreciate the subtle urgency of the subject matter. As he stresses over and over again, the impetus to investigate the history of political and philosophic thought—beyond a mere inventory of ideas—is the suspicion that our contemporary understanding of human life and action is somehow inadequate. On this point, the earnest concern to reassess the thought of the past is identical with the impetus of modern social science. It is the failure of "liberal clichés" to either understand or prevent contemporary threats to human flourishing that makes a scientific understanding of politics so urgent for Rothman. His somewhat grandiose exhortation to Promethean creativity is in fact an understandable plea to abandon the methods of the past in favor of a new path. Our human need to meet new modern challenges, according to this view, necessitates new methods. His cry for empirical certainty is genuine but is intermingled with an extra-scholarly concern to take up arms against political uncertainty.[25] Whereas Rothman places the blame for contemporary confusions on the tradition of political inquiry, the alternative is to wonder whether a more adequate view than our own existed in the past, albeit now obscured or forgotten. The search for an accurate understanding of the past is inextricably tied to the persistent need on the part of thoughtful human beings to search for more than the "shallow pieties" of their immediate surroundings (Dunn 1996).[26]

Our need to revisit earlier thinkers is more obvious in the case of fairly recent figures like Hobbes and Locke than in the case of the classical philosophers (*WIPP*, chaps. 7–8). Their possible intellectual influence over the modern world gives us a more vital and immediate interest in understanding them. Although less immediate at first, the stakes turn out to be just as high for earlier thinkers. In order to get some grasp of Hobbes and Locke, we would eventually need some knowledge of what came before them, and this is especially true if an integral part of their teaching and philosophy is a conscious attack on the entire tradition of political philosophy. We turn to Hobbes and Locke to understand their possible sway over us, only to find out they are a kind of pivot point or impetus to look back further.[27] In Strauss's interpretations of men like Xenophon, Farabi, and Maimonides, the connection between their reflections and our concern to gain self-understanding is never far from view. By reminding us of the reason for our palpable hope in turning to the study of history in the first place, Strauss's commentaries feel strikingly contemporary despite their ancient subjects.[28] The attack on contemporary social science and on our assumptions about historical inquiry in the opening chapters of *What Is Political Philosophy?* makes it impossible to dismiss Strauss's efforts of historical recovery as being merely antiquarian. Around every corner, as it were, we are given examples of current inadequacies followed by novel historical investigations. The cumulative effect of this procedure induces many readers to assume a political or moralistic purpose, "for what author would be so harsh as to begin a work so full of foreboding unless he somehow planned to offer relief?" (Ceaser 2011, 46–48).[29]

Strauss's writings are further complicated by his insistence on the vivid use of both the language and the manner of his historical subjects. When commenting on Plato and Aristotle, for example, he imitates their direct approach to political life by preserving their use of the ordinary language of the citizens and statesmen. Although this is not the end of the story, Strauss often begins from the perspective of commonplace praise and blame: noble and base, just and unjust, pious and impious. This imitative procedure can be so scrupulous that it becomes difficult to discern when Strauss speaks in his own voice (cf. 140–42). We are told, for example, that proper household management supplies knowledge of "the best possible ordering" of household affairs, or that the science of government supplies "knowledge of human happiness and the way towards its acquisition" (156). If both things are true, however, the perfection of both families and governments depends upon the rule of "wise men," or at least the existence of wise counselors in the halls of power (156). Depending on the point of view of Strauss's readers, statements such as these can either charm or repulse. Whether we agree with these declarations or sense the potentially horrific consequences of attempting to institutionalize them in the modern world, however, the point here is that they say nothing about Strauss's own political judgment. They are contained in a paragraph that summarizes Maimonides's statements, or what "he says" regarding the books of countless ancient philosophers (155–56).[30] This example is a relatively simple one, but there are many places in *What Is Political Philosophy?* where readers can be lulled into assuming entire paragraphs or sections express Strauss's own viewpoint. The alternation between exegetical summary and personal judgment can be invigorating because it gives Strauss's prose a dialectical or narrative quality, but it can also be very frustrating. There is a paucity of metadiscourse such as "I say" (93) or "I assert" (224), and following shifts in perspective can be difficult. Scholars usually keep their own voice at the forefront. There is something highly heuristic and consciously pedagogical in Strauss's writings, but this same quality obviously lends itself to being misunderstood. If he had the choice to write in the more straightforward style of the traditional scholarly treatise—less susceptible to being misunderstood—it is important to understand why he did not make his own views more explicit.

The initial consideration regards the necessity of historical exactness. A meaningful clarification of the issues raised by political life requires some experience of opinions, convictions, and cultures that are not identical to our present circumstances. It is historical knowledge above all else that serves as the initial safeguard against "mistaking the specific features of the political life" of our own time "for the nature of political things" as such (56–57). An honest examination of any question of justice, for example, requires an equally honest examination of our own views of the matter. We would also have to be acutely mindful of our own potentially prejudicial hopes in answering such questions. But is such an examination really possible? Returning to the impetus to study Hobbes and Locke given above, if either thinker is approached to gain a richer or more historically informed understanding of our own circumstances, we run the serious risk of overlooking those aspects of their thought that do not appear immediately relevant to us (174). The well-intentioned endeavor to discover how their doctrines might contribute to our current beliefs, or how we might salvage their teaching "given what we know now" (67), likely leads to a caricature of the past. The effort to examine our contemporary political views would seem to require at least the hypothetical abandonment of our current standards; otherwise the conclusion of all historical investigation is inevitable: so-and-so did not fully understand or anticipate our current knowledge. It would be silly to think that even the temporary suspension of our present concerns is an easy thing to do, but the difficulty of the endeavor does not diminish its necessity for the sake of genuine historical accuracy.[31]

For Strauss, the necessity of gaining a precise historical assessment, coupled with the extreme difficulty of doing so, demands the practice of approaching any particular thinker on his own terms. For example, "The right procedure consists in imitating, within reason, the movement of Hobbes's thought for which he has accepted responsibility" (173). If he remains within the horizon of the subject matter and has the courage and discretion to focus only on the issues for which an author takes responsibility, there will be many occasions where an interpreter must leave questions open, even urgent questions (269). No amount of interest in problems of the modern state will settle Plato's view of the matter, for example. The attempt to do so only saddles an author with intentions or positions he did not have (57) and errors he did not commit. Putting a premium on historical accuracy of this character, however, can place an interpreter in the precarious position of appearing to be a simpleminded advocate of the view in question. This is understandable because, for most of us, it seems to be humanly impossible to think about important problems or questions without being tempted to decide the issue or becoming inclined toward a solution (116). The disadvantage of Strauss's procedure should be obvious: to the degree he attempts to imitate the movement of an author's argument or question, there is a proportional tendency on the part of the reader to assume Strauss must also have a definitive answer. Despite this shortcoming, however, the attempt to meet an older author on his own terms has an undeniable benefit: *provocation*. Scrupulously following the movement of the thought of another increases the likelihood that we will encounter unsettling and sometimes even original insights.

Understanding the attempt to gain a historically accurate view leads us to another, more decisive reflection. The final consideration regarding Strauss's manner of writing is a distinctly theoretical one. In Strauss's presentation, the history of thought eventually forces readers to confront "outdated" concepts as genuine possibilities. The most serious question that arises during the attempt to discover what an author actually says or intends is "Is it true?" This unexpected theoretical question can arise only with genuine doubt with respect to what we already think we know. The attempt to understand current dilemmas or to approach the history of political thought without wondering whether we are adequate judges of either is doomed to issue in shallow subjectivity (e.g. 56, 173–77, 310–11). For most of us, this genuine doubt arises only after some uncomfortable prodding: we are asked to compare the ancient virtues of courage and moderation with the contemporary virtues of "toilet training" (171); we are induced to contrast our own easygoing and facile nihilism with the rewards and splendor of the arduous search for truth. These types of polemics can either charm or repulse individual readers, but they serve a purpose. They are necessary because no amount of lip service to the importance of historical knowledge can be effective unless readers have some suspicion about contemporary certainties. Currently, for example, one such view is that all human thought—and all human choice—is the dispensation of some "fated blindness" (Dunn 1996) or that our most deeply held values are the "merest contingencies of our peculiar history and social structure" (Skinner 1969). The same recorded history that provides the opportunity for some impartiality regarding current pieties has been transformed into the greatest evidence for the view that such impartiality is impossible. As if this is not sobering enough, however, Strauss prods even further by reminding us that the most consistent and philosophical adherent of the view that our fate is the inevitable outcome of historical dispensation not only submitted to but welcomed "the least wise and least moderate part of his nation while it was in its least wise and least moderate mood" (27).[32] But if this is true, then what are we to do? What is the best way for us to live?

By facing the simple Socratic question "What is political philosophy?" and attempting to think it through, Leo Strauss slowly induces us to face the obvious question that is so often ignored: why are we so intensely interested in understanding politics from a philosophic point of view? What promise do we expect philosophy to keep? Because Strauss wrote with a view to both the mind and the heart—by posing questions with the patience to resist the demand for easy answers—we become aware of the possibility of a life of the mind that does not stifle the voice of our hearts. The attempt to learn *from* the history of political philosophy instead of only *about* it can be a bewildering experience, but such an experience is imperative for any genuine education to begin. It is just such thought-provoking bewilderment that Strauss has in mind with a statement like the following: "The crucial issue concerns the status of those permanent characteristics of humanity, such as the distinction between the noble and the base . . . can these permanencies be used as criteria for distinguishing between good and bad dispensations of fate?" (26). That these apparently simple, nontechnical, and nonabstract *questions* can arouse so much ire or admiration testifies to their importance and to the lasting attraction of *What Is Political Philosophy?* as a whole:

It would not be easy to find another book touching on so many controversial topics of a political character which is equally remote from partisanship. It is written *sine ira et studio*, without sentimentality or vagueness, and with competence and a natural grace. The treatment is narrative and meditative rather than disputative or analytical. At times . . . the author, adapting himself to the character of his subject, seems to draw rather than to speak. (268)[33]

It is above all the attempt to understand the author—learning from him instead of about him—that unites the essays in the present volume. It is hard to imagine that someone who has attracted so much attention does not have something from which we can learn. We are in no position to judge what this might be, or whether it is true, however, until we read him for ourselves—without anger or zealousness.

Notes

I would like to thank Peter Lawler for his initial encouragement of this volume, and John Tryneski for aid and encouragement in seeing it through. Peter Ahrensdorf, Richard Ruderman, Laurence Nee, Edward Gramling, Svetozar Minkov, and the critical remarks of Christopher Bruell were all helpful in different ways.

1. For a description of the rumors surrounding the influence of Strauss and his students in the 1960s, see Kendall (1967).

2. All unspecified chapter and page references are to this edition. I occasionally use the abbreviation *WIPP* to specify pages in the same volume when also quoting pages from other works.

3. Also see, e.g., 282, 297, 301–2, 305.

4. For examples see Bruell (2011, 92ff.). For an overview of the themes that occupied Strauss's career, see Tarcov and Pangle (1987) and the focused account given by Meier (2006).

5. The book as a whole has a surprisingly "public" character. In addition to the "Sixteen Appraisals" of contemporaries at the conclusion of the volume, chapters 1 and 10 began as public addresses, chapters 7 and 8 are extended commentaries on contemporary scholarship, and chapters 4 and 9 are responses to criticisms of his own work. (See Janssens, chap. 9 below.)

6. For a striking nonpartisan assessment, see Ferrari (1997). Perhaps the most telling evidence is the number of recent articles on classical political philosophy that follow Strauss's once-controversial approach that have recently appeared in the pages of the *American Political Science Review*, a stark contrast to the 1970s and 1980s.

7. In the 1950s, Strauss was widely respected as a leading political theorist by behavioral political scientists and even contributed substantial aid to colleague Da-

vid Easton in the composition of the theoretical portions of *The Political System*. See Easton (1953, ix). His reputation among political theorists was even higher, e.g., "one of the few dominant figures" (Muller 1960, 257); "something to behold" (Gale 1961, 420); "few teachers . . . have had an influence comparable" (Deane 1961, 149); "methodical thoroughness and imaginative brilliance which an admiring generation . . . has come to expect" (Niemeyer 1961, 101); and "to avoid its reading because of disagreement with its theme would be scholarly dereliction" (Wasserman 1960, 840).

8. According to Robert Dahl (1961), the most meaningful intellectual influence on the successful "revolution" in political science was the attempt to redefine political science on the model of the natural sciences as described by Max Weber.

9. For a defense of traditional political science, see Crick (1959). For a more radical protest, see Cornforth (1952). Also see the stern response by Nagel (1952).

10. Schaar and Wolin (1963); Storing et al. (1963). The original critique was twenty-five pages of additional space added to the journal's normal length (far more than an average article of the time). In addition to defending the new behavioral political science, Schaar and Wolin also focused on what they perceived to be the "politically suspect" motives of Strauss and his students (Kettler 2006). The eleven additional pages allotted to Storing et al. to respond in the next issue of the journal amounted to far more than a traditional academic dust-up.

11. For the editorial posture of the *APSR* toward Strauss and his students before, during, and after the controversy, see Kettler (2006). For the precipitous decline of Strauss's reputation, see Behnegar (2003, chaps. 6–8); Major (2005, 478–79).

12. The reviews consulted include Barnes (1960); Deane (1961); Gale (1961); McRae (1960); Muller (1960); Niemeyer (1961); Raphael (1961); Rees (1962); Wasserman (1960).

13. The exception is Wasserman (1960).

14. As early as 1946 Strauss warned of the danger of assuming that Plato and Aristotle supplied ready-made answers to contemporary problems. There is no indication in Strauss's later writings that he changed his view. See Tarcov (1991).

15. Regarding the status or accuracy of the historicist critique of positivism in Strauss's thought, see Zuckert, chap. 2, and Shell, chap. 10 below.

16. According to this older view, on Strauss's reading, only "harmless doves" would be "guided by the belief that what was most desirable in itself should be put into practice in all circumstances." Such a view was more likely to be held by advocates of the "'abstract principles'" in the eighteenth century than by earlier thinkers who recognized a distinction between philosophical and political questions "as a matter of course" (61).

17. E.g., it may be necessary for any successful political constitution to claim some basis in "universal" principles, but this political fact is not necessarily a theoretical claim (cf. 303 with 222ff.).

18. This implicit concern with the beneficial uses of political science was present

for those political scientists in favor of the possibilities for liberal democracy and those scholars attempting to demonstrate a different form of scientific materialism. These predispositions were often "unself-conscious" products of contemporary strains of "liberal and Marxist forms of analysis" (Skinner 1969).

19. See Nagel's original thoughtful assessment of Strauss in "The Value Oriented Bias of Social Inquiry" (Nagel 1961, 485–502). Rothman's rehearsal of Strauss's argument is derived mainly from the first half of chapter 1 of *WIPP?*, although he also uses selections from *Natural Right and History* (Strauss 1953).

20. Rothman speculates extensively on Strauss's adherence to an antiquated "cosmology" as the cause of his error (compare *WIPP*, 38). Nagel, by contrast, does not include Strauss among those who are satisfied that the mere difficulty of scientific description makes social science impossible (Nagel 1961, 488–89).

21. This "methodological dispute" was continued in a systematic response by Cropsey (1962). Strauss's own public response to Rothman and Nagel can be found in the first three lectures of a 1962 class entitled "Natural Right" (Strauss 1962). For a retrospective assessment of the "epical failure" of modern social science to accomplish its goals, see chapter 1 of Dunn (1996).

22. Rothman asserts that Strauss's work "will place in power the philosopher king and the guardians, i.e., Strauss and his disciples" (Rothman 1962, 352). Rothman remarks that he makes his accusation "half-seriously." He does not specify which half.

23. In contrast to Rothman, Nagel attempts to meet Strauss on the merits of his argument, because for Nagel, Strauss represented a "more sophisticated" objection to the modern social science enterprise (Nagel 1961, 490).

24. This tactic of making incendiary accusations followed by convoluted and sometimes tortured proof of Strauss's ambition has been repeated most famously by Burnyeat (1985) and Drury (1988). For a detailed review of more recent accusations regarding Strauss's political ambition, see Zuckert and Zuckert (2006).

25. In this regard, Rothman (1962, 352), like Ernest Nagel (1952), was very concerned with the spread of communism and its perceived threat to human freedom and rational inquiry.

26. According to Dunn, however, the earnest examination of the history of political theory in an effort to understand "what it means for us" can arouse grave suspicions. Energetic inquiry can appear to undermine political life altogether or, alternatively, be suspected of providing a "careless stimulus" or even a "dishonest cloak" for political intrigue (Dunn 1996, 25, 31).

27. See Stauffer, chap. 7 below.

28. See Nadon, chap. 4 below.

29. For the history of Strauss's initial reception and abrupt abandonment by American conservatives, see Nash (1998). The best account of the understandable difficulties in interpreting Strauss's political views is Bruell (1993). The most extended reflection on interpreting Strauss's art of writing and its "preparatory" character can be found in Lenzner (2003).

30. The far more interesting historical and philosophical issue is whether Maimonides himself sides with the ancient philosophers. Cf. Parens, chap. 6, with Tanguay, chap. 5 below.

31. See Janssens, chap. 9 below.

32. See Shell, chap. 10 below.

33. This is Strauss's description of Karl Löwith's *Von Hegel bis [sic] Nietzsche*. The accuracy of Strauss's summary is questionable (see 270 top).

Works Cited

Barnes, Harry Elmer. 1960. "Review: *What Is Political Philosophy?*" *Annals of the American Academy of Political and Social Science*, 329: 204–5.

Behnegar, Nasser. 2003. *Leo Strauss, Max Weber, and the Scientific Study of Politics*. Chicago: University of Chicago Press.

Bruell, Christopher. 1993. "A Return to Political Philosophy and the Understanding of the American Founding." In *Leo Strauss: Political Philosopher and Jewish Thinker*, ed. Kenneth L. Deutsch and Walter N. Nicgorski, 325–38. Lanham, MD: Roman and Littlefield.

———. 2011. "The Question of Nature and the Thought of Leo Strauss." *Klesis—Revue philosophique* 19: 92–101.

Burnyeat, Myles F. 1985. "Sphinx without a Secret." Review of *Studies in Platonic Political Philosophy*, by Leo Strauss. *New York Review of Books*, 30 May, 30–36.

Ceaser, James W. 2011. *Designing a Polity: America's Constitution in Theory and Practice*. Lanham, MD: Rowman and Littlefield.

Cornforth, Maurice. 1952. *In Defense of Philosophy against Positivism and Pragmatism*. New York: International Publishers.

Crick, Bernard R. 1959. *The American Science of Politics: Its Origins and Conditions*. London,: Routledge and Kegan Paul.

Cropsey, Joseph. 1962. "The Revival of Classical Political Philosophy: A Reply to Rothman." *American Political Science Review* 56 (2): 353–59.

Dahl, Robert. 1961. "The Behavioralist Approach in Political Science: Epitaph for a Monument to a Successful Protest." *American Political Science Review* 55 (4): 763–72.

Deane, Herbert A. 1961. "Review: *What Is Political Philosophy?*" *American Political Science Review* 55 (1): 149–50.

Drury, Shadia B. 1988. *The Political Ideas of Leo Strauss*. New York: St. Martin's Press.

Dunn, John. 1996. *The History of Political Theory and Other Essays*. Cambridge: Cambridge University Press.

Easton, David. 1953. *The Political System: An Inquiry into the State of Political Science*. New York: Alfred A. Knopf.

———. 1966. *The Political System: An Inquiry into the State of Political Science*. New York: Alfred A. Knopf. Original edition, 1953.

Ferrari, G. R. F. 1997. "Strauss's Plato." *Arion* 5 (2): 36–65.

Gale, Richard M. 1961. "Review: *What Is Political Philosophy?*" *Philosophy and Phenomenological Research* 21 (3): 419–20.

Germino, Dante. 1963. "The Revival of Political Theory." *Journal of Politics* 25 (3): 437–60.

Gunnell, John G. 1986. "Texts in Context: Revisionist Methods for Studying the History of Political Theory; The Status and Appraisal of Classic Texts: An Essay on Political Theory, Its Inheritance, and the History of Ideas." *American Political Science Review* 80 (2): 631–39.

Kendall, Willmoore. 1967. "Review: Ancients and Moderns." *American Political Science Review* 61 (3): 783–84.

Kettler, David. 2006. "The Political Theory Question in Political Science, 1956–1967." *American Political Science Review* 100 (4): 531–37.

Lenzner, Steven. 2003. "Leo Strauss and the Problem of Freedom of Thought." Ph.D. diss., Harvard University.

Major, Rafael. 2005. "The Cambridge School and Leo Strauss: Texts and Context of American Political Science." *Political Research Quarterly* 58 (3): 477–85.

McRae, K. D. 1960. "Review: *What Is Political Philosophy?*" *Canadian Journal of Economics and Political Science* 26 (3): 497–99.

Meier, Heinrich. 2006. *Leo Strauss and the Theologico-Political Problem.* Trans. Marcus Brainard. New York: Cambridge University Press.

Muller, Steven. 1960. "Review: *What Is Political Philosophy?*" *Political Science Quarterly* 75 (3): 457–60.

Nagel, Ernest. 1952. "Review: *In Defence of Philosophy Against Positivism and Pragmatism* by Maurice Cornforth." *Journal of Philosophy* 49 (20): 648–50.

———. 1961. *The Structure of Science: Problems in the Logic of Scientific Explanation.* New York: Harcourt, Brace and World.

Nash, George H. 1998. *The Conservative Intellectual Movement in America, since 1945.* 1st softcover ed. Wilmington, DE: Intercollegiate Studies Institute.

Niemeyer, Gerhart. 1961. "Review: *What Is Political Philosophy?*" *Review of Politics* 23 (1): 101–7.

Raphael, D. D. 1961. "Review: *What Is Political Philosophy?*" *British Journal of Sociology* 12 (12): 85–86.

Rees, J. C. 1962. "Review: *What Is Political Philosophy?*" *Philosophy* 37 (142): 366–68.

Rothman, Stanley. 1962. "The Revival of Classical Political Philosophy: A Critique." *American Political Science Review* 56 (2): 341–52.

Schaar, John H., and Sheldon S. Wolin. 1963. "Essays on the Scientific Study of Politics: A Critique." Review of *Essays on the Scientific Study of Politics,* by Herbert J. Storing. *American Political Science Review* 57 (1): 125–50.

Skinner, Quentin. 1969. "Meaning and Understanding in the History of Ideas." *History and Theory* 8 (1): 3–53.

Smith, Steven B. 2009. *The Cambridge Companion to Leo Strauss*. Cambridge: Cambridge University Press.

Storing, Herbert J. 1962. *Essays on the Scientific Study of Politics*. New York: Holt, Rinehart.

Storing, Herbert J., Leo Strauss, Walter Berns, Leo Weinstein, and Robert Horwitz. 1963. "Replies to Schaar and Wolin: I–VI." *American Political Science Review* 57 (1): 151–60.

Strauss, Leo. 1946. "On a New Interpretation of Plato's Political Philosophy." *Social Research* 13 (3): 326–67.

———. 1953. *Natural Right and History*. Chicago: University of Chicago Press.

———. 1959. *What Is Political Philosophy? and Other Studies*. New York: Free Press.

———. 1962. "Natural Right." Ed. Nathan Tarcov. Leo Strauss Center.

Tarcov, Nathan. 1991. "On a Certain Critique of 'Straussianism.'" *Review of Politics* 53 (1): 3–18.

Tarcov, Nathan, and Thomas Pangle. 1987. "Epilogue: Leo Strauss and the History of Philosophy." In *History of Political Philosophy*, ed. Leo Strauss and Joseph Cropsey, 907–38. Chicago: University of Chicago Press.

Wasserman, Louis. 1960. "Review: *What Is Political Philosophy?*" *Western Political Quarterly* 13 (3): 839–40.

Zuckert, Catherine, and Michael Zuckert. 2006. *The Truth about Leo Strauss: Political Philosophy and American Democracy*. Chicago: University of Chicago Press.

CHAPTER ONE

Reading "What Is Political Philosophy?"

Nasser Behnegar

Characterizing the morbid state of political philosophy in the 1950s, Strauss writes: "Today, political philosophy is in a state of decay and perhaps putrefaction, if it has not altogether vanished."[1] For some, he implies, political philosophy has decayed into "weak and unconvincing protestations" against newfangled thoughts and ways; for others it has survived as "a matter for burial," that is, as a matter for historical inquiries that put to rest its unwholesome pretensions; but for most it has vanished altogether, being replaced by an unphilosophic political science. After establishing to his own satisfaction—and he was not a man who was easily satisfied—the possibility and the necessity of political philosophy, Strauss sought to change this state of affairs, and with some success too. Thanks to his efforts, today political philosophy is held in high, even highest regard, at least in small circles within the academy. To be sure, such success may turn political philosophy into a prejudice and destroy its vitality by obscuring questions that give urgency to thought. But among the best antidotes to these dangers are Strauss's own writings, which were designed to lead the demanding reader to a sharper understanding of the problem of man and therewith of the problem of political philosophy.

This certainly is the case with *What Is Political Philosophy?*, a collection of essays, chosen by himself, that appears to be an introduction to Strauss's lifelong activity. The eponymous essay that opens this collection is an introduction to this introduction.[2] Political philosophy like any other human activity can be defined adequately only in terms of its end, by what it tries to accomplish. Strauss defines political philosophy by the problem it seeks to solve: what is the good society? He does not state the character of this problem; instead he attempts to show to political human beings that this problem is implicit in all political controversies: beginning with the observation that all political action aims at either preservation or change, Strauss shows that this implies some thought of the good, asserts that that thought has the character of mere opinion, the awareness of which compels one to search for that thought of the good that is no longer questionable, and finally argues that this search must turn into the search for knowledge of the complete political good, for knowledge of the good life and the good society. The pivot of this argument is the assertion that while every political act assumes a thought about the good which the political actor no longer questions—otherwise he could not act—this thought upon reflection proves questionable, an assertion that is confirmed by the ubiquity of disputes in political life. Once he becomes aware of this fact, the serious political human being becomes in a way a political philosopher, for it does not suffice to pursue policies that only seem to be good. To determine the goodness of these policies, one must examine them in light of the ultimate political goal, the good society, and one cannot understand the good society without knowing the character of the truly good human life. All this means that one must pursue the question of the good society, and the connected question of the good human life, with the radicalism and comprehensiveness that are characteristic of philosophizing.

In this way, Strauss arrives at his first definition of political philosophy as the attempt "to acquire knowledge of the good life and of the good society" (10). This most provisional definition is modified after Strauss gives a provisional explanation of philosophy. According to Strauss, philosophy, as quest for wisdom, is an attempt to replace opinions about the whole with the knowledge of the whole. What men believe about God or gods necessarily implies some opinion about the whole (for instance, that it consists of "God, the world, and man"); philosophizing then necessarily involves the questioning of the prephilosophic view of divinity. Strauss suggests that philosophers identify the whole with "all things" because "the whole is not a pure ether or an unrelieved darkness in which one cannot distinguish one part from the other, or in which one cannot discern anything" (11). We see things, but what is harder to see is their nature, the unalterable characteristics of things that belong to the same class. Philosophy is the attempt to replace the opinions about the whole with the knowledge of the nature of all things. This definition of philosophy prepares Strauss's second definition of political philosophy, which is now understood as a branch of philosophy: "Political philosophy will then be the attempt to replace opinion about the nature of political things by knowledge of the nature of political things" (11–12). For the moment the question of the good society fades into the background as the nature of political things, the necessities that rule political things, surfaces. To understand this movement, we need to look at another aspect of his explanation of philosophy.

Strauss gives an account of the philosophic refusal to abandon questions to which there may not be adequate answers. This refusal belongs to the essence of philosophy, which is "essentially not possession of truth, but quest for truth." Strauss's account is based on a distinction between more or less important things, an important thing being one that affects many other things. By quoting Thomas Aquinas, he suggests that it is better to have a slight knowledge of God than certain knowledge of the least important thing, say a pebble (11). For clearly what God is or what he is not affects one's understanding of everything. This implies that one can have at least a slight knowledge of the most important things. Strauss explains this possibility and more by arguing that it is possible to know the nature of a thing (in the sense of a demarcation of its possibilities) without answering the fundamental question that concerns it: "For the clear grasp of a fundamental question requires understanding of the nature of the subject matter with which the question is concerned" (11). These reflections must be applied to political philosophy as a branch of philosophy. The political philosopher does not abandon the question of the good society because it is difficult or impossible to answer, for the clear grasp of this question may be sufficient for the acquisition of the knowledge of the nature of political things.

The above consideration explains the second definition of political philosophy, but it also indicates its incompleteness. According to Strauss, one cannot understand political things if they are examined in a disinterested manner, for in them there is an "explicit or implicit claim to be judged in terms of goodness or badness, of justice or injustice" (12). This reflection moves in the direction of the first definition of political philosophy, but in a richer or more complex manner, for it couples consideration of goodness with that of justice. Accordingly, we arrive at the third definition of political philosophy: "Political philosophy is the attempt truly to know both the nature of political things and *the right, or the good*, political order" (12, emphasis added). It is noteworthy that this insistence on understanding political things in terms of their claim to justice appears only after Strauss's discussion of philosophy. In his essay "On Classical Political Philosophy," Strauss explains this sequence: "it is ultimately because he means to justify philosophy before the tribunal of the political community, and hence on the level of political discussion, that the philosopher has to understand the political things exactly as they are understood in political life" (94). *Even* in "What Is Political Philosophy?," where the focus is fittingly on the ordinary meaning of political philosophy as the philosophic treatment of politics, we see the influence of the deeper understanding of political philosophy as "the political, or popular, treatment of philosophy" (93). *Even* here Strauss shows the meaning of political philosophy by showing its meaningful character, answering the question "What is political philosophy?" with the answer to the question "Why political philosophy?"

After defining political philosophy, Strauss distinguishes it from political thought in general, political theory, political theology, social philosophy, and political science. The last discussion is of special interest because it includes a rare discussion of the useful work done by members of political science departments, which "consists of careful and judicious collections and analyses of politically relevant data," an activity that he distinguishes from the "scientific" political science guided by the model of natural science. He begins by showing how "all political life is accompanied by more or less coherent and more or less strenuous efforts to replace political opinion by political knowledge" (15). Yet this movement to knowledge is not political philosophizing because by political opinion Strauss means not opinion about the nature of political things but "guesses, beliefs, prejudices, forecasts, and so on." In the past, the usual way of acquiring political knowledge was through political experience and the reading of good historians, but as societies governed by traditions gave way to dynamic mass societies, a need emerged for specialized scholars who follow the rapidly changing situations of the new increasingly complex societies. The need in question is a public-spirited one, for these scholars want to counteract the degeneration of the public into a mass that can be manipulated by unscrupulous men: "while even the most unscrupulous politician must constantly try to replace in his own mind political opinion by political knowledge in order to be successful, the scholarly student of political things will go beyond this by trying to state the results of his investigations in public without any concealment and without any partisanship: he will act the part of the enlightened and patriotic citizen who has no axe of his own to grind" (15–16). But Strauss notes that the unscrupulous political actor and the political scientist have one thing in common; for both of them "the center of reference is the given political situation, and even in most cases the given political situation in the individual's own country" (16). In contrast, "[i]t is only when the Here and Now ceases to be the center of reference that a philosophic or scientific approach to politics can emerge" (16).

It seems then that the dynamic character of mass society calls for a political science that is even more distant from political philosophy than the citizens and statesmen of traditional societies were. Yet Strauss sees a bridge that necessarily takes the more demanding political scientist to political philosophy: "All knowledge of political things implies assumptions concerning the nature of political things, i.e., assumptions which concern not merely the given political situation, but political life or human life as such" (16). For instance, Strauss observes that "[o]ne cannot know anything about a war going on at a given time without having some notion, however dim and hazy, of war as such and its place within human life" (16). This notion is apt to affect one's perception and evaluation of the war in question. If frontiers, patriotism, and wars are ultimate verities, one is apt to see in some wars "a kind of dignity and even nobility"; if they are not, war might appear "only as a nightmare interlude, something to be permanently avoided."[3] Or we may consider Strauss's example about domestic politics: "One cannot see a policeman as a policeman without having made an assumption about law and government" (16). If one assumes that laws and governments are instruments that only serve the interest of the ruling class, one will see a policeman differently than if one assumes that laws and governments are attempts to support moral action. Once the political scientist sees the import of different opinions about war and its place in human life, or of the assumptions about law and government, he will see the necessity of replacing these opinions or assumptions with knowledge about these matters; he will see the necessity of entering the ambit of political philosophy.

Strauss suggests that there is also another, if harder to see, reason that leads a political scientist to political philosophy. This reason is seen once a political scientist as a political scientist becomes self-conscious. While the center of reference of political science is the given situation at the time, political science does not "emerge if it has not been realized among other things that even such political matters as have no bearing on the situation of the day deserve to be studied" (15). In other words, political science as an organized discipline is possible only in a society that has recognized the goodness of science. This breeds an attachment on the part of the political scientist to the political order and society in which he exists, making him act the part of the enlightened and patriotic citizen. Yet, this state of affairs makes it difficult for a political scientist to examine the assumptions underlying the modern liberal society and his own activity. To see whether these assumptions are sound, to see whether his love of truth is merely a prejudice inculcated by a particular society, the political scientist has to think about society and human life in general; he has to think about the place of science in political life.

After articulating the character of political philosophy by distinguishing it from similar activities, Strauss examines two reasons that have led his contemporaries to reject the inquiry into the nature of political things and the good, or right, society as a reasonable pursuit. They are the claim of social science positivism that denies the possibility of objective value judgments and the claim of historicism that denies the permanence of important statements of fact or value. Strauss argues that positivism is theoretically indefensible and that its deficiencies are such that when thought through it transforms itself into historicism, which he judges to be the serious antagonist of political philosophy. In addition, he argues that the denial of the objectivity of value judgments puts the positivist social scientist in an indefensible political position in relation to his political community, an argument that anticipates "the post-behavioral revolution" in political science (18–20). As to historicism, he observes that thoughtful historicists do not deny the existence of "permanent characteristics of humanity, such as the distinction between noble and base" (26). They only argue that "their objective, common, superficial and rudimentary character" prevents them from being used as criteria for evaluating the social situations that fate has imposed on us. In describing the permanent characteristics of humanity recognized by thoughtful historicists, Strauss does not mention the distinctions between good and bad, and just and unjust. Perhaps this is because a historicist such as Heidegger (whom Strauss describes here as the radical historicist) respects nobility more than justice or advantage. Yet Heidegger has contempt for any efforts to derive from the idea of nobility a permanent standard. Strauss then seems to be suggesting that it was Heidegger's attraction to nobility together with his contempt for an analysis of nobility as a permanent characteristic that allowed him "in 1933 to submit to, or rather to welcome, as a dispensation of fate, the verdict of the least wise and least moderate part of his nation while it was in its least wise and moderate mood, and at the same time to speak of wisdom and moderation" (27). Both positivism and historicism find themselves in an indefensible political position precisely because they have given up on the questions of political philosophy.

There is, however, a third and older objection to political philosophy, which is almost invisible in Strauss's treatment because he chooses to address it in an indirect manner. The essay "What Is Political Philosophy?" is based on a series of lectures that Strauss gave in Jerusalem in 1954. It is divided into three parts: "the Problem of Political Philosophy," "the Ancient Solution," and "the Modern Solutions." Given that the eventual book includes essays on Farabi and Maimonides, we are struck by the absence of medieval political philosophy in the introductory chapter. Indeed, such a discussion would have been especially relevant in Jerusalem. Strauss comes close to explaining this omission in his opening paragraph, where he apologizes for speaking about political philosophy in Jerusalem. He excuses himself by appealing to necessity. After expressing his utter inability to convey to his audience "our prophets' vision," he writes:

> I shall even be compelled to lead you into a region where the dimmest recollection of that vision is on the point of vanishing altogether—where the Kingdom of God is derisively called an imagined principality—to say here nothing of the region which was never illumined by it. But while being compelled, or compelling myself, to wander far away from our sacred heritage, or to be silent about it, I shall not for a moment forget what Jerusalem stands for. (9–10)

While the subject matter certainly compels Strauss to wander away from his sacred heritage, he, it seems, compels himself to be silent about that heritage, and he does so evidently out of a deep respect for that heritage. In a related context a few pages later, he once again speaks of compulsion: "We are compelled to distinguish political philosophy from political theology" (13). These two types of teachings differ not only in their sources but also, as the immediate context of that passage indicates, in the substance of their moral teachings. Moreover, political philosophy emerges through a rejection of political theology inasmuch as it is essential to it "to be set in motion, and be kept in motion, by the disquieting awareness of the fundamental difference between conviction, or belief, and knowledge" (12). Conversely, political theology denies the usefulness of political philosophy, as we see from the traditional Jewish view according to which philosophic books on politics have been rendered superfluous by the Torah, a view that Strauss argues Maimonides rejected (157). Strauss's moral delicacy then explains his silence about his sacred heritage at least while lecturing in Jerusalem.

But it is his deep respect for Judaism that prevents him from forgetting about it even "for a moment." This respect is more than an expression of a residual loyalty to a community to which he was born; his words about

Jerusalem reveal a respect that has intellectual and moral content that can be recognized by Jews and non-Jews alike: "In this city, and in this land, the theme of political philosophy—'the city of righteousness, the faithful city'—has been taken more seriously than anywhere else on earth" (9). To be sure, philosophy emerged in Athens, but another community as a community devoted itself more seriously to a matter that is of central interest to political philosophy—righteousness or justice. Jerusalem presents a problem for philosophizing because its seriousness about justice cultivated and belonged to an attitude altogether different from that developed in Plato's *Republic*. Strauss brings out the relevance of the Bible to political philosophy by "repeating" the theme of the latter: "The theme of political philosophy is mankind's great objectives, freedom and government or empire—objectives which are capable of lifting all men beyond their poor selves" (10). The two statements of the theme of political philosophy are not unrelated. One cannot understand freedom and government or empire without also understanding justice or righteousness; and nothing lifts men above their poor selves more than the contemplation of the holy God of the Bible. Political philosophy must have a conversation with Judaism, a conversation that attends to its moral and theological seriousness, but it is also necessary for Jews to have a conversation with political philosophers. The very last sentence of the first section of this essay hints at this necessity. Discussing Heidegger's inability to take the true measure of Hitler, a failure that Strauss traces to this philosopher's rejection of political philosophy, Strauss writes: "The biggest event of 1933 would rather seem to have proved, if such proof was necessary, that man cannot abandon the question of the good society, and that he cannot free himself from the responsibility for answering it by deferring to History or *to any other power different from his own reason*" (17, emphasis added). This sentence (which occurs in the twenty-sixth paragraph of the essay, twenty-six being "the numerical value of the sacred name of God in Hebrew, of the Tetragrammaton")[4] indicates that Heidegger was not the only one who was in an impasse in 1933 and gives some support to those Jews, like Leon Pinsker and Theodor Herzl, who sought to protect themselves by learning from a political philosopher, in their case Spinoza (12).

The Naturalness of the Ancients

The title of the second part, "The Classical Solution," implies not only an agreement between Plato and Aristotle regarding the nature of political things and the best political order but also an evaluation of that agreement as the classical solution. Strauss begins the seventeen paragraphs devoted to this solution by following the lead of Johann Joachim Winckelmann's characterization of the classic as "noble simplicity and quiet grandeur," a characterization that was an attempt to articulate the "naturalness" of classical thought.[5] Strauss contrasts "the natural" not with the supernatural but with the "merely human, all too human," because he ultimately wants to distinguish classical political philosophy from the modern. Classical political philosophy is "natural" because its aim is the perfection of human nature. Classical political philosophy is also "natural" because it emerged in a time most free from traditional ideas: "Classical political philosophy is non-traditional, because it belongs to the fertile moment when all political traditions were shaken, and there was not yet in existence a tradition of political philosophy" (27). Instead of making it easier for us to see political things, the tradition of political philosophy acts like a screen between the philosopher and the political things, for it is easier to transmit answers to questions than the full reasoning that supports them, and the mere acceptance of the necessity of philosophy, a way of life that looks at all things as objects of contemplation, has a corrosive effect on seeing political things, which as such cannot be preserved in purely theoretical or "objective speech." This problem is magnified for those who have inherited the tradition of modern philosophy, which, finding the bedrock of certainty in one's consciousness of oneself, leads to a view of man that abstracts from one's communal existence and what is higher than oneself. Strauss denies that a mere rejection of modern philosophy can take one back to man's "natural situation." Referring to Martin Buber's effort to correct the problem of objectification by supplementing the I-It relation with the I-Thou relation, Strauss argues that such efforts to reach the concrete from the abstract fail because they accept the abstraction as the starting point (see also 79–80, 257–58, and Shell, chap. 10 below.). Buber's I-Thou-We relation is in fact an objectification of friendship: "By speaking of 'the Thou' instead of 'the friend,' I am trying to preserve in objective speech what cannot be preserved in objective speech" (29). The classics, however, understood that "adequate 'speaking about' in analytical and objective speech must be grounded in and continue the manner of 'speaking about' which is inherent in human life" (29). This approach has the advantage of seeing political life in its full richness including the contradictions inherent in political opinion, which insight initiates the movement from opinion to knowledge, from here and now to what is always or

eternal. It allows one to see the genuinely sublime without being blinded
by the fake:

> Hence their political philosophy is comprehensive; it is both political theory
> and political skill; it is as open minded to the legal and institutional aspects
> of political life as it is to that which transcends the legal and institutional; it is
> equally free from the narrowness of the lawyer, the brutality of the technician,
> the vagaries of the visionary, and the baseness of the opportunist. It reproduces,
> and raises to its perfection, the magnanimous flexibility of the true statesman,
> who crushes the insolent and spares the vanquished. It is free from all fanati-
> cism because it knows that evil cannot be eradicated and therefore that one's
> expectations from politics must be moderate. (28)

In speaking of the "noble simplicity and quiet grandeur" of the classics,
Winckelmann primarily had in mind the capacity of Greek artists and
writers to portray men who endure life's great sufferings with composed
minds, artists who could draw such portraits because they themselves were
such men. Strauss shares this admiration, but he makes it clearer that this
capacity was due to insights that bring with them a measure of happiness, a
happiness that stands in the midst of ineradicable evil. Accordingly, drop-
ping "noble simplicity" and reformulating "quiet grandeur," he characterizes classical political philosophy by its "serenity or sublime sobriety" (28;
compare 43, 49). And in a later essay, he frees Winckelmann's formulation
from its romantic assumption by suggesting that the classics can be more
adequately characterized by their "noble reserve" than by their "noble
simplicity" (104).

Strauss illustrates the character of classical political philosophy by
first turning to Plato's *Laws*, which he describes as "his political work *par
excellence*," and even as "*the* Platonic dialogue about politics and laws."
In this work, an old Athenian philosopher attempts to transform a less
civilized but more law-abiding society into a civilized society that will be
superior to Athens in the important respect that its piety laws will tolerate
philosophers. The Athenian stranger carries out this extraordinary task
by proceeding cautiously with deep knowledge of the importance of law-
abidingness to political life. His delicate and slow steps are necessary because his enterprise is a radical one: in order to reform the Cretan laws, he
has to show that the laws of Crete were not given by a god. It does not suffice to cast doubt on the stories that trace these laws to Zeus; he must show
that the laws are man-made, and he does so by testing them according to

the standard that "a code given by a god, by a being of superhuman excellence, must be unqualifiedly good" (30). He attempts to answer a theological question by shifting the question onto the moral and political plane.
Plato's *Laws*, in Strauss's reading, goes beyond showing that Cretan or
Spartan laws are not divine; it shows that no "other code can be the work
of a god."[6] This thesis is the foundation of classical political philosophy
insofar as its guiding theme is the *politeia*, the regime, for Strauss makes
the ground-breaking observation that the very notion of the regime, a notion that traces the character of the whole social and political order to the
ruling body, maintaining that all laws are derivative from the character and
aspirations of men who make them, rests on the premise that all laws are
man-made.[7] Accordingly, "there are a number of Biblical terms which can
be properly translated by 'law'; there is no Biblical equivalent to 'regime' "
(34). Although regimes are in actuality more fundamental than the laws,
one needs the study of the laws in order to establish this fact. Thus, Plato's
Republic, which has as its theme the regime, stands higher than his *Laws*,
but the latter is both more political and more fundamental in the order of
inquiry.

The classics discerned in human life a tendency toward social life, and
in social life a tendency toward political organization or governance of
society by human beings who embody the goal of society. As a result of
this domination, what gives society its character is the form of life as living together: political life is essentially hostile to privacy. The notion of
regime signifies that whole, which we today on account of the influence
of liberal theory view "primarily in a fragmentized form": "regime means
simultaneously the form of life of a society, its style of life, its moral taste,
form of society, form of state, form of government, spirit of laws" (34).
The classics, however, see cracks in political life that eventually become
openings to the most private life. There is a variety of regimes, each making general claims that contradict those of the others, and this fact forces
the question of the best regime. The classical analysis leads to the conclusion that the goal of political life is virtue and that the best regime is an
aristocracy. Plato's best regime depends on chance, because it involves
the coincidence of philosophy and political power, "things which have a
natural tendency to move away from each other" (34). It is telling that it is
in the more realistic Aristotle that Strauss finds the ultimate reason for the
utopian character of the classical notion of the best regime: human beings
by nature have desires found in beasts as well as desires fitting for gods,
but the nature of most people is such that the high desires cannot domi-

nate the low ones, and these more powerful many will resist any attempt to direct society as a whole to the higher desires, any attempt to establish a genuine aristocracy. The classics accepted this utopian solution or did not attempt to overcome chance, because they did not believe it is wise to conquer nature. Although this solution is utopian, Strauss observes that it has a practical meaning. It shows that there is a tension between one's society and the best regime or between one's own and the good, a tension that leads Strauss to write the saddest sentence of the whole essay: "All human love is subject to the law that it be both love of one's own and love of the good, and there is necessarily a tension between one's own and the good, a tension which may well lead to a break, be it only the breaking of a heart" (35). The classical thinkers understood that one ought to choose the good over one's own, which understanding turns the sad truth into a liberating one, freeing them to pursue the highest of which human nature is capable.

Strauss ends his discussion of classical political philosophy by considering two objections to it. The first is the moral-political objection that classical political philosophy is not democratic. Strauss does not deny that classical political philosophy favors aristocracy over democracy, but he denies that this preference rests on obliviousness to the advantages of democracy; the classical thinkers favored aristocracy because under ancient economic conditions it best served the ends of political stability and the cultivation of virtue. And they did not attempt to change these economic conditions because they had misgivings about the emancipation of technology from moral and political control. Moreover, Strauss argues that classical political philosophy can help modern democracy by offering an education that cultivates nonconformist and even rugged individualists. In other words, the very fact that the education provided by classical political philosophy is nondemocratic—Strauss even goes so far as to say that it is "an understatement to call it royal education"—makes it of service to democracies because it provides the education that thoughtful modern theoreticians of democracy have judged necessary for the health of democracies.

The second is the objection that classical political philosophy rests on an antiquated teleological understanding of nature. Strauss denies that classical political philosophy rests or depends on "a specific cosmology." Here he traces the origin of classical political philosophy to Socrates, who "was so far from being committed to a specific cosmology that his knowledge was knowledge of ignorance" (38). He interprets this to be the knowledge of the inadequacy of the authoritative opinions of his society about the nature of whole. Unlike the modern social scientist, who looks at man in the light of the subhuman, Socrates looked at man "in the light of the mysterious character of the whole" (39). Shortly afterward, in an extraordinary gloss on Plato's ideas, Strauss says that Socrates viewed "man in the light of the unchangeable ideas, i.e., of the fundamental and permanent problems" (39). The whole is not as mysterious as it first appears because we can understand the nature of our ignorance of the whole.

But what are the fundamental and permanent problems? Strauss mentions here one such problem, the problem of cosmology. This problem is permanent because its solution is "not at our disposal" and fundamental because uncertainty about its solution affects all human knowledge. He elevates this problem above the ontological and the theological problem by suggesting that it constitutes the essence of philosophy: "To articulate the problem of cosmology means to answer the question of what philosophy is or what a philosopher is" (39; see 248). To begin with, he suggests, the problem is that we have knowledge of the parts but not of the whole. Since we do not have knowledge of the whole, we cannot fully know the parts: our knowledge of parts is essentially partial. In particular, not knowing the whole, our knowledge of parts suffers from "a dualism which has never been overcome" (39): the knowledge of homogeneity and the knowledge of heterogeneity. The former, which manifests itself originally in mathematics and productive arts, understands things in light of their essential sameness. The latter, which manifests itself in politics, understands things in light of their qualitative differences or the different ends that each thing pursues. Strauss suggests that a philosopher feels the desire of combining these two forms of knowledge without succumbing to that desire. As one who wants to replace opinions about the whole with the knowledge of the whole, the philosopher feels this desire, for "[i]t seems that knowledge of the whole would have to combine somehow political knowledge in the highest sense with knowledge of homogeneity" (39). But as one who knows the difference between knowledge and ignorance, the philosopher resists such a combination because it is not truthfully at our disposal. There are two ways of combining these two forms of knowledge. One may derive from knowledge of homogeneity the ends of man as Spinoza seems to have done in his *Ethics*, deriving a moral teaching from his notion of God understood as a single substance that underlies everything. Or one may derive from knowledge of heterogeneity a particular interpretation of nature, as someone might derive a worldview from his belief in a personal God:

Men are constantly attracted and deluded by two opposite charms: the charm of competence which is engendered by mathematics and everything akin to mathematics, and the charm of humble awe, which is engendered by meditation on the human soul and its experiences. Philosophy is characterized by the gentle, if firm, refusal to succumb to either charm. It is the highest form of the mating of courage and moderation. (40)

In resisting the charm of competence, the philosopher moderates his longing for knowledge; in resisting the charm of humble awe, the philosopher exercises his courage in the face of fearsome threats and entreaties. Yet Strauss suggests that all this means that the philosopher never reaches his goal of acquiring knowledge of the whole and thus philosophizing appears as a high but a "Sisyphean or ugly" activity. Strauss, however, suggests that philosophizing does not deprive one of the pleasures of beauty, for "it is necessarily accompanied and elevated by *eros*" (40). He implies that human *eros* involves a longing for eternity and that the philosopher's contemplation of the fundamental and permanent problems is accompanied by pleasures that are natural to a being that has such a longing.

Modernity and the Denaturing of Man

In the third part, Strauss speaks of "the Modern Solutions." The plural is justified, for Machiavelli's hardheaded republicanism, Hobbes's peace-loving despotism, Locke's economic liberalism, Rousseau's totalitarian republicanism, Hegel's postrevolutionary state, Marx's classless and stateless society, and Nietzsche's planetary aristocracy are clearly different answers to the question of the right political or social order. Strauss describes all these solutions as modern not for chronological reasons but because there is a fundamental agreement among them and others in their class. What the new political philosophers have in common is their opposition to the old: "rejection of the classical scheme as unrealistic" (40). Beginning with this negative formulation, Strauss arrives at a positive answer to the question of the essence of modernity, an answer that shakes the common view of modernity as the secularization of Christianity.

Strauss devotes more space to Machiavelli, the founder of modern political philosophy, than to any other modern thinker, paying homage to his discovery of a wholly new political teaching and to his success in persuading almost all future philosophers of the soundness of a break with the whole tradition of political philosophy. According to Strauss's Machiavelli,

"there is something fundamentally wrong," wrong from a political perspective, "with an approach to politics which culminates in a utopia, in
the description of the best regime whose actualization is highly improbable" (41). Machiavelli, in contrast, attempts to reduce the dependence of
politics on chance; he attempts to conquer chance. He does this by identifying the goal of politics with objectives which are actually pursued by
all societies: "freedom from foreign domination, stability or rule of law,
prosperity, glory or empire" (42). This is a radical step because in actuality these objectives had always been pursued in contexts that recognized
higher objectives. Accordingly, Machiavelli's approach can work only if
the classics were wrong in assuming that morality is "a force in the soul
of man" (41). Although this assumption is supported by observations of
men in normal life, one may wonder whether human nature might reveal
itself only in extreme circumstances. Reflection on these circumstances,
especially on the founding of societies, led Machiavelli to conclude that by
nature man is directed neither to society nor to morality; man is by nature
selfish, and selfishness is the cause of man's morality and sociality. If man
is by nature selfish, the very power of sociality and morality in men living
in society ceases to be evidence in favor of the ancient view of man and
becomes evidence for a new thesis that man is much more malleable than
the ancients supposed. Thus, it becomes possible to conceive of a new kind
of morality that consciously identifies virtue with "patriotism, or devotion
to collective selfishness," a morality that is to be taught to men by a new
prince who himself is motivated by the selfish passion of glory. Although
Machiavelli's hardheaded republicanism is not generally accepted today,
Strauss observes that his underlying view of human nature and his principle of solving political problems by appealing to self-interest have become
utterly respectable: "The shift from formation of character to the trust in
institutions is the characteristic corollary of the belief in the almost infinite
malleability of man" (43).

After sketching Machiavelli's critique of classical political philosophy,
Strauss brushes aside that criticism by asserting: "there is in the whole
work of Machiavelli not a single true observation regarding the nature
of man and of human affairs with which the classics were not thoroughly
familiar" (43). But the main point of Strauss's move is to draw attention
to Machiavelli's familiarity with something that was unknown to the classics: the Bible. In this way, he explains how Machiavelli's narrowing of
the human horizon (his lowering of the goals of human life) appeared as
an enlargement of that horizon. He observes that in Machiavelli's times

the classical tradition had been transformed by Christianity with the contemplative life moving to monasteries and moral virtue being replaced by
Christian charity, which by infinitely increasing man's responsibility to his
fellow men led to "courses of action which would have appeared to the
classics, and which did appear to Machiavelli, to be inhuman and cruel"
(44; also see Parens, chap. 6 below). One could have argued that religious
persecution is unchristian, but this option was closed to Machiavelli because he "seemed to have diagnosed the great evils of religious persecution
as the necessary consequence of the Christian principle, and ultimately of
the Biblical principle" (44). Strauss implies that Machiavelli judged that
the victory of the Christian principle along with the consequent "increase
in man's inhumanity is the unintended but not surprising consequence of
man's aiming too high" (44). He suggests that Machiavelli lowered the
goals of human life because he was animated by an "anti-theological ire."
Strauss's presentation suggests that this ire is a moral response to the practical consequences of the biblical principle: Machiavelli lowered the goals
of human life because he hated the inhumanity and cruelty that result
when human beings aim too high. Yet there are reasons to think that this
is not the whole or the final explanation of Machiavelli's "anti-theological
ire" as Strauss understood it. Strauss mentions that in Machiavelli's time
the contemplative life "found its home in monasteries." Devotion to God
replaced philosophizing as the highest human activity. Was this transformation necessary? Strauss suggests that Machiavelli believed that this
development, with the consequent elevation of charity, was not in itself
necessary, but rather "the unintended but not surprising consequence of
man's aiming too high" (44). Accordingly, he sought an alternative to the
classical solution. He attempted to construct a society on the basis of principles that were consistent with his view of the cosmos, a view that Strauss
charmingly describes as "decayed Aristotelianism"—Aristotelian because
of its denial of providence, decayed because it was free from the scholastic
notion of natural ends (47). If Machiavelli and his heirs succeed in constructing such a society, and if the new society turns out to be a better
habitation for human beings, Machiavelli's view that man is not naturally
directed to God is vindicated. In this reading of Strauss, "anti-theological
ire" is interpreted literally. It is Machiavelli's anger against discourse about
God, anger at the persistence of such discourse despite the strong, if not
compelling, evidence against God.[8] According to this reading, which was
first introduced by Christopher Bruell, Machiavelli's "anti-theological ire"
is ultimately the result less of his aversion to cruelty than of his love of

philosophy, a love distorted by a certain uneasiness about the possibility of philosophy.

Regardless of whether his motive was chiefly moral or philosophical, Machiavelli sought to replace the Christian order or the rule of man by God with a this-worldly political order or the rule of man by man.[9] One advantage of Strauss's interpretation is that it explains why "[n]o earlier philosopher had thought of guaranteeing the posthumous success of his teaching by developing a specific strategy and tactics for this purpose" (46). It explains the Enlightenment, which Strauss traces back to Machiavelli. While this movement lowers the goal of political life, it also raises philosophical expectations and expectations for philosophic rule. Accordingly, Strauss describes the great travails of this enterprise through the image of waves borrowed from Plato's *Republic*, an image that represents the situation of men who propose a solution that turns out to be tantamount to being swept out to sea. Machiavelli, Rousseau, and Nietzsche are the initiators of the three waves of modernity, thinkers whose solutions become problems for their successors, each problem becoming increasingly more difficult. They are thinkers who are aware to a high degree of the problematic character of their solutions, so much so that in the case of Rousseau and Nietzsche the very idea of a political solution to the problem of man becomes questionable. More generally, each change in political solution is made necessary by the desire to actualize Machiavelli's primary intention while responding to difficulties in the preceding solution. There is a common theme to the difficulties that initiate changes both within and between waves: moral dissatisfaction. Machiavelli's solution was too revolting to be effective, Hobbes's too fear-inspiring, Locke's too cold, Montesquieu's too corrupting, Rousseau's too questioning of the dignity of social life, Hegel's too easygoing, and Nietzsche's too controlling (172). Are these changes not themselves a witness to the classical view that morality is a force in the human soul?

Machiavelli initiated a political founding to test the truth of his thesis about the nature of man, and we have the results of the test, which in Strauss's interpretation speak against the truth of that thesis. First, the belief that man is infinitely malleable led Nietzsche to be "certain of the tameness of modern western man," which belief allowed him to "preach the sacred right of 'merciless extinction' of large masses of men" (54–55). Yet Western men proved not so tame, and it seems it was, in part at any rate, Hitler's appeal to a kind of political virtue that attracted so many misguided youths to him and his regime (280).[10] Second, granting the need for virtue, one cannot promote virtue by appealing to selfish passions. In his discussion of Hegel, Strauss observes that the very thought that the right order is established by means that contradict the right order, the main thesis of the philosophy of history, undermines that order: "The delusions of communism are already the delusions of Hegel and even of Kant" (54). We may wonder whether the same difficulty does not afflict democracy insofar as the case for it rests on the possibility of universal education, which in turn is made possible by the wealth generated through "emancipation of technology, of the arts, from moral and political control" (37). Finally, Strauss observes that the difficulty inherent in Nietzsche's attempt to explain the fluidity of all human thought through the doctrine of will to power led to Heidegger's rejection of that doctrine and therewith to the explicit renunciation of the very notion of eternity, and he observes that in this respect Heidegger's radical historicism merely makes conscious what was implied in the attempt to master nature, for domination of nature presupposes the denigration of the natural order in favor of the order that originates in man: "For oblivion of eternity, or, in other words, estrangement from man's deepest desire and therewith from the primary issues, is the price which modern man had to pay, from the very beginning, for attempting to be absolutely sovereign, to become the master and owner of nature, to conquer chance" (55). Since such primary issues as friendship, love, and justice cannot be understood apart from man's longing for happiness, a longing tied to man's longing for eternity, and if an adequate analysis of these issues is the most certain path to philosophy as Plato seems to have thought, the conquest of nature leads to a twofold impoverishment of human life. Thus one can understand why Strauss wondered whether Machiavelli's world is "fit for human habitation" (40). Nonetheless, Strauss must have been grateful to Machiavelli for helping to eliminate religious persecution from parts of the globe, for "the subtlety of his speech" and "the intrepidity of this thought," and for inspiring a vital philosophic tradition that even in its failure allows one to see important things more clearly.

The opening essay of *What Is Political Philosophy?* unmistakably and unambiguously sides with the ancients against the moderns. But it behooves us to look at the later essays for a fuller statement of this quarrel, and not least his essay on Locke, which discusses that philosopher's understanding of nature with an appreciation that contrasts with his treatment of Locke in *Natural Right and History* (see also Nadon, chap. 4; Stauffer, chap. 7; and Zuckert, chap. 8 below).[11] While Strauss certainly favored the ancients over the moderns, there are reasons to doubt that the issue is as uncomplicated as the impression left here. One of these reasons is the way he introduces the objections to classical political philosophy: "Classical political philosophy is today exposed to two very common objections, the raising of which requires neither originality nor intelligence, nor even erudition" (36). That Strauss thought it necessary to disarm these objections by such a rhetorical device is a sign that, in his own mind, his response to them in this essay, however substantive, is insufficient. Confirming this suggestion is that Strauss himself belonged to the lowly class of those who made one or the other of these objections, for in a rather prominent place he had argued that "[n]atural right in its classic form is connected with a teleological view of the universe" and that this view seemed to have been refuted by modern science by the kind of evidence that Aristotle himself would have acknowledged.[12] The discoveries of modern natural science may not affect Socrates's basic insights, but they do have a bearing on one's understanding of human things. And perhaps something can be said, after all, in favor of Machiavelli's "decayed Aristotelianism."

Notes

1. Strauss (1959, 17). All unspecified references are to this text. The current essay is a corrected and expanded version of an earlier essay (Behnegar 2010). The author wishes to thank the anonymous reviewers of the University of Chicago Press and Robert Bartlett, Alice Behnegar, David Bolotin, Christopher Bruell, Daniel Burns, Rafael Major, Susan Shell, Devin Stauffer, and Nathan Tarcov for their helpful comments on this and the earlier version of the essay.

2. In "What Is Political Philosophy?" Strauss explains political philosophy as the philosophic treatment of politics. In "On Classical Political Philosophy," Strauss refers to the deeper meaning of political philosophy as "the political, or popular, treatment of philosophy" (93). As Nathan Tarcov points out (chap. 3 below.), this explains why "What Is Political Philosophy?" is placed before "On Classical Political Philosophy." This is not the only case where a statement in the opening essay calls for comparison with a statement in a later essay.

3. Keynes (1951, 67).

4. Strauss (1983, 223). The name YHWH occurs in the fourth chapter of Genesis, which happens to have twenty-six verses. As the above reference (which is from an interpretation of Machiavelli) and the essays on Farabi and Maimonides in *WIPP* show, Strauss sometimes made "somewhat playful" use of numerology in interpreting certain (but of course not all) philosophers (165); it also seems that he himself sometimes crafted his writing with numerology in mind (see nn. 5, 9, and

11 below). Although this is not the most important aspect of either his interpretations or his own writings (166), it could help one see the central theme of an essay. The ultimate standard, however, is always the content of the writing. To return to our case, consider the bearing of statements made on 9–10, 11, 13, 21–22, and 23 on the theme of God. Another of Strauss's essays in *WIPP*, "On the Basis of Hobbes's Political Philosophy," also has twenty-six paragraphs, and a consideration of its content supports the view that this is not a coincidence.

5. In a letter to Alexandre Kojève, Strauss identifies seventeen as the number designating nature (Strauss 1991, 275). According to Christopher Bruell, who does not share Strauss's taste for numerology, Strauss explained the reasoning behind this tradition by noting that there are seventeen consonants in the Greek alphabet and that consonants like nature herself are relatively mute while tradition requires audibles for its transmission.

6. Strauss (1955, 122). The quotation comes from the English summary, but I cannot ascertain that Strauss himself wrote the summary, though he does refer to it in his preface to *WIPP* without suggesting that it was written by anyone other than himself (7).

7. It seems that Strauss arrived at a full understanding of the notion of regime rather late. In "On Classical Political Philosophy," an essay originally written in 1945 that is also included in *WIPP*, Strauss does not even use the word "regime." In *Natural Right and History* he speaks of regimes ruled by priests and speaks of the dependence of laws on human beings only in the sense that "laws have to be adopted, preserved, and administered by men" (Strauss 1953, 136–37).

8. For the clearest statement of Strauss in support of this interpretation of modernity in general (though it was made prior to his discovery of Machiavelli as the founder of modernity), see his introduction to *Philosophy and Law* (1995, 21–39).

9. It might not be an accident that the part devoted to the modern solutions contains twenty-three paragraphs. Twenty-two is the number of revelation, because Hebrew, the language in which biblical revelation was given, has twenty-two letters. According to an old tradition, the language of the eternal revelation has twenty-three letters, the extra letter signifying the insufficiency of the given revelation. Thus, twenty-three is a number that signifies opposition to the existing revelation. "Three Waves of Modernity," which covers the same ground as the third section of "What Is Political Philosophy?," also happens to have twenty-three paragraphs (in Strauss 1989). Strauss also writes "How Farabi Read Plato's *Laws*," an essay included in *WIPP*, in twenty-three paragraphs, thus indicating that there was an opposition to revelation that came from the classical tradition. He indicates an important difference between Farabi and Maimonides by writing "Maimonides' Statement on Political Science," another essay in *WIPP*, in twenty-two paragraphs.

To summarize this use of numerology: God poses a problem for political philosophy; the classics attempt to solve this problem by turning or ascending to nature, the moderns by rejecting God and the goodness of created nature untouched by human art.

10. Also see Strauss (1999, 352–78).

11. As Michael Zuckert observes (chap. 8 below), Strauss changes the paragraphing of "Locke's Doctrine of Natural Law" from twenty-eight in the version published in *APSR* to seventeen in the version in this volume, a change that did not involve substantial subtractions or additions (according to Zuckert, Strauss dropped section headings and made few minor stylistic changes). By revising his essay in this way and in this context, Strauss, it seems to me, hints at an alternative view of nature to the classical view (see also 166; n. 5 above.).

12. Strauss (1953, 7). If my suggestion here seems far-fetched, consider the following statement from his essay on Hobbes in *WIPP*: "The most satisfactory section of Polin's study is his critique of the attempt to trace in Hobbes's writings a development from an earlier recognition of 'honor' as 'aristocratic virtue' to a later rejection of this principle" (195). A reader unfamiliar with Strauss's work could not know that here Strauss is praising Polin for his criticism of Strauss's Hobbes book. (See Stauffer, chap. 7 below.)

Works Cited

Behnegar, Nasser. 2010. "Reading 'What Is Political Philosophy?' " *Perspectives on Political Science* 39 (2): 66–71.

Keynes, John Maynard. 1951. "Mr. Churchill on the War." In *Essays in Biography*, 53–67. New York: Horizon Press.

Strauss, Leo. 1953. *Natural Right and History*. Chicago: University of Chicago Press.

———. 1955. "Hebrew Translation with English Summary of 'What Is Political Philosophy?' " *IYYUN: Hebrew Philosophical Quarterly* (Jerusalem) 6 (2).

———. 1959. *What Is Political Philosophy? and Other Studies*. New York: Free Press.

———. 1983. *Studies in Platonic Political Philosophy*. Ed. Thomas Pangle. Chicago: University of Chicago Press.

———. 1989. *An Introduction to Political Philosophy: Ten Essays*. Culture of Jewish Modernity. Ed. Hilail Gildin. Detroit: Wayne State University Press.

———. 1991. *On Tyranny*. Ed. Victor Gourevitch and Michael S. Roth. New York: Free Press. Original edition, 1948.

———. 1995. *Philosophy and Law: Contributions to the Understanding of Maimonides and His Predecessors*. Trans. Eve Adler. Ed. Kenneth Hart Green. SUNY Series in the Jewish Writings of Leo Strauss. Albany: SUNY Press.

———. 1999. "German Nihilism." *Interpretation* 26 (3): 352–78.

CHAPTER TWO

"Political Philosophy and History"

Catherine Zuckert

In the first and title essay of the collection, "What Is Political Philosophy?," Strauss observed that political action concerns preservation or change, and that to decide what to preserve and what to change, people require a standard of good and bad. Since the question that animates and guides political philosophy is what is the best regime (or what is the standard of good and bad in politics), political philosophy remains not merely relevant but central to political life. In the twentieth century political philosophy nevertheless became an incredible endeavor, because people had come to believe that it was impossible to have knowledge of what is good and bad or just and unjust. The first and most powerful support for that belief was the "positivist" claim that natural science constitutes the only form of human knowledge, that scientific knowledge is based on empirical data or "facts," and that statements of "value" about what is "good" or "just" are, therefore, merely expressions of subjective feeling. Responding to the "positivist" challenge, Strauss pointed out that natural science is a human endeavor that presupposes a judgment that science itself is good. That judgment, moreover, has been made in the West and in modern times, but not at all times and in all places. Strauss thus concluded that the "historicist" claim that judgments of good and bad vary according to time and place constituted the more fundamental challenge to the possibility of political philosophy. In the second essay in the collection, "Political Philosophy and History," he therefore responded to the historicist challenge.

Strauss's critique of historicism has led many commentators to fault him for ignoring history.[1] As the second essay in *What Is Political Philosophy?* shows, that charge as stated is simply not true. What is true is that Strauss understands history differently both from conservative critics who

cling to tradition qua tradition and from the contextualists or "historicists" who see history as setting boundaries to what any given individual
could think at any given time. In this essay Strauss first explains briefly how
"historicism" arose and shows that many of the reasons the contention
that all thought is historically "conditioned" has become widely accepted
cannot withstand critical scrutiny. In the process he thus responds, in advance as it were, to many of his critics. Rather than argue that the circumstances in which past philosophers wrote are irrelevant to understanding
their thought, Strauss contends that the relation between a philosopher's
doctrine and his historical situation is not a simple or unambiguous one.
It differs not only from individual philosopher to philosopher but also
from time to time and place to place. Both medieval and modern political
philosophers took their basic concepts from classical political philosophy.
Medieval political philosophers adapted those concepts in the process of
applying them in different circumstances, but modern political philosophers transformed the basic concepts in fundamental ways—partly in
reaction to the medieval scholastic adaptations. In order to uncover the
foundations of modern political philosophy, it thus becomes necessary
for us to study the history of political philosophy. In contrast to the "historicists," however, Strauss limits the necessity of fusing philosophy with
history to modern political philosophy. It does not apply to classical political philosophy or the "philosophy of the future."

In making this argument Strauss solves what might appear to be
a paradox, if not an outright contradiction in his own work. He begins
this essay by declaring that "political philosophy is not a historical discipline. The philosophic questions about the nature of political things and
of the best, or the just, political order are fundamentally different from
historical questions, which always concern individuals. . . . In particular,
political philosophy is fundamentally different from the history of political
philosophy" (56).[2] Yet, as any reader of *What Is Political Philosophy?* can
see, Strauss's own writings clearly constitute studies of the history of political philosophy. "Political Philosophy and History" appears, therefore, to
constitute not merely the rationale for, but also an explanation of, the distinctive way in which he approaches the history of political philosophy.[3]

The "Traditional View" and the "Historicist" Challenge (¶¶1–2)

In "the traditional view," Strauss emphasizes, political philosophy and
history constitute two essentially different kinds of inquiries about essen-

tially different kinds of objects. Political philosophers ask "about the nature of political things and of the best, or the just, political order," whereas
historical questions "always concern individuals: individual groups, individual human beings, individual achievements, individual 'civilizations' . . .
and so on."[4] But, he immediately adds, that does not mean "that political
philosophy is absolutely independent of history" (56). Even in the traditional view, historical knowledge plays two important, if preliminary, aux-
iliary roles in the development of political philosophy: First, the question
that animates political philosophy, the question of the nature of political
things and the best order, would never arise "without the experience of the
variety of political institutions and convictions in different countries and
at different times." And, second, "only historical knowledge can prevent
one from mistaking the specific features of the political life of one's time
and one's country for the nature of political things" (56–57).[5] Contrary
to the assertions of many of his critics, we thus see at the outset of this
essay, Strauss does not deny the importance of historical knowledge for
the study of political philosophy. He merely, if emphatically, insists that
historical and philosophical knowledge are not the same.

Strauss recognizes, however, that his traditional view has been challenged by what he calls "historicism," i.e., "the assertion that the fundamental distinction between philosophic and historical questions cannot in
the last analysis be maintained" (57). Indeed, he concedes, the "historicist"
challenge may appear "to go deeper to the roots, or to be more philosophic, than the political philosophy of the past." By raising doubts about
whether "the very questions of the nature of political things and of the
best, or the just, political order" can ever be answered, for all times and
places, historicism brings the very possibility of political philosophy into
question; and it thus "creates an entirely new situation for political philosophy." Like a historicist, Strauss links the precarious condition of political
philosophy in our time to an unprecedented historical "situation."

Strauss's Explanation of the Rise and Widespread Acceptance of Historicism (¶¶ 3–8)

Strauss doubts that the fusion of philosophy and history advocated by
"historicists" has been or ever can be achieved. But, he concedes, such a
fusion appears to be the natural goal of the victorious trends of the political thought of the nineteenth and early twentieth centuries. He thus briefly
describes that development. It begins in the sixteenth century when the

opposition to previous political philosophy is marked by a novel emphasis on history.[6] That early turn to history was "absorbed by the 'unhistorical' teachings of the Age of Reason," so that by the end of the seventeenth century it became customary to speak of 'the spirit of a time.'" The term "philosophy of history" was coined in the mid-eighteenth century (by Voltaire); and "the teaching of the outstanding philosopher of the nineteenth century, Hegel, was meant to be a 'synthesis' of philosophy and history" (58).[7] The "historical school" of the nineteenth century then brought about the historicization of previously unhistorical or ahistorical sciences like jurisprudence, politics, and economics. But these historicists were, in turn, criticized by their twentieth-century successors for losing themselves in a passive contemplation of the past. "The typical historicism of the twentieth century demands that each generation reinterpret the past on the basis of its own experience and with a view to its own future" (59). As a result, the questions of traditional political philosophy concerning the nature of political things, of the state, and of the nature of man have been replaced by questions about the modern state, about the present political situation, and so on, as if we could know what the modern state is without knowing what a state is. More thoughtful historicists thus admit that it is not possible to abandon the universal questions of traditional philosophy, but they insist that any answer to them is dependent on the specific situation in which it is suggested and cannot, therefore, be universally valid.

Strauss suggests that the most fundamental historicist claims can thus be summarized in two widely shared assumptions: (1) that the object of historical knowledge, "History," is a "field" or "world" fundamentally different from "Nature," and (2) that "restorations of earlier teachings are impossible, or that every intended restoration necessarily leads to an essential modification of the restored teaching" (60).[8]

Strauss's Critique of Historicism (¶¶ 9–15)

Strauss admits that he cannot disprove these widespread historicist assumptions without giving a full critical analysis of modern philosophy. In this essay he thus limits himself to giving reasons why his readers should not take either of these historicist claims for granted.

He begins by attempting to dispel a popular misunderstanding and moves step by step to addressing the deepest philosophical claims made on behalf of the historicist thesis. This widespread misunderstanding can be traced back to the attacks of early historicism on the political philosophy that led to the French Revolution.[9] People often claim that earlier philosophers conceived and proposed a "right" or "rational" political order that could be implemented at any time and any place. It is not the philosophers, Strauss counters, but their critics who fail to distinguish properly between the abstract character of a philosophical definition of the best regime and the limitations placed upon its practical implementation by the concrete circumstances. Philosophers know "that all political action, as distinguished from political philosophy, is concerned with individual situations" (61).[10] They never expected that their account of the best regime would be put into practice without regard for specific conditions and traditions.

Many people accept the historicist thesis, Strauss suggests, simply on the grounds that what comes later must be better. He thus presents three reasons why this simple thought is problematic. First, he reminds his readers that unless we worship mere success, we will not identify the victorious cause with the truth. Second, even if we identify the truth with the actual outcome, we do not know how history will end. We do not and cannot know what is true, therefore, on the basis merely of what comes later; we have to know what will come last. Strauss thus observes, third, that "those who prefer historicism to non-historical political philosophy because of the temporal relation of the two, interpret then that relation in a specific manner: they believe that the position which historically comes later can be presumed, other things being equal, to be more mature than the positions preceding it" (62). In the case of political philosophy, specifically, historicists take the scandalous disagreements among the philosophers, especially the failure of earlier philosophers to formulate answers to the fundamental questions that their successors could accept, to show that there are no answers valid for all times and all places.

Rather than teaching us that the political philosophies of the past refute each other, Strauss responds, history shows us merely that they contradict each other. Just as historical knowledge of the differences among regimes gave rise to the question that animates political philosophy—namely, what is the best regime—so historical knowledge about the variety of answers to that question offered by political philosophers over the ages ought to give rise to the question, which is right or true. "If the 'anarchy of systems' exhibited by the history of philosophy proves anything, it proves our ignorance concerning the most important subjects (of which ignorance we can be aware without historicism), and therewith it proves the necessity of philosophy" (62).

Strauss concedes, however, that historicists do not argue that there are no universally valid answers to the traditional questions merely because of the variety of conflicting past philosophical doctrines. They point to the close relation that can be found between each political philosophy and the situation in which it emerged. Strauss thus responds to this central historicist contention by observing that historical evidence of the connection between any given philosophical doctrine and its historical setting has a much more limited bearing on the question of whether there can be universally valid answers to enduring questions than historicists think. Strauss does not deny that there is a connection. He contends rather that the meaning of the connection is not as unambiguous as the historicists seem to think. First, he observes, the historicists do not pay sufficient attention to the possibility that political philosophers in the past deliberately adapted their views to the prejudices of their contemporaries. Many political philosophers do not present their teachings in scientific treatises proper; they write what might be called "treatise-tracts." These philosophers do not restrict themselves to expounding truth; they combine their exposition of what is true with what they consider desirable or feasible in the circumstances in which they find themselves, or what they think will be intelligible on the basis of generally received opinion. Those who wish to know what Strauss did or did not claim should note that Strauss does not relate the attempts of past philosophers to adapt the expression of their views to the circumstances and opinions of their contemporaries to a desire to avoid persecution. Observing that some philosophers were attempting to affect the political opinions and thus the practices of their contemporaries, Strauss recognizes the "performative" character of the "tract-like" aspects of their writings that Quentin Skinner, explicitly incorporating J. Austin's notion of a "speech act," emphasizes.[11] By explicitly acknowledging that some political philosophers sought to make their arguments intelligible to their readers by adapting the expression of those arguments to the opinions of their contemporaries, Strauss also recognizes their use of the linguistic conventions that, following analytic linguistic philosophy, J. G. A. Pocock stresses.[12] Strauss differs from these historicists not in denying that there is a connection between a philosophy and the historical situation in which it is articulated but in pointing out that this relation may not be the same under all historical circumstances. "The obvious possibility is overlooked that the situation to which one particular doctrine is related, is particularly favorable to the discovery of *the* truth, whereas all other situations may be more or less unfavorable" (64). One cannot stop at ascertaining, loosely, that there is "a relation" between a philosophical argument and its historical origins. One has to determine more specifically what that relation is; and to discover what the relation is, one has to try to determine whether the doctrine in question is true or false. The fundamental problem with historicism and the reason that it does not, in fact, raise the most radical questions about the possibility of political philosophy, Strauss concludes, is that it cuts off inquiry into the question of the truth or falsity of any philosophical argument from the very beginning by insisting that the truth or validity of any doctrine is limited to its particular time and place. Without examining it, historicists deny from the outset that any argument or doctrine articulated by a philosopher in the past can be true now.

Strauss's Critique of Historicism as History (¶¶16–22)

Strauss indicates the difference between his own understanding and the traditional view by observing that "the old-fashioned, not familiar with the ravages wrought by historicism, may ridicule us for drawing a conclusion which amounts to the truism that we cannot reasonably reject a serious doctrine before we have examined it adequately" (64). He thus leads his readers to ask why, more precisely, historicists claim that past doctrines cannot possibly be true now. The answer he gives "briefly, and in a most preliminary fashion," is that historicists observe that the particular political phenomena about which political philosophers in the past wrote, particularly classical political philosophers, no longer exist. How can what they claimed about the "*polis*," which Strauss himself admits no longer exists, be true about the modern state?

Strauss responds to this "most important example," first, by observing generally that "every political situation contains elements which are essential to all political situations."[13] If not, how could we "intelligibly call all these different political situations 'political situations'?" (64). The concept embedded in the linguistic conventions Pocock emphasizes speak against the conclusion that they are completely limited temporally and spatially. Second, and in some ways more significantly, Strauss argues that classical political philosophers did not contend that the "city" was the most perfect form of political organization merely because they had inherited it from their ancestors and were ignorant of other possible forms of political organization. On the contrary, these philosophers argued that the "city" was superior to the two basic alternatives known to them, the tribe and the Eastern monarchy, on the basis of two standards or desiderata

derived from those two alternatives—the freedom that "we can say tenta-
tively" characterized the tribe but was destroyed by the monarchy, and the
"civilization (high development of the arts and sciences)" in the monarchy
but absent in the tribe. And, Strauss observes, "this preference was not a
peculiarity bound up with their particular historical situation. Up to and
including the eighteenth century, some of the most outstanding political
philosophers quite justifiably preferred the city to the modern state which
had emerged since the sixteenth century, precisely because they measured
the modern state of their time by the standards of freedom and civilization." Only in the nineteenth century did the modern state become able to
claim that it was superior to the Greek city on these very grounds. Strauss
does not deny "that the emergence of modern democracy in particular
has elicited, if it has not been the outcome of, such a reinterpretation of
both 'freedom' and 'civilization' as could not have been foreseen by classical political philosophy." In other words, he is not claiming that classical
political philosophy is simply true or simply superior to modern political
philosophy. Indeed, he acknowledges that "there are definite reasons for
considering that reinterpretation intrinsically superior to the original version" (66). Those reasons do not, however, include the "fact" that "modern democracy has superseded earlier forms of political association" or
that "it has been victorious," because it has not always or everywhere been
victorious. Some philosophers have questioned the validity of these standards, moreover. Even in antiquity, some classical political philosophers
preferred the Eastern monarchy to the city.[14] Strauss insists merely that
we cannot know which, if any, of the philosophers has stated the truth
about such political matters until we have subjected their doctrines to a
philosophic critique.

   In order to subject past doctrines to a philosophic critique concerning their truth or falsity, Strauss insists, it is necessary to understand the
thought of a philosopher exactly as he understood it himself. "All historical evidence adduced in support of historicism presupposes as a matter of
course that adequate understanding of the philosophy of the past is possible on the basis of historicism." However, "this presupposition is open
to grave doubts" (66).

   Ironically, historicists are guilty of exactly the same error they pointed
out in earlier, explicitly "progressive" history. Because they assumed that
current thought is superior to the thought of the past, "progressive" historians understood past thought only as a preparation for the present. In
studying a doctrine of the past, they "did not ask primarily, what was the

conscious and deliberate intention of its originator? They preferred to ask, what is the contribution of the doctrine to our beliefs?" By asking what a past doctrine meant "in the light of later discoveries or inventions," such historians "took it for granted that it is possible and even necessary to understand the thinkers of the past better than those thinkers understood themselves." Strauss thinks that the historicists were right to object to "progressive" history:

> The "historical consciousness" rightly protested in the interest of historical truth, of historical exactness. The task of the historian of thought is to understand the thinkers of the past exactly as they understood themselves, or to revitalize their thought according to their own interpretation. If we abandon this goal, we abandon the only practical criterion of "objectivity" in the history of thought. (67)

Strauss admits that "the same historical phenomenon appears in different lights in different historical situations; new experience seems to shed new light on old texts"; and that observations of this kind seem to suggest that the claim of any one interpretation to be *the* true interpretation is untenable." But, he insists, observations of that kind do not justify this suggestion. "For the seemingly infinite variety of ways in which a given teaching can be understood does not do away with the fact that the originator of the doctrine understood it in one way only, provided that he was not confused" (67). All other "interpretations" of his doctrine represent, basically, attempts to understand his thought better than he did.

"Historicism is constitutionally unable to live up to the standards of historical exactness which it might be said to have discovered," Strauss concludes. "For historicism is the belief that the historicist approach is superior to the non-historical approach, but practically the whole thought of the past was radically 'unhistorical'" (68).

Strauss's Critique of Historicism as Philosophy (¶¶23–28)

Contrary to the beliefs of many historians, Strauss argues, the historicist thesis cannot be proved solely on the basis of historical evidence. The most a historian qua historian can show is that all political philosophies are related to specific historical settings, or that only people living in a specific historical situation will be apt to accept a given political philosophy.

He cannot prove that the historical setting of one particular political philosophy is not the ideal condition for the discovery of *the* political truth without determining that no political philosophy articulated in the past is true.

On the basis of the historicist assumption that the validity of every political philosophy is limited to its particular time and place, a contemporary student of the history of political philosophy might be tempted to inquire not about the best regime per se but only about the "operative ideals which maintain a particular type of state."[15] But, as A. D. Lindsay points out, any thorough discussion of those ideals must eventually raise the question of the absolute worth of those ideals. "Nor," Strauss adds, "can the question of the best political order be replaced by the question of the future order." Even if we knew with certainty that the future will bring a communist world society, we would know only "that the communist world society is the only alternative to the destruction of modern civilization, and we should still have to wonder which alternative is preferable" (69). It is not possible to replace the fundamental questions of traditional political philosophy about the best regime with questions about present and future possibilities. What historicists can reasonably claim is not that the questions change from time to time, but that no answer to the universal questions is going to be valid for all times and places, because all the answers are "historically conditioned."

"The historicist thesis amounts then to this, that there is an inevitable contradiction between the intention of philosophy and its fate."[16] The contradiction is inevitable, because thinkers will continue not only to raise the fundamental questions that arise, naturally, as it were, out of human existence, but also to find satisfactory, which is to say, universal answers to those questions. That attempt will necessarily fail, however, if all human thought is enthralled by opinions and convictions that differ from historical situation to historical situation. Philosophers who come to this conclusion would not be able to believe that any answer they found or formulated could be simply true. Moreover, they would not be able to know the precise reason why their answers were defective, because that reason would be found in the deepest prejudice of their time, which would be hidden from them. Such philosophers could not help but raise the fundamental questions that occur to all thoughtful people, but they would have to join their philosophic effort to coherent reflection on their historical situation in order to free themselves as much as possible from the prejudices of their age. "That historical reflection would be in the service of the philosophic effort proper, but would by no means be identical with it" (70).[17]

Historicist philosophy claims to be superior to nonhistorical philosophy for three reasons. Strauss disputes all three. He initially concedes that the attempts of historicist philosophers to identify the connection not only between past philosophies and their historical situations but also and even preeminently between their own philosophy and the current situation might appear to be at a higher level of reflection and thus more truly philosophic than the "naïve," nonhistorical philosophy of the past. By casting doubt on the adequacy of any answers, such reflections might appear to make historical political philosophy less apt to degenerate into dogmatism than its nonhistorical predecessor. But, he retorts, "a moment's reflection suffices to dispel that delusion" (71). For nonhistorical philosophers, all the answers suggested in former ages are potentially true until proven otherwise; historicist philosophers dogmatically exclude all the answers suggested in former ages before examining them. Nor does reflection on their historical situation necessarily mean that historicist philosophers are thinking more deeply or at a higher level than their nonhistorical predecessors, who were not greatly concerned with their historical situation. "For it is quite possible that the modern philosopher is in much greater need of reflection in his situation because, having abandoned the resolve to look at things *sub specie aeternitatis*, he is much more exposed to, and enthralled by, the convictions and 'trends' dominating his age" (71). In fact, Strauss proceeds to argue, that is the case.

The second reason historicist philosophy claims to be superior to past nonhistorical philosophy is that it proceeds explicitly in light of an unknown future and thus has an "open horizon," whereas past, nonhistorical philosophy occurred within a closed horizon, restricted to the possibilities known at the time. But, Strauss objects, "the possibilities of the future are not unlimited as long as the differences between men and angels and between men and brutes have not been abolished." (And, he could have added, historicist philosophers like Martin Heidegger and Hans-Georg Gadamer continue to affirm these differences.) Moreover, it may be impossible to foresee all possible developments, even within the limitations imposed by human nature, but it is equally impossible to say anything about possibilities that are at present not even imagined. "We must leave it to the political philosophers of the future to discuss the possibilities which will be known only in the future" (72).

The third and most fundamental reason historicist philosophy claims to be superior to nonhistoricist philosophy is that historicist philosophers know that the fundamental questions cannot be answered, whereas previous philosophers thought that they could. Strauss responds to this claim by observing that every philosophic position implies that there are answers to fundamental questions that are final and true for all times. Historicism merely replaces one kind of finality by another kind of finality, "by the final conviction that all human answers are essentially and radically 'historical.'" Historicism could claim to have done away with all pretense to finality only if it presented the historicist thesis not as simply true but as true for the time being only. In fact," Strauss concludes, "if the historicist thesis is correct, we cannot escape the consequence that that thesis itself is 'historical' or valid, because meaningful, for a specific historical situation only" (72).

Historicism as the Truth of Our Time, but Not of the Past or Future (¶¶ 28–36)

If the historicist thesis is applied to itself, Strauss concludes, "it will . . . reveal itself as relative to modern man; and this will imply that it will be replaced, in due time, by a position which is no longer historicist." Strauss admits that some historicists would see such a development as a manifest decline; but, he argues, in doing so they would be ascribing "to the historical situation favorable to historicism an absoluteness which, as a matter of principle, they refuse to ascribe to any historical situation" (73).

Applying the historicist thesis to itself, Strauss asks what it is about the modern situation that leads modern people, in contrast to premodern, to be so concerned about history. And to answer that question he gives the argument in favor of the fusing of philosophic and historical studies he finds most convincing. "Political philosophy is the attempt to replace our opinions about political fundamentals by knowledge about them. Its first task consists therefore in making fully explicit our political ideas, so that they can be subjected to critical analysis." The problem for modern political philosophers is that "our ideas" are partial abbreviations or residues of the thoughts of past thinkers. "These thoughts were once explicit and in the center of consideration and discussion. It may even be presumed that they were once perfectly lucid. By being transmitted to later generations they have possibly been transformed, and there is no certainty that the transformation was effected consciously and with full clarity." So, Strauss concludes, "if we want to clarify the political ideas we have inherited, we must actualize their implications, which were explicit in the past, and this can be done only by means of the history of political ideas." Thus "the clarification of our political ideas insensibly changes into and becomes indistinguishable from the history of political ideas. To this extent the philosophic effort and the historical effort have become completely fused" (73).[18] Despite his insistence on the need for a historical "prolepsis," the fundamental thrust and character of Strauss's understanding of philosophy remains recognizably Socratic.

Once we recognize our need to engage in historical studies in order to clarify our own ideas, Strauss adds, we also become aware of the fact that premodern political philosophers perceived no such need. "The most natural, and the most cautious explanation of this paradoxical fact would be, that perhaps our political ideas have a character fundamentally different from that of the political ideas of former ages" (74). In earlier ages, Strauss observes, political ideas were based, like our ideas of things like dogs, on firsthand experience. The idea of the modern state is not like that, however. "It emerged partly owing to the transformation, or reinterpretation, of more elementary ideas, of the idea of the city in particular. Ideas which are derived directly from impressions can be clarified without any recourse to history; but ideas which have emerged owing to a specific transformation of more elementary ideas cannot be clarified but by means of the history of ideas" (74).[19]

Strauss does not rely solely on his own observations of the evident difference between premodern and modern political philosophers with regard to the importance of history, however, or the reasons he gives for this difference. He also quotes the first and foremost "philosopher of history," G. W. F. Hegel:

> "The manner of study in ancient times is distinct from that of modern times, in that the former consisted in the veritable training and perfecting of the natural consciousness. . . . philosophizing about everything it came across, the natural consciousness transformed itself into a universality of abstract understanding which was active in every matter and in every respect. In modern times, however, the individual finds the abstract form ready made."[20]

Strauss glosses Hegel's statement by observing that classical philosophers articulated the fundamental concepts of political philosophy by starting from political phenomena as they present themselves to "the natural consciousness," which is a prephilosophic consciousness.[21] "These concepts can, therefore, be understood and their validity tested by direct reference to the phenomena as they are accessible to 'the natural consciousness.'"

These concepts remained the basis of the philosophic efforts of the Middle Ages and were "partly taken for granted and partly modified by the founders of modern political philosophy. In a still more modified form they underlie the . . . political science of our time." Because "modern political philosophy emerges not simply from 'the natural consciousness,' but by way of a modification of . . . a tradition of political philosophy, its fundamental concepts cannot be fully understood until we have understood the earlier political philosophy from which, and in opposition to which, they were acquired, and the specific modification by virtue of which they were acquired" (75).

It is not merely the fact that modern political philosophy is "dependent" on earlier philosophy that requires philosophers now to study the history of philosophy, Strauss emphasizes. Medieval philosophy was dependent upon ancient philosophy, but the relation between medieval and ancient philosophy was different from that between modern and premodern. For medieval philosophers, "Aristotle was *the* philosopher." However a medieval philosopher "might deviate from Aristotle in details, or as regards the application of the true teaching to circumstances which Aristotle could not have foreseen [including, most importantly, the rise of religions that claimed to be universally true, as opposed to the gods of the ancient cities], the basis of the medieval philosopher's thought remained the Aristotelian teaching" (76). Because the medieval philosopher thought that Aristotle's teaching was the true teaching, the basis of the medieval philosopher's thought was present to him; and because the basis of his thought was present to him, the medieval philosopher did not need to engage in a historical study, for example, of Aristotle.

The kind of dependency modern political philosophy has on ancient philosophy is different, precisely because the basis of modern political philosophy in ancient philosophy is no longer present to modern philosophers. Because "modern thought is in all its forms, directly or indirectly, determined by the idea of progress," modern thinkers assume that they can build on foundations that have already been laid without going back and reexamining the truth or validity of those foundations. As a result, the foundations or basis of modern political philosophy gradually become covered over. If we are to understand the basis of the ideas we have inherited and to determine whether those ideas are well-founded or not, we have to unearth the bases of these ideas in earlier philosophy. "This philosophic inquiry is the history of philosophy or of science" (76).

Such a philosophic inquiry into the origins of modern philosophy and science is necessary in order to revive an appreciation of the distinction between "inherited knowledge, . . . a man takes over from former generations" and "independently acquired knowledge, . . . the philosophic or scientific knowledge a mature scholar acquires in his unbiased intercourse, as fully enlightened as possible as to its horizon and presuppositions" (76–77). That distinction has unfortunately been clouded if not covered over in our time by talk about a "body of knowledge" or "the results of research," in which people "tacitly assign the same cognitive status to inherited knowledge and to independently acquired knowledge" (77). Strauss concludes that "modern political philosophy or science, as distinguished from pre-modern political philosophy or science, is in need of the history of political philosophy or science as an integral part of its own efforts, since . . . it consists to a considerable extent of inherited knowledge whose basis is no longer contemporaneous or immediately accessible." But, he insists, "the recognition of this necessity cannot be mistaken for historicism. For historicism asserts that the fusion of philosophic and historical questions marks in itself a progress beyond 'naïve' non-historical philosophy, whereas we limit ourselves to asserting that that fusion is . . . inevitable on the basis of modern philosophy, as distinguished from pre-modern philosophy or 'the philosophy of the future'" (77).

Strauss's somewhat ironical evocation of Nietzsche's call for a "philosophy of the future" at the conclusion of this essay highlights the fundamental issue, as Strauss understood it. Will there be political philosophy in the future? Will philosophers continue to raise the fundamental questions? Or, if they continue to raises these questions, will they be discouraged from vigorously pursuing answers by a historicist conviction that they will never find an answer whose validity is not "historically conditioned" and thus limited in a way they themselves will never be able to perceive? By the mid-1930s Strauss had become convinced that in his attempt to recapture ancient virtue Nietzsche had not sufficiently freed himself from the idea of progress that is fundamental to all modern thought and was implicit in Nietzsche's call for a "philosophy of the future."[22] What was needed, Strauss suggested in the title of a series of talks he gave a few years later, was not an attempt to make further "progress" on the basis of past achievements but rather, first, an attempt to "return" to understanding past thinkers as they understood themselves.[23] In the essays that follow "Political Philosophy and History" in this collection, Strauss sought to demonstrate that political philosophy in its original meaning is still possible, even though he argued in a Socratic manner that political philosophy now requires a preliminary historical critique of received opinions. In chapter 3, "On Classical Political Philosophy" he explained that the purpose of his remarks was "to discuss especially those characteristic features of classical political philosophy which are in particular danger of being overlooked or insufficiently stressed by the schools that are most influential in our time." In particular, he emphasized the way in which classical political philosophy was directly related to political life and so based on firsthand experience. In his "Restatement on Xenophon's *Hiero*" in chapter 4, he then showed how the concepts first articulated by classical political philosophers are needed to understand contemporary political phenomena like tyranny, even though the present-day manifestations of these phenomena are fundamentally different. In chapters 5 and 6 he analyzed the way in which medieval political philosophers (Farabi and Maimonides) adapted classical political philosophy, which they considered to be the truth, to the changes brought about in their circumstances by the emergence of revealed religions that claimed to be universally true. (See especially pp. 144 and 159). In chapters 7 and 8 he then showed that contemporary commentators on the works of Hobbes and Locke failed to see the ways in which these modern political philosophers not only appropriated concepts they took from classical political philosophers but also transformed those concepts as a result of their opposition to earlier Christian scholastic appropriations and reinterpretations, because these contemporary commentators imposed their own current notions, rather than first seeking to understand Hobbes and Locke as they understood themselves. In chapter 9 Strauss responded to two critics of his own approach. And in chapter 10 he presented an extremely sympathetic account of Kurt Riezler's attempt but ultimate failure to recapture the truth of ancient philosophy and so to move beyond Heidegger and his historicism. So long as we attempt to move beyond the achievements of past philosophers, rather than first seeking to move back and to recover the foundations of their thought, Strauss suggested, we will continue to be not only animated, but also limited, by the modern prejudice in favor of progress. We need to study the history of political philosophy in order to learn what political philosophy originally was—and still can be. In *What Is Political Philosophy?* he demonstrated how that study should be conducted. By way of contrast, in the sixteen critical book reviews with which he concluded this collection of essays, he showed not only how widely historicist assumptions were to be found in contemporary studies of the history of political philosophy but also the deleterious effects of those assumptions.

Notes

1. Examples of such critiques include Skinner (1969) and Ryn (2005). Grant Havers (2005, 5) defends Strauss from conservative critics on the basis of his perceived rejection of history but argues that "Strauss did not share the conservative enthusiasm for the application of biblical ideas to politics." Paul Norton (1981) provides an explication and defense of Strauss's argument. Emil Kleinhaus (2001, 95) argues that "Strauss was a historian who bridged the gap between history and philosophy by extracting the universal from the particular."

2. The in-text page citations that follow are to Strauss (1959).

3. Strauss first published this essay in 1949 in a well-known and highly respected journal, the *Journal of the History of Ideas,* before he published *Persecution and the Art of Writing* in 1953 and *Natural Right and History* in 1954. It is, therefore, surprising that none of Strauss's critics even refers to this essay. These critics include conservatives like Ryn (2005) and Gottfried (1986); "historicists" like Skinner (1969); and more recent commentators like Major (2005) and Ward (2009), who try to show that Strauss and Skinner are closer to each other than they think.

4. Strauss seems to be referring to Aristotle's famous statement in the *Poetics* (9.1451b6–7) that poetry is more philosophical than history, because it depicts types rather than particular instantiations, but the "traditional" view is, of course, not limited to Aristotle. One of the notable characteristics of this particular essay, in contrast both to the first and to many of the essays that follow it in this collection, is that in this essay Strauss rarely associates particular arguments with particular philosophers or locates their origin in particular works.

5. If so, the main political and philosophic function of historical studies, according to Skinner (1969, 53), does not require or depend upon the "historicist" claim that all political thought is tied to the particular time and place where it was first expressed.

6. Strauss would appear here to be referring particularly to the work of Machiavelli, who urged his readers to study ancient history, but not ancient philosophy.

7. In claiming that "Strauss's way of dealing with the problem of history indicates that some of the most important ideas of modern philosophy are largely unknown to him" and that Strauss's "reductionist construct 'historicism' . . . precludes attention to the philosophically crucial idea of *synthesis*," Ryn (2005, 36) ignores Strauss's response to the Hegelian and other secularized versions of a purported "synthesis" between the Greek and scriptural roots of Western civilization in Strauss's "Progress or Return" (1989).

8. Strauss indicated some of the grounds of this assumption in his account of the "modern solutions" in chap. 1, when he observed that "the second wave of modernity" that includes both German idealistic philosophy and romanticisms of all kinds "consisted in the first place in a return from the world of modernity to pre-modern ways of thinking. Rousseau returned from the world of finance, from

what he was the first to call the world of the *bourgeois*, to the world of virtue and the city, to the world of the *citoyen*. Kant returned from Descartes' and Locke's notion of ideas to the Platonic notion. Hegel returned from the philosophy of reflection to the 'higher vitality' of Plato and Aristotle. And romanticism as a whole is primarily a movement of return to the origins. Yet in all these cases, the return to pre-modern thought was only the initial step of a movement which led, consciously or unconsciously, to a much more radical form of modernity." The reason these returns to premodern thought led to more radical forms of modernity, Strauss suggests, is that the return in all cases took place on the basis of modern principles. For example, he observes that "Rousseau returned from the modern state as it had developed by his time to the classical city. *But he interpreted the classical city in light of Hobbes's scheme*" (Strauss 1959, 50, emphasis added). And later, "The right order may have been as loftily conceived by Hegel as it was by Plato, which one may doubt. It certainly was thought by Hegel to be established in the Machiavellian way, not the Platonic way; it was thought to be established in a manner which contradicts the right order itself" (54). In a famous letter to Karl Löwith in 1935 Strauss reported that he had broken with Nietzsche, because he did not think that Nietzsche had succeeded in recapturing the ancient view of human excellence, because Nietzsche had not freed himself sufficiently from modern concepts and concerns (Löwith and Strauss 1988, 183). As we shall see in this essay, Strauss himself tried to avoid the problems these modern political philosophers experienced in returning to premodern institutions and concepts by understanding all political philosophers, but especially the classics, as they understood themselves (and not through modern lenses).

9. Here Strauss seems to be referring to Edmund Burke (Strauss 1953, 294–323).

10. Ryn (2005) accuses Strauss of this kind of abstraction, partly on the basis of his critique of Burke in Strauss (1953, 294–323).

11. Skinner (1969, 45–46). In emphasizing the commonality between Skinner, who argues that it is necessary to study history, because "some writers voluntarily convey their meaning with deliberate obliqueness," and Strauss's (in)famous argument in *Persecution and the Art of Writing* that "many authors deliberately engage in the 'metaphoric' practice of 'writing between the lines,'" Major (2005) misses the performative element of Skinner's argument that makes Skinner look at past authors in terms of their possible effect on their contemporaries, given current opinions and circumstances, and not on posterity. Both Tarcov (1992) and Zuckert (2002) emphasize this difference and its effects on the way Skinner and Strauss, respectively, interpret texts.

12. Pocock (1962, 184–85; Pocock (1972); Pocock (1973); Pocock (1975, viii, 3–5, 57–58, 83–84); Boucher (1985).

13. Strauss takes the example from Collingwood (1939, 59–62). He agrees with Collingwood that 'polis' is not the same thing as a modern 'state' or 'city' and should not be translated by 'state' or 'city-state.' He suggests that 'commonwealth'

may be the nearest equivalent. See Strauss (1964, 30); Strauss (1965, lectures 4, 6, 7, and 10).

14. Strauss's preliminary consideration of this most important example here indicates the reasons why he takes up "classical political philosophy" in the next chapter and the relevance or applicability of that philosophy to politics in the second half of the twentieth century in his "Restatement on Xenophon's *Hiero*" in the fourth chapter (see Nadon, chap. 4 below)

15. Strauss quotes A. D. Lindsay (1943, 1: 45).

16. Strauss examines this position more fully in his concluding essay on Kurt Riezler (see Shell, chap. 10 below.)

17. Strauss seems here to have what he later calls "radical historicism" (Strauss 1953, 26–29) or Heidegger (Strauss 1991, 251) in mind. At times, e.g., in "The Age of the World View" (Heidegger 1977 [1952], 115–54), Heidegger appears, like other "historicists" such as Collingwood, to argue that the questions change from era to era. For example, in this essay Heidegger suggests that the ancients asked "why?" whereas the moderns ask "how?" Both in *Being and Time* and in his later work, however, Heidegger argues that the "truth" disclosed by the entire history of Western philosophy has been limited by its original experience and definition of "being" as presence. By arguing that "being" is, in fact, temporal, since the "present" is merely a transition from "past" to "future," and thus that "being" is fundamentally historical, Heidegger claims to have disclosed the limitations of previous philosophy and so to have opened the possibility of a "new beginning" for which he calls in both his infamous *Rector's Address* and his posthumously published *Beiträge zur Philosophie* (Heidegger 1999). But, Heidegger concedes, the new, "historical" understanding of being to which he has come is and will necessarily also be limited. In contrast to less philosophically rigorous historicists, Strauss argues in a later essay (Strauss 1983), Heidegger not merely confronted the possibility that all ages are not equal with regard to the disclosure of truth; indeed, like Hegel, Marx, and Nietzsche before him, Heidegger argued (and had to argue) that the truth about the historical character of the disclosure of the truth had become evident only at his time.

18. In the course "Introduction to Political Philosophy." Strauss (1965, lecture 7) indicates that he agrees with Collingwood that there must be a certain kind of "fusion" of history, but he explains that he has something quite different in mind. Whereas Collingwood argued that all modern individuals are products of an accumulation of ideas they inherited from the past (and so they cannot take or study the works of past authors seriously or carefully, since Collingwood looked at past historians, ironically, the way "progressive" historians did, merely as contributors to the present), Strauss insists that modern philosophers have to investigate the sources or grounds of the ideas they have inherited, which means that they have to investigate the truth or validity not only of those grounds but also of the modern transformations of earlier, "premodern" ideas. He presented a fuller, more de-

tailed critique of Collingwood in "On Collingwood's Philosophy of History" (Strauss 1952). In the course transcript a student asks: "As far as I understand, you agreed with Collingwood in saying that it was necessary today that there be a rapprochement between history and philosophy. Do you mean that in contrast to the premoderns, we simply have more obstacles to overcome? Or did you mean something else, more than that?" And Strauss responds, "I meant it in the first place as a strictly empirical assertion, in the old sense of the word, where an empirical assertion means I know that it is so, and I do not know the reason. What they call a 'hard fact.' A hard fact is a fact where you do not know the reason, because if you know the reason, it is no longer so hard, yes? *(Laughter.)* That is so that whenever I read something, an analysis of some of the fundamental concepts with which political scientists are concerned—of course, the mere historical knowledge which is thoughtless and undigested is of no value; I am speaking only of the other way around—but if someone does not go into the genesis of these concepts, then he is simply a superficial analyst. One can state it formally, and therefore simply, as follows. As men of science, we are all concerned with knowledge about the things of which we have primarily only opinions. And if we want to proceed in a perfectly above-board and cleanly manner, we must first make clear to ourselves what our opinions are. We must clarify our opinions. Now, if we begin to do that, we see very soon that our opinions are in very large part opinions which we share with our contemporaries, and even more, inherited opinions. But think of a thing like political freedom. While there are some features, perhaps, which have emerged in the last generation, fundamentally that concept is an inheritance. Now if we want to clarify our opinion, we must therefore also go into this whole history of, quote, 'political liberty.' So the strictly philosophic concern with clarifying our opinions changes necessarily and even insensibly into historical study. This is, I think, an empirical fact which every one of us who is doing some thought, some reflection about it, simply experiences."

19. That was the reason Strauss suggested earlier that we need to recapture a sense of the original meaning of the 'polis,' even though there are no longer any *poleis* to be observed directly, in order to understand what we still mean by "politics" or "the political."

20. To bring the intention of Hegel's remark out more clearly, Strauss notes, he has changed the translation he quotes from Hegel's *The Phenomenology of Mind* (1931, 94). For a more precise analysis Strauss refers his readers to Jacob Klein's *Greek Mathematical Thought and the Origin of Algebra* (1968).

21. Stanley Rosen, a sometime student of Strauss, challenges both Strauss and his teacher Edmund Husserl by arguing that there is no such thing as a "natural consciousness" (Rosen 2002, 54–93, 135–58). Like a historicist, Rosen argues that people at all times see and interpret their experiences through a particular, usually inherited understanding of their "world."

22. Löwith and Strauss (1988, 183).

23. As Hilail Gildin notes, the first two parts of "Progress or Return?" were "published in *Modern Judaism* 1 (1981, 17–45) and represent an edited version of two of three lectures Leo Strauss delivered at the Hillel House, University of Chicago, in November 1952. Part three, the third lecture, was published as 'The Mutual Influence of Theology and Philosophy' in *The Independent Journal of Philosophy* 3 (1979, 111–118). The text of the original lecture was edited slightly to bring it into line with a published Hebrew translation (in *Iyyun. Hebrew Philosophical Quarterly* 5, no. 1 January 1954)" (in Strauss 1989, 248). In other words, Strauss gave these talks three years after he first published "Political Philosophy and History" and three years after he presented his Walgreen lectures (1949), which he later published as *Natural Right and History* in 1953.

Works Cited

Boucher, David. 1985. "Language, Politics and Paradigms: Pocock and the Study of Political Thought." *Polity* 17: 761–76.

Collingwood, R. G. 1939. *Autobiography*. Oxford: Oxford University Press.

Gottfried, Paul Edward. 1986. *The Search for Historical Meaning: Hegel and the Post-war American Right*. DeKalb: Northern Illinois University Press.

Havers, Grant. 2005. "Leo Strauss, Willmoore Kendall, and the Meaning of Conservatism." *Humanitas* 18: 5–25.

Hegel, Georg Wilhelm Friedrich. 1931. *The Phenomenology of Mind*. Trans. J. B. Baillie. 2nd ed. London: G. Allen and Unwin.

Heidegger, Martin. 1977 [1952]. "The Age of the World View." In *The Question concerning Technology and Other Essays,* trans. William Lovitt, 115–54. New York: Harper and Row.

———. 1999 [1989]. *Contributions to Philosophy [From Enowning]*. Trans. Parvis Emad and Kenneth Maly. Bloomington: Indiana University Press.

Klein, Jacob. 1968 [1934]. *Greek Mathematical Thought and the Origin of Algebra*. Trans. Eva Brann. Cambridge: MIT Press.

Kleinhaus, Emil A. 2001. "Piety, University, and History: Leo Strauss on Thucydides." *Humanitas* 14: 68–95.

Lindsay, A. D. 1943. *The Modern Democratic State*. New York: Oxford University Press.

Löwith, Karl, and Leo Strauss. 1988. "Correspondence." *Independent Journal of Philosophy* 5/6: 183.

Major, Rafael. 2005. "The Cambridge School and Leo Strauss: Texts and Context of American Political Science." *Political Research Quarterly* 58: 477–85.

Norton, Paul. 1981. "Leo Strauss: His Critique of Historicism." *Modern Age* 25: 143–54.

Pocock, J. G. A. 1962. "The History of Political Thought: A Methodological Enquiry." In *Philosophy, Politics and Society,* 2nd series, ed. P. Laslett and W. C. Runciman, 184–85. Oxford: Basil Blackwell.

———. 1972. *Politics, Language and Time.* London: Methuen.

———. 1973. "Verbalizing a Political Act: Toward a Politics of Speech." *Political Theory* 1: 35–41.

———. 1975. *The Machiavellian Moment.* Baltimore, MD: Johns Hopkins University Press.

Rosen, Stanley. 2002. *The Elusiveness of the Ordinary: Studies in the Possibility of Philosophy.* New Haven: Yale University Press.

Ryn, Claes G. 2005. "Leo Strauss and History: The Philosopher as Conspirator." *Humanitas* 18: 31–58

Skinner, Quentin. 1969. "Meaning and History in the History of Ideas." *History and Theory* 8: 3–53.

Strauss, Leo. 1949. "Political Philosophy and History." *Journal of the History of Ideas* 10: 30–50.

———. 1952. "On Collingwood's Philosophy of History." *Review of Metaphysics* 5: 559–86.

———. 1953. *Natural Right and History.* Chicago: University of Chicago Press.

———. 1959. *What Is Political Philosophy? and Other Studies.* New York: Free Press.

———. 1964. *The City and Man.* Chicago: Rand McNally.

———. 1965. *Introduction to Political Philosophy.* Audiotape of lectures 4, 6, 7, and 10 [18, 25, 27 January and n.d.]. Leo Strauss Center, http://leostrausscenter. uchicago.edu/course/introduction-political-philosophy-winter-quarter-1965.

———. 1983. "Philosophy as a Rigorous Science." In *Studies in Platonic Political Philosophy,* ed. Thomas L. Pangle, 29–37. Chicago: University of Chicago Press.

———. 1989. "Progress or Return? The Contemporary Crisis in Western Civilization." In *An Introduction to Political Philosophy: Ten Essays by Leo Strauss,* ed. Hilail Gildin, 249–310. Detroit: Wayne State University Press.

———. 1991. *On Tyranny.* Ed. Victor Gourevitch and Michael S. Roth. New York: Free Press.

Tarcov, Nathan. 1992. "Quentin Skinner's Method and Machiavelli's Prince." *Ethics* 92: 692–709.

Ward, Ian. 2009. "Helping the Dead Speak: Leo Strauss, Quentin Skinner and the Arts of Interpretation in Political Thought." *Polity* 41: 235–55.

Zuckert, Michael. 2002. "Appropriation and Understanding in the History of Political Philosophy." In *Launching Liberalism,* 57–81. Lawrence: University Press of Kansas.

CHAPTER THREE

Leo Strauss's "On Classical Political Philosophy"

Nathan Tarcov

Although "On Classical Political Philosophy" is the oldest or first pub-lished of the articles collected in *What Is Political Philosophy? and Other Studies*,[1] it appears as the third chapter. The two chapters preceding it, "What Is Political Philosophy?" (1955) and "Political Philosophy and History" (1949), are treatments of political philosophy both classical and modern. This chapter on classical political philosophy in turn precedes three chapters with premodern authors in their titles (Xenophon, Farabi and Plato, and Maimonides), followed by two on modern authors, Hobbes and Locke.

Strauss admits at once that his purpose in this study is "to discuss espe-cially those characteristic features of classical political philosophy which are in particular danger of being overlooked or insufficiently stressed by the schools that are most influential in our time," not "to sketch the out-lines of an adequate interpretation of classical political philosophy," but to point to the only way, "as it seems to me," whereby it can eventually be reached "by us" (78).[2] This unusual density of uses of the first person plural and singular ("our," "me," and "us") draws the reader's attention to "our time" with its influential schools and the dangers they pose to the understanding of classical political philosophy and to Strauss as an indi-vidual opposed to those schools.[3] The two features of classical political philosophy that Strauss stresses both concern its relation to political life but are quite different: that it was related to political life directly and that it transcended political life. The first is emphasized in the first twenty-eight paragraphs (78–90); the second in the last eight paragraphs (90–94).[4] The omission in this essay of explicit treatments of the themes of "Jerusalem and Athens," natural right, and exotericism, so prominent in others of Strauss's writings, highlights its focus on the twofold relation of classical political philosophy to political life.

I. The Direct Relation of Classical Political Philosophy to Political Life

As in the opening of the section on the classical solution in "What Is Political Philosophy?" (27–28), Strauss opens "On Classical Political Philosophy" by contrasting classical political philosophy's direct relation to political life with the more remote relation of later political philosophy, presumably ancient and medieval as well as modern, which was "related to political life through the medium of a tradition of political philosophy" (78–79). Although Strauss sometimes gives the impression of being and is often taken to be a defender of "The Great Tradition" or Western tradition,[5] he praises classical political philosophy first of all for being nontraditional, for seeing political life freshly rather than through taken-for-granted, inherited concepts. The subsequent tradition of political philosophy took for granted the necessity and possibility of political philosophy; traditions as such take for granted what they inherit.[6] Classical political philosophy's direct relation to political life entailed that, in contrast to later political philosophy, it did *not* take for granted the necessity and possibility of political philosophy. Strauss returns to this crucial issue of the necessity and possibility of (political) philosophy only toward the end of the study.

Whereas the tradition of political philosophy, even modern political philosophy that otherwise tried to reject traditional political philosophy, took for granted the necessity and possibility of political philosophy, present-day ("empirical") political science, Strauss reports, believes that it achieves the most direct relation to political life by rejecting or emancipating itself from political philosophy altogether (79). It is one of the influential schools in our time that make it difficult to understand the true character of classical political philosophy, in particular its direct relation to political life. It fails, however, Strauss claims, to reestablish a direct relation to political life since its relation is mediated through both modern natural science and taken-for-granted concepts inherited from the philosophical tradition. It goes even further than modern political philosophy in departing from a direct relation to political life by abandoning concern with the guiding question of classical political philosophy, that of the best political order, and focusing instead on questions of method.

Strauss writes that classical political philosophy "attempted to reach its goal by accepting the basic distinctions made in political life exactly in the sense and with the orientation in which they are made in political life, and by thinking them through, by understanding them as perfectly as possible" (79–80). He does not at this point address whether thinking those distinctions through and understanding them as perfectly as possible leads classical political philosophy to move beyond their sense and the orientation with which they are made in political life. He does not say at this point what the goal of classical political philosophy was. By contrasting it with "a science that is not itself essentially an element of political life" (present-day political science), he implies but does not actually affirm that classical political philosophy was "essentially an element of political life." He asserts that it followed the articulation "inherent in, and natural to, political life and its objectives" but does not say that its goal was identical with the objectives of political life.

The primary questions, the terms, and even the method of classical political philosophy were not specifically philosophic but already present in political life (80). Strauss presents the view of the political philosopher as the umpire in the controversies of paramount and permanent importance among opposed partisan claims that characterize political life, the arbitrator who tries to "give each party what it truly deserves" (80–81). By characterizing this view of the function of the political philosopher as "of political origin," Strauss may suggest that this is how the political philosopher "first comes into sight" to the good citizen rather than that this is simply how the political philosopher understands himself. Strauss describes the partisan claims among which the classical political philosopher umpires as based on "opinions of what is good or just." This description is neither "idealist" nor "realist." He writes: "Those who raise a claim usually believe that what they claim is good for them. In many cases they believe, and in most cases they say, that what they claim is good for the community at large. In practically all cases claims are raised, sometimes sincerely and sometimes insincerely, in the name of justice." Strauss thereby implies that in *most* cases partisans believe that their claims are good for themselves but not for the whole community (which "realists" since Thrasymachus claim is *always* the case), though in many cases they believe both, and in some cases they even believe that their claims are good for the community at

large but not for themselves (which "realists" deny is ever the case or treat
as mistakes). Strauss here distinguishes between justice and the good of
the community at large but leaves open their relation and the possibility of
opposition between them.[7] This function of serving as umpire among the
parties derives from "the duty of the good citizen to make civil strife cease
and to create, by persuasion, agreement among the citizens" (81), so that
the political philosopher "first comes to sight as a good citizen."[8] Strauss
does not explain here why the patriotic duty to make civil strife cease
should have priority for the political philosopher over aiding the partisans
of justice, virtue, or the common good to defeat their partisan enemies.
The implication seems to be that each of the parties (normally?) has some
grasp but none of them has a full grasp of justice or the common good. (In
chapter I Strauss writes that "Aristotle says in effect that the partisan sees
deeper than the patriot but that only one kind of partisan is superior to the
patriot; this is the partisan of virtue" [35]).[9] To fulfill this duty of a good
citizen the political philosopher has to raise "ulterior questions . . . never
raised in the political arena" (distinct from his "primary questions," which
are raised in political life), but he never abandons "the orientation inherent in political life," again in contrast to the methodological orientation
of present-day political science (81). Strauss does not explain here why
the political philosopher's ulterior questions are never raised in political
life or what constitutes the orientation inherent in political life, though
he suggests it is concerned with what is to be done in a particular political
community in a particular situation and in the light of accepted opinions
about what is good or just.

Political philosophy differs from political life in that it is concerned
primarily with "what is essential to all political communities" rather
than with an individual community and individual situations (81). Nonetheless "there is a straight and almost continuous way leading from the
pre-philosophic to the philosophic approach": the "political science" or
prudence of the excellent statesman is applicable to all political communities; the skill of rhetoric, political science "in a more precise sense," is yet
more universal; classical political philosophy founded "political science in
the final and precise sense of the term" by raising the whole of it (deed as
well as speech) "as far as possible or necessary" to the level of generality
reached by the rhetoricians (81–83). The classical political philosopher
who reached his goal did this by acting as the teacher of legislators, who
legislate the frameworks within which statesmen act and who raise fundamental and universal political questions, most fundamentally that of the

best political order, of who should rule (83–84). Thus the almost continuous way ascends from the good citizen to the excellent statesman to the
rhetorician to the legislator to the political philosopher. Strauss writes
that "the political philosopher who has reached his goal is the teacher of
legislators," but they may be only characters in his books or hypothetical readers rather than actual particular legislators. This does not imply
that his goal is to teach legislators: that may be merely a by-product of his
reaching his goal.

Strauss explains that because of its orientation toward the fundamental
political controversy over who should rule, the classics are "not primarily
concerned with the question of whether and why there is, or should be,
a political community; hence the question of the nature and purpose of
the political community is not the guiding question for classical political
philosophy" (84). This statement implicitly contrasts the guiding question
of classical political philosophy most sharply with the starting point of
modern thinkers such as Hobbes, Locke, or Rousseau, who start with the
state of nature as the absence of a political community. Though the nature
and purpose of the political community were not its *guiding* questions or
primary concerns, classical political philosophy ultimately must answer
"the question of the nature of political things" (94).[10]

Given recent controversy over Strauss's supposed influence on U.S.
foreign policy despite the paucity of passages on the subject in his writing, it is worth pausing over his remark here that since "the survival and
independence of one's political community . . . the ultimate aim of foreign policy is not essentially controversial," classical political philosophy
was concerned primarily not with questions concerning the political community's external relations but with its inner structure, controversy over
which "essentially involves the danger of civil war" (84–85). This remark
suggests that controversy over foreign policy is only over means to the
political community's survival and independence, not over those ends. If
one thinks, however, of Strauss's phrase in chapter 1, "mankind's great
objectives, freedom and government or empire" (10), elaborated later in
that chapter with reference to Machiavelli (42), one is reminded that there
are sometimes controversies over whether to pursue empire rather than
mere survival and independence. Strauss's understanding of the stance of
classical political philosophy toward that issue is made clear by the conclusion of the paragraph in *Natural Right and History* that invokes "freedom
and empire": "the end of the city is peaceful activity in accordance with
the dignity of man, and not war and conquest."[11] The primary concern of

classical political philosophy with the inner structure of the political community reflects that rejection of conquest as the end of the city. Nevertheless Strauss admits in *The City and Man* that for a city not on the verge of civil war or in it, "the most important questions concern its relations with other cities." It is therefore "not without reason" that Thucydides makes his Diodotus call freedom (from foreign domination) and empire "the greatest things," as generally speaking foreign policy is primary "for us," "for the citizen." Classical political philosophy, however, ascends to what is "first by nature" from what is first for us "understood as adequately as possible in the manner in which it comes to sight prior to the ascent," from questions concerning foreign policy to the question of the best political order.[12]

In explaining how political controversies over the best political order for a given political community tend to express themselves in universal terms as competing answers to the question of the best political order as such, Strauss gives the examples of "a man who rejects kingship for Israel" and "a man who defends democracy in Athens," as well as the fact that monarchy is the best political order for Babylon (85). He seems to allude to Samuel's warning the people of Israel (on God's instructions) of the disadvantages of kingship (cf. 188) and perhaps to Pericles's praise of Athenian democracy in his funeral oration.[13] This is as close as Strauss comes in this essay to referring to his famous topic of "Jerusalem and Athens."[14] (He does not refer in this chapter as he does in chapter 1 to the conflict between philosophy and the city regarding the gods of the city [32]). In this presentation Jerusalem and Athens are united in rejecting kingship, though not in defending democracy (Samuel rejected kingship on behalf of theocracy). This openness of political life to the question of the best political order, despite its immediate concern with the best order for a given community and its recognition that the best political order may not be best for an inferior situation, contrasts with the later denial (e.g., by the historical school) that the question makes sense owing to the primacy of particularity (26, 60–61).[15]

Strauss presents "aristocracy" (the rule of "the good," the best, or men of merit) as the natural answer to the natural question of the best political order given not only by classical political philosophy but by "all good men"—the only example he adduces is Thomas Jefferson—indeed as "the pre-philosophic answer" (85–86). By "aristocracy" here Strauss means neither anything as crude as a hereditary nobility nor anything as sublime as philosopher-kings, but the general preference in political life for "courageous and skilful generals, incorruptible and equitable judges, [and] wise and unselfish magistrates." He does not make an explicit effort in this chapter as he does in chapter 1 to defend this answer and classical political philosophy against the obvious objection that they are antidemocratic (36–38).[16] The general preference in prephilosophic political life for good rulers who prefer the common interest to their private interest and who do the noble and right thing because it is noble and right is accompanied, however, by "further questions of almost overwhelming political significance" or "formidable objections" or "more or less 'sophisticated' attacks made by bad or perplexed men," that desirable results can be achieved by men of dubious character or by unfair means, that the just and the useful are not identical, and that "virtue may lead to ruin." (Though the last phrase suggests Machiavelli, Strauss thereby asserts that this was known to prephilosophic political life and to classical political philosophers long before Machiavelli.)[17] Classical political philosophy especially "goes beyond" prephilosophic political life paradoxically by defending the prephilosophic political answer to the question of who should rule ("the good") against these objections or attacks (86). The Maimonidean term "perplexed" suggests a degree of sympathy for at least some of those attacking the rule of virtue, without whom the classical political philosopher would not be compelled to address the ulterior questions about virtue that compel or enable him to transcend the dimension of prephilosophic political life (90, 94).[18] Such men may be genuinely perplexed by the "radical insufficiency" of the common opinions about virtue (90–91). Strauss does not explain here how classical political philosophers defended the prephilosophic answer against these formidable objections.

Strauss continues by explaining that the classical political philosopher becomes the teacher of legislators primarily by answering the question of what conditions and institutions most favor "the rule of the best," a question that becomes most urgent (only) when that answer to the fundamental political question is accepted (86–87). He can thereby assist the legislator in compromising between what is most desirable in itself and what less favorable circumstances permit. Contrary to the view recently attributed to Strauss in the media—namely, that liberal democracy should be imposed everywhere—he stresses that institutions and laws must fit the circumstances, including the character of the people, their traditions, and economic conditions. He denies, however, that for the Greek political philosophers either the best political order or philosophy itself was intrinsically or necessarily Greek (87–88).

Strauss contrasts classical political philosophy as essentially "practical" (his quotation marks) or primarily concerned with the guidance of political life and the quest for the best political order with purely descriptive or analytical modern political philosophy or "theory" (again his quotation marks) (88–89). This contrast would seem to apply to Hegel (the only modern political philosopher mentioned here) and to present-day political science rather than to such modern political philosophers as Machiavelli, Hobbes, or Locke. Strauss's statement here that Hegel's demand that political philosophy "understand the present and actual state as something essentially rational, amounts to a rejection of the *raison d'être* of classical political philosophy" suggests not only that classical political philosophy's primary concern was the right guidance of political life but that it regarded the actual state as essentially less than rational judged by its standard of the best political order.[19]

Classical political philosophy started from the moral distinctions of everyday life as sufficient "for all practical purposes," that is, for most cases, which is to say not for all or rare cases or for theoretical purposes (89). It knew the "formidable theoretical objections" to them "better than the dogmatic skeptic of our time" (presumably the value-free social scientist who denies the rationality of all value judgments). These formidable theoretical objections seem related to but distinct from "the formidable objections" that "belong to pre-philosophic political life" (86), available via pre-Socratic philosophy, the Sophists, and classical conventionalism.[20] Classical political philosophy addressed its political teaching, which had recourse to myths, primarily to decent men who took everyday moral distinctions for granted. Classical political philosophy did this not because it took those distinctions for granted but, on the contrary, because it knew that in their politically relevant sense they are indemonstrable and exposed to grave theoretical doubts, that "the well-being of the political community requires that its members be guided by considerations of decency or morality," and that the political community therefore cannot tolerate a political science that loosens the hold of moral principles (89–90). This "political teaching" of classical political philosophy was, however, distinguished from its "theoretical teaching." Strauss's claim that classical political philosophy was "essentially 'practical' " and that its "primary concern" was guiding political life (88) does not imply that classical political philosophy had no theoretical teaching or even that its ultimate concern was giving political guidance. The attitude of classical political philosophy was "always akin" (but not identical) to that of the enlightened statesman rather than that of the detached zoologist, the social engineer "who thinks in terms of manipulating or conditioning rather than in terms of education or liberation," or the prophet "who believes that he knows the future" (90). The last of these contrasts is, like the earlier allusion to Samuel, as close as Strauss comes in this essay to explicit reference to the theological-political problem he later designated as *the* theme of his investigations.[21] The *enlightened* statesman may differ from other statesmen in his focus on education or liberation and in his own liberation from such illusions as that he knows the future.

The discussion of the direct relation of classical political philosophy to political life (78–90) concludes with a summary paragraph repeating that the purpose of classical political philosophy was to settle the most fundamental political controversy in the spirit of a good citizen and "in accordance with the requirements of human excellence" (90). This last addition prepares the reader for the shift in emphasis in the next section.[22]

II. Classical Political Philosophy's Transcendence of Political Life

In the section on classical political philosophy's transcendence of political life, Strauss specifies one of the "ulterior questions" never raised in political life that the classical political philosopher raises (90–91; cf. 81): "What is virtue?" or rather what is the virtue that gives one the highest right to rule. Strauss now admits that the classical political philosopher whose direct relation to political life he emphasized earlier is "compelled to transcend not merely the dimension of common opinion, of political opinion, but the dimension of political life, as such; for he is led to realize that the ultimate aim of political life cannot be reached by political life, but only by a life devoted to contemplation, to philosophy." This implies that philosophy as a way of life offers "as it were, the solution to the problem that keeps political life in motion." Strauss does not here identify that ultimate aim or that problem: he does not mention happiness here (cf. 117); the preceding paragraph suggests the problem is who has the right to rule, but beyond that may lie the question of the right way of life or happiness. Paradoxically and contrary to the impression given earlier in the chapter that classical political philosophy was essentially practical in the sense of being concerned with the fundamental controversy of political life, Strauss now admits that ultimately political philosophy is "no longer concerned with political things in the ordinary sense of the term."

No difference between classical and modern political philosophy is "more telling" than this ultimate concern with the philosophic life (91). We can add that nothing may more clearly distinguish Strauss from his contemporaries than his own focus on the philosophic life as the highest subject of political philosophy. Yet even this concern with the philosophic life is not unrelated to political life, Strauss argues, given the popular appreciation of the greater freedom and higher dignity of private life.

In "What Is Political Philosophy?" Strauss had to explain philosophy as the attempt to replace opinions about the whole or about all things by knowledge of the whole or the natures of all things before explaining political philosophy provisionally as the branch of philosophy that attempts to replace opinions about the nature of political things by knowledge of them, though even there he first briefly argued for the intrinsic directedness of political life toward political philosophy (10–12). In contrast, in "On Classical Political Philosophy," only after an extensive account of the direct relation of classical political philosophy to political life does Strauss turn to philosophy as an attempt to rise from opinion to science and as itself posing an "almost overwhelming difficulty which had to be overcome before philosophers could devote any serious attention to political things, to human things" (92).[23] Strauss reminds us that political philosophy was "at first exclusively concerned with the natural things" as distinguished from the human things. Political philosophy thus is almost overwhelmed by difficulties from both sides: from prepolitical (pre-Socratic) philosophy as well as from the formidable objections of "almost overwhelming political significance" arising from prephilosophic political life (86). Pre-Socratic philosophy considered the natural things to be "absolutely superior in dignity" to the human or political things and so was concerned "only negatively, only accidentally" with politics, presumably by its denial of the natural status of the political things, above all law and justice (92).[24] In *The City and Man* Strauss therefore concludes that "philosophy must be compelled to turn back toward the human things from which it originally departed."[25]

Strauss argues, however, that philosophy is not only negatively and accidentally but necessarily and essentially concerned with the nature of political things.[26] It must be so concerned to understand fully its own purpose and nature, because as the attempt to rise from opinion to knowledge, its essential starting point is the essentially political sphere of opinion (92). Strauss is distinguished from his contemporaries not only by his focus on the philosophic life as the highest subject of political philosophy but also by his insistence on the political character of philosophy. Not only must political philosophy be concerned with the philosophic life, but philosophy must be concerned with political life. Philosophers are compelled to ask the practical question "Why philosophy?"—why is it needed by political life, why is it good and right (92–93). The need to answer this question and show the necessity of philosophy for the political community made moral and political reflection a necessity for philosophy. The question of the necessity of political philosophy raised near the beginning of the chapter thus has two sides: philosophy's practical need to show the political community's practical need for political philosophy, and philosophy's theoretical need for political philosophy. (The question of the possibility of philosophy, less explored in this essay than that of its necessity,[27] also has two sides in that both philosophers and some nonphilosophers become aware of its possibility through reflection on the philosophers' own doings [92]. The possibility of philosophy can mean either its theoretical validity or its practical existence.) Classical political philosophy did not take for granted the necessity and possibility or the goodness and rightness of philosophy. Strauss concludes, "This question calls philosophy before the tribunal of the political community; it makes philosophy politically responsible."[28] Philosophy must provide a political justification for itself and show how the well-being of the political community depends on philosophy (cf. 126). It must do so not only to answer the question of why philosophy is good and right but also to protect itself against the distrust and hatred of many citizens. Strauss gives the impression here that this distrust and hatred are a mere prejudice owing to the general failure to understand the meaning of philosophy rather than to philosophy's lack of belief in the gods of the city as in "What Is Political Philosophy?" (32).

In "What Is Political Philosophy?" Strauss provisionally explains that "in the expression 'political philosophy,' 'philosophy' indicates the manner of treatment: a treatment which goes to the roots and is comprehensive; 'political' indicates both the subject matter and the function: political philosophy deals with political matters in a manner that is meant to be relevant for political life; therefore its subject must be identical with the goal, the ultimate goal of political action," and he seems to suggest there that the goal is freedom or empire (10). Something close to that is the understanding of political philosophy presented in the first section of "On Classical Political Philosophy," but it is radically revised in the shorter last section where the philosophic life itself is said to be what reaches the ultimate goal of political life: "From this point of view the adjective 'political' in the expression 'political philosophy' designates not so much a subject matter as a manner of treatment; from this point of view, I say, 'political philosophy' means primarily not the philosophic treatment of politics, but the political, or popular, treatment of philosophy, or the political introduction to philosophy" (93). (This is as close as Strauss comes in this essay to explicit mention of his famous distinction between exoteric and esoteric philosophic teachings.) The unusual interjection "I say" emphatically identifies Strauss with this revised explanation of political philosophy, which he immediately refers to as the "deeper meaning of 'political philosophy'" in contrast to its ordinary meaning (94).[29] Strauss arranged the book *What Is Political Philosophy?* so that the deeper answer to the question in the title of the book is given only in this third chapter rather than in the first chapter entitled "What Is Political Philosophy?," which provides only the ordinary or provisional answer.

In both of its meanings, political philosophy culminates in praise of the philosophic life (94). Political philosophy in the ordinary meaning praises the philosophic life as the means to reach the goal of political life; in its deeper meaning it praises the philosophic life in an attempt to lead those qualified away from the political life to the philosophic life (94, 125). The stress on the direct relation to political life of classical political philosophy in the first section of the third chapter is revealed in its final section to be ultimately for the sake of the political justification of philosophy.[30] Political philosophy as a practical discipline (cf. 88) must primarily ask essentially practical questions, but it thereby achieves "insight into the limits of the moral-political sphere as a whole" ultimately for the sake of theoretical understanding.

Notes

1. It was first published in 1945 in *Social Research*; some of the notes on books were published earlier. Cf. Leo Strauss, *What Is Political Philosophy? and Other Studies* (Strauss 1959, 5–6). Parenthetical references are to page numbers in this book. This essay benefited from the comments of André Abranches, Nasser Behnegar, Steven Lenzner, Jennifer London, and Rafael Major and the assistance of Brandon Sward.

2. The version Strauss published in the book omits the first four paragraphs from the original article, which present the "very precise meaning" of political philosophy in the past as the "attempt to replace opinions about political fundamentals by genuine knowledge" and trace "the present crisis to political philosophy" and the misinterpretation of classical political philosophy to positivism and

historicism (Strauss 1945, 98–99). These issues were dealt with more extensively in "The Problem of Political Philosophy," the first part of chapter 1, and in chapter 2. The version in the book occasionally treats positivist political science but not historicism. The book also omits the original epigraph from Swift's *Battle of the Books*, which seems to suggest that the ancients would "not only give license, but also largely contribute" to modernity, that an admirer of the ancients need not reject modernity.

3. Strauss substituted "as it seems to me" for "I believe" in the original article and added "by us." The latter addition may point to Strauss's future work on classical political philosophy. He also changed "a truly historical interpretation" to "an adequate interpretation," as he had omitted the preceding explanation that a historical interpretation, in contrast to a historicist one, tries to understand the philosophy of the past as it understood itself. The first word of the original article ("today") immediately drew attention to our time.

4. The original article was divided into two numbered but untitled parts corresponding to paragraphs 2–31 and 32–36 of the chapter in the book. Cf. Burns (2002 149–50).

5. Cf. Strauss (1958, 59–60, 120; 1966, 3, 7; 1970, 83; and 1989, 72–73). In the last of these Strauss admits that speaking of "the Western tradition" cannot withstand precise analysis.

6. Cf. Strauss (1953, 31): "it is of the essence of traditions that they cover or conceal their humble foundations by erecting impressive edifices on them." This point is more fully developed in the book than in the original article.

7. Cf. Strauss (1953, 160–61).

8. Strauss writes here of "the political philosopher" and not specifically of classical political philosophy: he cites Hume and Tocqueville as well as Xenophon and Aristotle (81 n. 2). The quotation from Tocqueville was added to the note from the original article. We might add that the concern with avoiding civil strife (see also 85) is less emphatic and explicit in classical political philosophy than in Hobbes or than one might expect from Strauss's presentation.

9. See also Strauss (1964, 47).

10. See also Strauss (1964, 138). One might say that the question of why there is a political community or its nature and purpose is the opening question of book 1 of Aristotle's *Politics*; Strauss, however, must consider the question of who should rule that comes to the forefront in book 3 to be the work's guiding question.

11. Cf. Strauss (1953, 133–34), citing Thucydides 3.45.6. There may also be conflicts between survival and independence (as experienced for example by the Melians, Thucydides 5.84–116), to which classical political philosophy might have something to contribute.

12. Strauss (1964, 239–40).

13. 1 Samuel 8; Thucydides 2.37.

14. Cf. e.g., "Jerusalem and Athens," in Strauss (1997, 377–405).

15. Strauss (1953, 13–16).

16. See also Strauss (1964, 35–41).

17. Machiavelli, *The Prince,* chap. 15.

18. Strauss (1964, 25–27).

19. See Strauss (1964, 22–23; 2007, 521–22).

20. Cf. Strauss (1953, chap. 3). "On Classical Political Philosophy" obviously differs from the presentation of classical political philosophy in chapters 3 and 4 of *Natural Right and History,* "The Origin of the Idea of Natural right" and "Classic Natural Right," in that it does not present, let alone focus on, the dialogue between classical political philosophy and conventionalism, the ancient philosophy that asserted that all justice is conventional rather than natural. A related and even more obvious difference is that "On Classical Political Philosophy" does not mention natural right or what is by nature just; it hardly mentions justice, merely noting that opposed claims in political life are made in "the name of justice" (80) and that the political works of the classical political philosophers attempt to supply a "political justification of philosophy" (93–94).

21. Strauss (1997, 453). Cf. Meier (2006).

22. In chapter 1 Strauss contrasts the excellence of man (philosophy) with the excellence of the citizen (32).

23. Strauss omits from the book chapter the statement at this point in the article that philosophy originally was "an attempt to replace opinions about the nature of the whole by genuine knowledge of the nature of the whole" (Strauss 1945, 115).

24. Strauss (1964, 14; 1953, 93–123).

25. Strauss (1964, 13–14, 18).

26. In *The City and Man* Strauss writes that "political philosophy broadly understood is the core of philosophy" and that Socrates starts from and transcends the accepted opinions but "there is no unqualified transcending, even by the wisest man as such, of the sphere of opinion" (Strauss 1964, 20).

27. This may be because the essay does not directly address either of the two most powerful denials of the possibility of philosophy: divine law and historicism.

28. Cf. Strauss (1995, 132).

29. Cf. Gourevitch (1968, 64–65).

30. In "What Is Political Philosophy?" Strauss writes that the philosopher's acceptance of the political perspective, his adoption of the language of political man, is an "obfuscation," an exercise of the virtue of moderation as virtue not of thought but of speech (32).

Works Cited

Burns, Timothy. 2002. "Ancient and Modern Political Rationalism in the Thought of Leo Strauss." In *Gladly to Learn and Gladly to Teach: Essays on Religion and Political Philosophy in Honor of Ernest Fortin, A.A.,* ed. Michael P. Foley and Douglas Kries, 145–62. Lanham, MD: Lexington Books.

Gourevitch, Victor. 1968. "Philosophy and Politics, I." *Review of Metaphysics* 22 (1): 58–84.

Meier, Heinrich. 2006. *Leo Strauss and the Theologico-Political Problem.* Trans. Marcus Brainard. Cambridge: Cambridge University Press.

Strauss, Leo. 1945. "On Classical Political Philosophy." *Social Research* 12 (1): 98–117.

———. 1953. *Natural Right and History.* Chicago: University of Chicago Press.

———. 1958. *Thoughts on Machiavelli.* Glencoe, IL: Free Press.

———. 1959. *What Is Political Philosophy? and Other Studies.* New York: Free Press.

———. 1964. *The City and Man.* Chicago: Rand McNally, 1964.

———. 1966. *Socrates and Aristophanes.* New York: Basic Books.

———. 1970. *Xenophon's Socratic Discourse.* Ithaca: Cornell University Press.

———. 1989. *The Rebirth of Classical Political Rationalism: An Introduction to the Thought of Leo Strauss: Essays and Lectures by Leo Strauss.* Ed. Thomas L. Pangle. Chicago: University of Chicago Press.

———. 1995. *Philosophy and Law: Contributions to the Understanding of Maimonides and His Predecessors.* Trans. Eve Adler. Albany: SUNY Press, 1995.

———. 1997. *Jewish Philosophy and the Crisis of Modernity: Essays and Lectures in Modern Jewish Thought.* Ed. Kenneth Hart Green. Albany: SUNY Press.

———. 2007 "What Can We Learn from Political Theory," *Review of Politics* 69 (1): 515–29.

CHAPTER FOUR

Philosophic Politics and Theology

Strauss's "Restatement"

Christopher Nadon

It is surprising how little Leo Strauss's "Restatement on Xenophon's *Hiero*" has to say about Xenophon's *Hiero*. Then again this is the same Leo Strauss who wrote to his friend Jacob Klein in October of 1939, "I have been engaged with a book, about which I could believe *a priori* that it is indispensable for understanding the *Timaeus*: Hesiod's *Theogony*. Naturally it is not a theogony as the title already shows (what good author shows the subject in the title, instead of letting the reader find it?)."[1] Strauss seems to have put this practice into effect himself when he wrote the "Restatement on Xenophon's *Hiero*."[2] The essay is worlds away from the book it would seem to reprise. *On Tyranny* contains a long and detailed analysis of one of Xenophon's shortest works and operates at an almost microscopic level. The "Restatement" contains a quite short interpretation of Xenophon's longest work, *The Education of Cyrus*, and takes a telescopic view ranging over classical, medieval, and modern epochs. More to the point, Strauss's explicit restatement of his "contention" in *On Tyranny* takes up but one paragraph of the "Restatement" (96). And while he grants that what "seems to be the chief objection to which my study is exposed" can be found in "the gist" of his critics' objections, he states that objection in his own terms, terms foreign to his critics, Eric Voegelin and Alexandre Kojève: namely, that "the attempt to restore classical social science" would seem to be utopian "since it implies that the classical orientation has not been made obsolete by the triumph of the biblical orientation" (95–96). Strauss, according to this formulation, would seem to have forgotten that Athens has apparently given way not to the modernity of London or Florence but somehow to Jerusalem or perhaps even Rome. If this alleged triumph of the biblical orientation is the primary issue Strauss is concerned with in the "Restatement," then the essay is less, as it has often been taken, a defense of classical political philosophy over and against its modern counterpoint than an example of Strauss's abiding and overriding concern with what he once called the theological-political problem, from which perspective the quarrel between ancients and moderns appears more as an intramural squabble than a fundamental conflict. By following this strand of the "Restatement," one sees how it serves as a kind of introduction to his *Thoughts on Machiavelli*, where the relation between politics, religion, and philosophy becomes a central and explicit theme. Certainly its conclusion leads to a more nuanced and perhaps even sympathetic understanding of the origins of Machiavelli's project than what one might get from a cursory reading of *What Is Political Philosophy?* as a whole.[3]

What does Strauss consider to be the classical orientation that may or may not have been made obsolete by the triumph of the biblical orientation? And what does he mean by the triumph of the biblical orientation? Some remarks by Voegelin on Xenophon's *Cyropaedia* provide Strauss with the opportunity to give a remarkably succinct interpretation of that work whose implicit teaching he finds in harmony with Plato's explicit teaching in the *Republic*: the gentleman in the political or social sense is *not* a true gentleman.[4] Strauss understands this proposition to imply that "There is no adequate solution to the problem of virtue or happiness on the political or social plane" (100). If this insight is what Strauss means by the classical orientation, it makes sense that the essay would contain a response to Kojève. Following Hegel, Kojève holds that the best regime, understood as the universal and homogeneous state, can be established to the satisfaction of all, a development that would indeed make the classical orientation obsolete by proving it to have been wrong. In what is the most, or perhaps only, rigorously argued section of the essay (127–33), Strauss disputes this claim in order to show that it is the modern solution that "is utopian in the sense that its actualization is impossible" (132). He goes so far as to argue that inasmuch as the attempt to achieve the modern ideal results in the state of Nietzsche's last man, "Kojève in fact *confirms* the classical view that unlimited technological progress and its accompaniment, which are the indispensable conditions of the universal and homogeneous state, are destructive of humanity" (129, emphasis added; cf. 96). There is an uncharacteristic absence of qualifications from Strauss's

conclusion that the modern solution is impossible (132). If that alleged
solution is what stands in the way of a restoration of the classical view,
it would seem to be an obstacle overcome without great theoretical difficulty, even if opposing it in practice remains hard (133).

Yet is it correct to equate the modern solution with "the triumph of
the biblical orientation"? A Hegelian might hold that modern philosophy,
"which is the secularized form of Christianity" (128), makes possible the
establishment of "the Kingdom of Heaven" in the here and now through
the providential working of History.[5] Thus Strauss claims that for Kojève
"the classical frame of reference must be modified radically by the introduction of an element of Biblical origin." This element "is supplied by
the Biblical morality of Slaves or Workers" (108). Yet this description of
modern philosophy and its solution occur in paragraphs devoted to re-
stating Kojève's views. In his own name, however, Strauss first denies the
exclusively biblical origin of Worker morality and then claims the classics
had a superior understanding of this phenomenon: "What Kojève calls
the pleasure of doing one's work well or from realizing one's projects or
one's ideals, was called by the classics the pleasure deriving from virtuous or noble activity. The classical interpretation would seem to be truer
to the facts" (110; cf. 122). Strauss, in opposition to Kojève,[6] describes
Hegel's thought not as a synthesis of classical and biblical morality but as
a radicalization of certain elements in the tradition of modern philosophy
itself, a nonmiraculous "synthesis of Socratic and Machiavellian or Hobbian politics" that "encourages all statesmen to try to extend their authority over all men in order to achieve universal recognition" (111; cf. 58).[7]
Kojève himself describes his atheistic philosophy as "the *negation* of religious Christianity," a tributary of Paul not because of the Bible's triumph
but only in the sense that having been "negated" it must have been presup-
posed. It is ultimately surpassed. For while History may still be providential, its slaughter-bench operates on a different principle or plane than the
particular providence characteristic of the Bible (e.g., Genesis 13:15–17,
Matthew 10:30). It seems then that we must look elsewhere to find what
Strauss meant by "the triumph of the biblical orientation."

Voegelin also claims that the classical orientation has been made obsolete, but on grounds different from Kojève's. Tyranny as a term of classification and condemnation may well have worked before "the breakdown
of constitutional forms in the city-state," but it was inadequate for the new
political situation confronting Xenophon "when democracy had ceased
to function effectively." Xenophon's shift over the course of the *Hiero*
from using the word "tyrant" to "ruler" suggests he saw the need to drop

an inadequate term, yet he failed to come up with one that could move "beyond the distinction of king and tyrant that is politically significant only before the final breakdown of the republican constitutional order." The "luck" of this discovery was to be Machiavelli's.[8] Therefore not only does Voegelin deny the relevance of the classical frame of reference for understanding "modern tyranny,"[9] he thinks it was inadequate even to the task of understanding the immediate political situation faced by the classical authors themselves, and all this without any mention of the triumph of the biblical orientation.

Strauss defends the classics against Voegelin's charge of obsolescence by defending the adequacy of their understanding of "the phenomenon of Caesarism." Properly understood it is "a sub-division of absolute monarchy." Certain situations can arise where the establishment of absolute rule is the best to be hoped for and therefore cannot be justly blamed. Here Strauss could well have cited chapter and verse from Aristotle or even Xenophon.[10] Instead, he admits that Voegelin's characterization of the classics is in an important respect true: the classics, unlike Machiavelli, did not do much in the way of this line of thought. "The classics could easily have elaborated a doctrine of Caesarism or of late kingship if they had wanted, but they did not want to do it," i.e., they did not do it, even though, as Strauss grants, it is a "true doctrine" based on a "true distinction" (99, 98).[11] Where Strauss and Voegelin differ is in their account of the reasons behind this omission. For Voegelin, the historical situation of the classical authors forced them to grope without success for a doctrine of Caesarism. For Strauss, the failure to state clearly the truth about this aspect of political life was not the result of blindness or bad luck but an act of political responsibility or moderation.

> To stress the fact that it is just to replace constitutional rule by absolute rule, if the common good requires that change, means to cast doubt on the absolute sanctity of the established constitutional order. It means encouraging dangerous men to confuse the issue by bringing about a state of affairs in which the common good requires the establishment of their absolute rule. The true doctrine of the legitimacy of Caesarism is a dangerous doctrine. The true distinction between Caesarism and tyranny is too subtle for ordinary political use. (98)

In the sense in which "the adjective 'political' in the expression 'political philosophy' designates not so much a subject matter as a manner of treatment"—the "deeper meaning of 'political philosophy' "—the classical authors would then be more political; they are more fully self-conscious of their complicated and fragile relation to society at large than an apparently morally obtuse, if not inaccurate, Machiavellianism.[12]

Of course, Machiavellians are not alone in their moral obtuseness; and not all obtuseness stems from accuracy. According to Strauss, certain kinds of historicism share this obtuseness. "The current concept of Caesarism," as opposed to the phenomenon of Caesarism, derives from "19th century historicism" since it is based on the belief that the particular historical situation of any political action is "more fundamental" than whether that action is good or bad. It is inherently relativistic when it also refuses to make any distinction between good and bad historical situations. Thus, like other historicist concepts, it has nothing to say about which is better or more fundamental, the constitutional or postconstitutional situation. In this way, historicism, like the doctrine of Caesarism, casts doubt on the absolute sanctity of the established constitutional order. But historicism is worse than the doctrine of Caesarism. Whereas the doctrine of Caesarism connects the phenomenon to a corrupt people, a low level of political life, and a decline in society, the concept of Caesarism denies the essential character of such distinctions (97–98). Of course, to show that an insight has a corrosive effect on society hardly establishes its falsehood, most especially for Strauss. For him the truth, but not only the truth, can have subversive effects. But while he firmly rejects Kojève's modern solution as "impossible," Strauss leaves the challenge of historicism in suspense by changing the terms of the debate. The question to which he turns, whether "the historical meaning of a work" is to be determined by the historical situation or by the conscious intention or understanding of the author, is a different question, and even this Strauss answers with an ad hominem punt:

> But we cannot be better judges of that situation if we do not have a clearer grasp than he had of the principles in whose light historical situations reveal their meaning. After the experience of our generation, the burden of proof would seem to rest on those who assert rather than on those who deny that we have progressed beyond the classics. (101)

If Voegelin's "19th century historicism" represents "the triumph of the biblical orientation" that makes the classics obsolete, then Strauss's defense here is inadequate. Yet while Strauss admits historicism as a serious antagonist to political philosophy simply, he is equally emphatic that it is a product of modern thought whose origins lie in Machiavelli, not the biblical orientation ("What Is Political Philosophy?," 26, 55, 40). Or might some element of the biblical orientation triumph in modernity through the medium of Machiavelli? Something along these lines would seem to be Voegelin's view.

In his review of *On Tyranny*, Voegelin describes Machiavelli as moving beyond the classics through the introduction of "the non-classical conception of the ruler as the avenger of the misdeeds of a corrupt people," the "apocalyptic" figure of "*the profeta armato*" who takes on "a specific tone through the absorption of such mediaeval-Christian antecedents as the Joachitic *dux*, Dante's *veltro*, and the realization of these ideas in the savior-tribunate of Rienzo."[13] Or, as Strauss summarizes Voegelin's position, "According to Voegelin, it was Machiavelli, as distinguished from the classics, who 'achieved the theoretical creation of a concept of rulership in the post-constitutional situation,' and this achievement was due to the influence on Machiavelli of the Biblical tradition" (101). Voegelin's position stands in considerable opposition to the portrait of Machiavelli in the title essay, "What Is Political Philosophy?" There Strauss admits that while Machiavelli may have imitated Christian means or methods, he did so animated by "anti-theological ire" with the aim of superseding Christianity, of conquering chance, and thereby controlling the future ("What Is Political Philosophy?," 44–46).[14] Sufficient unto the day is the evil thereof was likely not his motto. Thus Machiavelli's innovation consists, not in the transmission or redirection of apocalyptic hopes for a Messiah into secular channels, but in "the rejection of classical political philosophy" and "the abandonment of the contemplative ideal," with all that this entails (103). Yet in the final paragraph of the section of the "Restatement" directed to Voegelin, Strauss is unwilling to close the question of biblical influence altogether. "It is impossible to say how far the epoch-making change that was effected by Machiavelli is due to the indirect influence of the Biblical tradition, before that change has been fully understood in itself" (103), he writes, thus foreshadowing the investigation he was to make in *Thoughts on Machiavelli*: "One cannot see the true character of Machiavelli's thought unless one frees himself from Machiavelli's influence. For all practical purposes this means that one cannot see the true character of Machiavelli's thought unless one recovers for himself and in himself the pre-modern heritage of the western world, both Biblical and classical."[15] Yet the "Restatement" itself contains some indications as to what Strauss might have meant by "the indirect influence of the Biblical." These indications, in turn, shed light on the basis of Machiavelli's "anti-theological ire" and why, despite "the intrepidity of his thought, the grandeur of his vision, and the graceful subtlety of his speech," he was apparently willing to share in and certainly encourage the kind of moral obtuseness that came to be characteristic of nineteenth-century historicism.[16]

Classical political philosophy was not morally obtuse because it understood philosophy to pose a danger to the common opinions necessary for political life. This insight eventually led the classics to engage in philosophic politics, not through the active pursuit of the best regime in which wisdom rules, but instead by

> satisfying the city that the philosophers are not atheists, that they do not desecrate everything sacred to the city, that they reverence what the city reverences, that they are not subversives, in short, that they are not irresponsible adventurers but good citizens and even the best of citizens. (126)

In the essay "What Is Political Philosophy?," Strauss calls Socrates's most impressive contribution to this cause—the decision to sacrifice his life in order to preserve philosophy in Athens—"a political choice of the highest order" (33). In the "Restatement," he claims Plato continued the effort with "a resounding success."

> What Plato did in the Greek city and for it was done in and for Rome by Cicero, whose political action on behalf of philosophy has nothing in common with his actions against Catiline and for Pompey. It was done in and for the Islamic world by Farabi and in and for Judaism by Maimonides. (126–27)

In light of this passage, it is not surprising that the two chapters following the "Restatement" deal with Farabi and Maimonides. Based on the historical outline given in "What Is Political Philosophy?," we might have expected a chapter devoted to Machiavelli (40–49). Instead we have treatments of Hobbes and Locke. But these substitutions make sense. Hobbes "mitigated" Machiavelli's scheme so as to guarantee the success of "Machiavelli's primary intention"; and Locke mitigated Hobbes's "fundamental scheme" to make it more acceptable to common opinion ("What Is Political Philosophy?," 47–48). What is surprising is the absence of a chapter devoted to Thomas Aquinas (or any scholastic), the obvious answer to the obvious question implicitly raised by the sequence of authors Strauss describes in this passage: Did no philosopher perform this political function in and for Christendom?

Aquinas is by no means absent from Strauss's considerations in the book as a whole, nor from the "Restatement" in particular, although he is admittedly not mentioned by name in the latter. The passage most relevant to our question occurs in the review of Anton Pegis's edition of *The Basic Writings of Saint Thomas Aquinas*. While agreeing with Pegis that the fundamental issue at stake in Aquinas is " 'the nature of philosophy itself,' " Strauss thinks this is true only in the sense that "Thomas, in order 'to make the Philosopher a worthy vehicle of reason in Christian thought,' had to give to philosophy itself a meaning fundamentally different from its Aristotelian (or Platonic) meaning: in Thomas, as distinguished from the classical philosophers and certainly from their greatest follower in the Islamic world (Farabi), philosophy is divorced from the conviction that happiness can be achieved only by, or essentially consists in, philosophy" (285). Strauss elsewhere distinguishes Aquinas's view of the natural law from "*the* philosophic view" and wonders whether it might not be better to consider it "as the view of the kalâm or, perhaps, as *the* theological view."[17]

Yet, according to Strauss, "political philosophy" must be distinguished from "political theology," the one based on reason, the other on divine revelation ("What Is Political Philosophy?," 13). By divorcing philosophy from happiness, Aquinas would seem to deprive it of its character as "a way of life," thus making it instrumental and hence more likely to decay into a "teaching" or dogmatic prejudice (91, 109–10, 113, 115–16, 200).[18] Kojève, after all, is not the only or even the first to claim to have synthesized the Bible and classical philosophy in a manner that makes the best regime attainable, to believe that our deepest love can be for a being simply because he is, and to consider satisfaction within the reach of all regardless of their philosophic dispositions.[19] "Syntheses effect miracles," declares a skeptical Strauss when faced with Hegel's system (111). Yet so too do miracles effect syntheses, and perhaps more plausibly so given the power that stands behind them. Not Hegel but Aquinas, or perhaps Christian scholasticism more generally, represents "the triumph of the Biblical orientation" that Strauss thinks may have made the classical orientation obsolete. For, according to Strauss, the synthesis of faith and reason, or the direction and submission of reason to an end disclosed by revelation, means the triumph of faith.[20] Philosophy so understood, no longer standing in opposition to politics and religion, can become genuinely respectable. But this result turns out to be not altogether in harmony with the "class interest of the philosophers qua philosophers."[21] Or, as Strauss elsewhere describes the practical or effective truth of this theoretical state of affairs,

> The official recognition of philosophy in the Christian world made philosophy subject to ecclesiastical supervision. The precarious position of philosophy in the Islamic-Jewish world guaranteed its private character and therewith its inner freedom from supervision. The status of philosophy in the Islamic-Jewish world resembled in this respect its status in classical Greece.[22]

Had Machiavelli understood Christianity simply to have made the world effeminate and thereby contributed to an increase in man's cruelty and inhumanity, had he thought that its deleterious effects were limited to the political sphere, he apparently could have remained within the classical tradition and reinterpreted religion after the fashion of Averroes so as to remedy its political defects, much as Strauss says Maimonides did when the Jews had embraced astrology to the neglect of military discipline (102–3). Yet "by Machiavelli's time the classical tradition had undergone profound changes. The contemplative life had found its home in monasteries" (43). This meant that if the most fundamental difference between the political man and the philosopher is with respect to happiness (117), the most fundamental difference between the philosopher and the man of faith, who could also be a political man, comes to be with respect to eternal beatitude. Faced with this historical situation, Machiavelli rejected "classical political philosophy" and "the contemplative ideal," not simply to protect politics from philosophy and its offspring, but to protect philosophy from what it had become. His antitheological ire would have been motivated at bottom by a prophilosophic love or a clear-sighted pursuit of his genuine class interest.

For Machiavelli to reject "the contemplative ideal" meant for him to change the character of wisdom so that it no longer had "a necessary connection with moderation" (103). Many of Strauss's writings are devoted to exploring the consequences of this separation and to wondering whether it was in fact necessary, and, if not, whether a return to the classical understanding is possible or desirable. The "Restatement" confirms what he stated more explicitly elsewhere: that he considered the biblical claim to supply "that sufficient knowledge of the idea of the good which is indispensable for the actualization of the perfect social order" to be the chief obstacle to such a return.[23] But the "Restatement" also shows Strauss to be mindful of the role the classics played in creating the conditions that led to their rejection, and thus perhaps more sympathetic to Machiavelli's rejection of their authority than is often understood.

If Aquinas's synthesis of faith and reason eliminated or diluted the tension between religion and politics on the one hand, and philosophy on the other, [24] and in doing so obscured the question "What is the right way of life?," this dilution by means of synthesis seems to have been anticipated by Aristotle's "natural right teaching," of which it "can safely be said" that it maintains that "there is no fundamental disproportion between natural right and the requirements of political society."[25] But Aristotle's teaching must be viewed in light of his desire to treat "each of the various levels of beings, and hence especially every level of human life, on its own terms." He differs from Plato, who "never discusses any subject—be it the city, or the heavens, or numbers —without having in mind the elementary Socratic question, 'What is the best way of life?'" This means that when Aristotle "discusses justice, he discusses justice as everyone knows it and as it is understood in political life, and he refuses to be drawn into the dialectical whirlpool that carries us far beyond justice in the ordinary sense of the term toward the philosophical life." But this sobriety comes at a price. For it leads us not to light but rather twilight, although humanely and responsibly so, since it is "twilight which is essential to human life as merely human."[26]

If Aristotle's synthesis of "natural right and the requirements of political society" may have anticipated Aquinas's synthesis of reason and faith, Strauss suggests in the "Restatement" that both may find a common source or inspiration in Plato. Strauss first declares Plato's "defense of philosophy before the tribunal of the city a resounding success," which ultimately became "a full success" (126–27). He then immediately wonders "whether it has not been too successful," that is, not altogether a success. Strauss helps us to see more clearly what he understood by Plato's success with a reference to the account found in Plutarch's *Life of Nicias* (126).

> People would not then [in Nicias's day] tolerate natural philosophers, and thinkers, as they then called them, about things above, as lessening the divine power, by explaining away its agency into the operation of irrational causes and senseless forces acting by necessity, without anything of Providence or a free agent. Hence it was that Protagoras was banished, and Anaxagoras cast in prison, so that Pericles had much difficulty to procure his liberty; and Socrates, though he had no concern whatever with this sort of learning, yet was put to death for philosophy. It was only afterwards that the reputation of Plato, shining forth by his life, *and because he subjected natural necessity to divine and more excellent principles*, took away the obloquy and scandal that had attached to such contemplations, and obtained these studies currency among all people.[27]

If Plato's submission of natural necessity to divine and more excellent principles was not his considered view but rather a political act intended to protect philosophy by taking away the obloquy and scandal attached to it at some particular time and place, a similar submission within a different historical context might no longer protect but even threaten philosophy. This seems to have been what happened in the Christian world, according to Strauss, where the official recognition of philosophy—to say nothing of the prevalence of a "popular" understanding of the "philosophic attitude" as detachment from "all things which are exposed to the power of chance"—made it possible to blur the distinction between philosopher and saint, between thinking and believing (122). While such a development can no doubt help to take away the obloquy and scandal attached to philosophy, the approval of society that it makes possible turns out to be a danger even greater than that of banishment and prison, given society's greater power to compromise the potential philosopher's "inner freedom."[28] Perhaps no other example than this "too successful" success of making philosophy an integral part of the established order better illustrates the view that no solution to the relationship between philosophy and political life can be definitive. Pathological, if unintended and unforeseen, consequences are not the exclusive preserve of the moderns.[29] The only things permanent are problems.

A more conspicuous example in the "Restatement" of a philosophic doctrine that undermines philosophy is that of the "world state." In the original version of the essay published in *De la tyrannie*, Strauss devoted a paragraph to sketching how Kojève goes about proving that "the only non-tyrannical regime is the universal and homogeneous state."[30] According to Strauss, Kojève begins from the principle of justice understood as "equal opportunity" or "from each according to his capacity, to each according to his merit." But as there is no good reason for assuming the capacity for meritorious action to be bound up with sex, beauty, race, country of origin, wealth, and so on, discrimination on the basis of sex, ugliness, and so on is unjust. Therefore, "only a state which is not only homogeneous but universal as well, can be simply just or non-tyrannical. In fact, only the universal state can be truly homogeneous or 'classless.' "[31] Strauss cut this "proof" of Kojève's thesis from the essay when he published it as the "Restatement" in *What Is Political Philosophy?* But he did not discard it. He reworked it into the chapter "Classical Natural Right" in *Natural Right and History*. Yet there he presents the thesis not as Kojève's but as the view of the classics, and in particular that of Plato. Plato, however, understood the thesis not as the sound basis on which to found universal politics but instead as a deduction showing that the problem of justice "obviously transcends the limits of political life" and that no human society can avoid "self-contradiction."[32] Or, as Strauss wrote in *De la tyrannie*, if the *Republic* "represents the closest approach in classical thought to an understanding of a non-tyrannical state," it nevertheless remains at some distance from the ideal.[33] Indeed, that ideal itself would seem to be a perfection or purification not of justice simply but of "the justice of the city," which as such remains, like Aristotle's natural right teaching, on the same level as the city rather than being transformed "by the dialectical whirlpool that carries us far beyond justice in the ordinary sense of the term toward the philosophic life." The ideal is therefore not one that Plato, or even Aristotle,[34] worked to attain. Were philosophers to pursue the actual establishment of the world state, they would present the sorry spectacle of philosophy working to destroy itself, or at least the conditions that make it possible or more likely, for the sake of achieving an ideal never intended to be realized in practice.

This explains why Strauss's most emphatic criticism of the universal and homogeneous state is that it would bring about "the end of philosophy on earth," that is, it would prove unjust in the extraordinary or precise sense of the term (133). His characterization of Kojève as a philosopher and not an intellectual—he "belongs to the very few who know how to think and who love to think" (104)—allows Strauss to play the Marxist card against him, playfully implying that he suffers from false consciousness and in fact betrays his own true class.[35] More seriously, Kojève fails "to distinguish between philosophic politics and the political action which the philosopher might undertake with a view to establishing the best regime or the improvement of the actual order" (127). This distinction is crucial for understanding Strauss's own politics.

If "opinion is the element of society," and the diffusion among the unwise of genuine knowledge "inevitably transforms itself into opinion, prejudice, or mere belief" (122), then society will remain forever mutable, almost infinitely so.[36] And if "philosophic politics" consists in satisfying society that "the philosophers are not atheists, that they do not desecrate everything sacred to the city, that they reverence what the city reverences, that they are not subversives, in short, that they are not irresponsible adventurers but good citizens and even the best of citizens," then philosophic politics must itself be similarly flexible. Or, as Strauss describes the situation, "the problem of what the philosopher should do in regard to the city remains, therefore, an open question, the subject of an unfinishable discussion" (127). Strauss comes close here to articulating a historicist or contextualist understanding of the philosophers' politics. And it is a mistake to think that he is primarily interested in praising or blaming the actions of a Machiavelli, an Aquinas, or a Plato. But he does not think the embrace of philosophic trimming need lead to the kind of moral obtuseness or relativism he considered characteristic of "19th century historicism." For Strauss, in contrast to this kind of historicism, still maintains that there are better or worse historical situations or epochs, by which he means better or worse for philosophy. A cave beneath a cave is worse than a cave.[37] This latter consideration provides a standard for evaluation and at least one of the principles by whose light "historical situations reveal their meaning" (101; cf. "Political Philosophy and History," 63, 66).

It would be odd if Strauss, who wrote as he read, did not also practice what he preached with regard to philosophic politics. In the "Restatement" itself, Strauss makes an effort in the direction of the Platonic "solution" of harmonizing divine and natural necessities when he gives a "popular and hence unorthodox" account of the philosopher's apparently disinterested and beneficent urge to educate those with the same potential. He asserts that the souls of men are "most akin" to the eternal order, and a good or healthy soul reflects that order more than one that is chaotic or disordered. Now precisely because the philosopher "has had a glimpse of the eternal order," he is intensely pleased or pained by the aspect of a healthy or disordered soul "without regard to his own needs or benefits." And since "the good order of the soul is philosophizing," he therefore has the urge to educate potential philosophers simply because he cannot help loving well-ordered souls. What could be more decent or less subversive than encouraging well-ordered souls to be in harmony with "the eternal cause or causes of the whole"? Yet having shown himself aware of the problems to which this kind of Platonizing can give rise, and also aware that such "pre-Victorian *niaiseries*" will find little purchase in contemporary society, Strauss immediately retracts his assertion that the well-ordered soul is more akin to the eternal order than is the chaotic soul. He characterizes such claims as boasting, and "we know how ugly or deformed a boaster's soul is" (121–22). In other words, "political philosophy" understood as the apologetic or political, or popular, treatment of philosophy should not prevent or unduly interfere with "political philosophy" understood as "the attempt to lead the qualified citizens, or rather their qualified sons, from the political life to the philosophic life" ("On Classical Political Philosophy," 94).

Strauss's presentation of Socrates in *On Tyranny* provides a different example of his philosophic politics, indeed, one that attempts to harmonize the apologetic and propaideutic aspects of political philosophy without recourse to divine principles. Political philosophy ought to satisfy the city that the philosophers are good citizens. What better way to do so than to present Socrates, in contrast to the wandering stranger Simonides, as emphatically a "citizen-philosopher,"[38] and to defend oneself "the prosaic maxim that the just is identical with the legal" (101)? But this also means that Socrates could not "with propriety be presented as praising tyranny under any circumstances," or entrusted with a "discussion of the problematic character of 'the rule of law.'" Important as they may be, these issues are better handled by a noncitizen. Thus, according to Strauss, "Simonides fulfills in the *Corpus Xenophonteum* a function comparable to that fulfilled in the *Corpus Platonicum* by the stranger from Elea."[39]

Strauss gives grounds even in *On Tyranny* to doubt whether he actually thought Socrates was essentially a "citizen-philosopher." After all, it is the tyrant Hiero who proves to be "at bottom a citizen."[40] And while the citizen as such would not accept the view that a nonpolitical good such as friendship is more valuable than the city, Strauss states that "it remains to be considered whether it was acceptable to citizen philosophers."[41] In *On Tyranny*, Strauss limits himself to showing that the exile Xenophon esteemed certain things more highly than Greece.[42] The "Restatement" contains a more direct consideration of Socrates's relation to the city that confirms this doubt and in doing so might well provide the essay's most important supplement or corrective to *On Tyranny*.

According to the "Restatement," the classics did not regard the conflict between philosophy and the city as tragic. Or "Xenophon at any rate seems to have viewed that conflict in the light of Socrates' relation to Xanthippe" (127). Yet if, as Socrates himself suggests, there is no essential difference between the city and the family, and if, as Strauss affirms, "the thesis of Friedrich Mentz, *Socrates nec officiosus maritus nec laudandus paterfamilias* (Leipzig, 1716), is defensible," then Socrates would also seem to have been a bad citizen (116). Or worse, since Xenophon refrains in his *Symposium* from counting Socrates among the married men, even though that dialogue contains a lengthy discussion of his relations to Xanthippe, Socrates would appear not to have been a citizen at all. Indeed, the stranger from Elea, whom Strauss distinguished from Socrates and associated with Simonides in *On Tyranny*, turns out, in *What Is Political Philosophy?*, to be indistinguishable from Socrates, at least when Socrates takes to the road ("What Is Political Philosophy?," 33).

Is political philosophy then, at least as understood and practiced by Strauss, simply misleading? This seems to me to go too far, or at any rate

to miss the difference between leading and misleading. Any political solution to the relation between philosophy and politics is necessarily incomplete and imperfect. But this does not mean that there are not better
or worse efforts to be made even if such efforts are conditional or relative to the times. Strauss praises Xenophon's use of the maxim that the
just is identical to the legal, but he refrains from employing it himself.
Contemporary conditions make it untenable or even counterproductive.[43]
Yet, according to Strauss, "if one is concerned with understanding the
problem of justice, one must go through the stage in which justice presents itself as identical with citizen-morality and one must not merely rush
that stage."[44] The presentation of Socrates as citizen-philosopher in *On
Tyranny*, while admittedly incomplete, serves as a check on our merely
rushing through that stage and therefore as an obstacle to our too quick
embrace or premature ascent to cosmopolitan political principles such as
those professed by Kojève, perhaps even to universal professions or doctrines of any kind. For "every faith that lays claim to universality, i.e., to
be universally accepted, of necessity provokes a counter-faith which raises
the same claim" (112). If so, Strauss's "Restatement" combines political
rhetoric with philosophic pedagogy in a manner different from but worthy of his "*spezieller Liebling*," Xenophon, whose own presentation of
philosophy has the merit of having given rise to no particular faith at all
(Strauss 2001, 567).

Notes

1. Strauss (2001, 581).

2. Chapter 4 of *What Is Political Philosophy?*, first published in the French translation of *On Tyranny* along with Alexandre Kojève's *Tyrannie et sagesse* (1954).

3. See, e.g., the reviews of *What Is Political Philosophy?* by Louis Wasserman
(1960, 289), Steven Muller (1960, 458), and Gerhart Niemeyer (1961, 103).

4. Cf. Strauss (2001, letter 97, 18 August 1939), "The agreements [of Xenophon]
with Plato are astounding, sometimes so astounding that astounded one asks: are
Xenophon and Plato two different persons?"

5. See Kojève's "Tyranny and Wisdom" (Strauss 1991, 172–73).

6. "In fact, the *universal* State is the one goal which *politics*, entirely under the
twin influence of ancient pagan *philosophy* and Christian *religion*, has pursued,
although it has so far never attained it" (Strauss 1991, 173).

7. This sentence "repeats" an earlier description of Kojève's view but replaces
the phrase "genuine synthesis" with "synthesis" (105). Strauss also says that to
present Hegel as a synthesis of biblical and classical morality requires Kojève "to
suppress his better knowledge" (111).

8. Voegelin (1949, 241–42).

9. Voegelin (1949, 243).

10. E.g., Aristotle *Politics*, 1285b29–33, 1287b36–11288a5; but cf. 1284a3–10, 1284b25–34. Also see Xenophon, *Education of Cyrus*, 8.1–3.

11. Thus Strauss is tempted to adopt Voegelin's version of the distinction, "post-constitutional," to describe Salazar's rule in Portugal (107).

12. Strauss (1959, 93–94, cf. 10).

13. Voegelin (1949, 243).

14. "The *only* element of Christianity which Machiavelli took over was the idea of propaganda. This idea is the *only* link between his thought and Christianity. . . . It goes without saying that Machiavelli's *imitatio Christi* was *limited to this point*" (Strauss 1959, 45, emphasis added).

15. Cf. Strauss (1958, 12) with Strauss (1959, 288, 289, 297).

16. Strauss (1958, 13).

17. Strauss (1952, 97–98).

18. See Meier (2006, 59).

19. While it is true that "neither Biblical nor classical morality encourages *all* statesmen to try to extend their authority over all men in order to achieve universal recognition," the Christian synthesis of both might have encouraged some one to do so (111, emphasis added). Again, Strauss would seem to have the papacy in mind when he writes of the improbability (not impossibility) of convincing the people to submit "to perpetual and absolute rule by a succession of wise men" rather than a code of laws (113).

20. "For a philosophy based on faith is no longer philosophy" (Strauss and Cropsey 1987, 279).

21. Strauss (1953, 143). On overcoming the antipathy between philosophy and politics, consider Strauss's remarks in his essay on John Wild: "[Wild's] admission that philosophy has an essentially fragmentary character is merely the prelude to a suggestion that philosophy must be subordinate to theology. *Only* on the basis of such a suggestion can he maintain within the Platonic framework the natural harmony between philosophy and politics and at the same time deny the possibility of direct and adequate knowledge of 'the supreme principle'; for what cannot be achieved by philosophy left to itself may be achieved by philosophy illumined by theology. Divine revelation, and not philosophy, supplies that sufficient knowledge of the idea of the good which is indispensable for the actualization of the perfect social order" (Strauss 1946, 362–63, emphasis added).

22. Strauss (1952, 21).

23. Strauss (1946, 363).

24. In the French version of the "Restatement," Strauss wrote: "le rapport entre la moralité, le droit de la cité, et la religion est si clair qu'il est inutile d'insister" (Strauss 1954, 333).

25. Strauss (1953, 156).

26. Strauss (1953, 156–57).

27. Plutarch's *Life of Nicias* (n.d., section 23 emphasis added).

28. "According to Socrates, the greatest enemy of philosophy, the greatest Sophist, is the political multitude" (Strauss 1983, 88; cf. 1959, 39).

29. Strauss was concerned with this difficulty or weakness in classical political philosophy at least as early as 1933–34. "Hobbes founded his political science in opposition to two frequently but not always allied traditions: the tradition of philosophic politics, whose originator was for him *Socrates*, and the tradition of theological politics, which appeals to revelation. . . . If order and peace were finally to come about, what was required, as it seemed, was a politics resting solely on the self-sufficient reflection of man. Such a politics had been elaborated by classical philosophy. But the philosophic politics that rested on the foundations conceived by Socrates had not only not refused an association with theology; it had also not *been able* to refuse this; in any case it had provided theological politics with some of its most dangerous weapons" (Strauss 2011, 26, 28, emphases in the original).

30. Strauss (1954, 309, my translation).

31. Strauss (1954, 311).

32. Strauss (1953, 149–51).

33. Strauss (1954, 310). This also suggests that the real title of *On Tyranny* that the reader is to find for himself might perhaps be *On the Nature of Political Society*.

34. Strauss (1953, 23).

35. "Philosophers as philosophers do not go with their families" (Strauss 1953, 143).

36. Strauss (1952, 222).

37. Strauss (1995, 136, 58; 1952, 155)

38. Strauss (1991, 77, 104, 87, 105).

39. Strauss (1991, 77).

40. Strauss (1991, 76).

41. Strauss (1991, 97–98).

42. Strauss (1991, 98).

43. Cf. Strauss (1953, 4 n. 2; 1964, 76).

44. Strauss (1953, 150 n. 24).

Works Cited

Aristotle. 1984. *The Politics*. Trans. Carnes Lord. Chicago: University of Chicago Press.

Meier, Heinrich. 2006. *Leo Strauss and the Theological-Political Problem*. Cambridge: Cambridge University Press.

Muller, Steven. 1960. "Review: *What Is Political Philosophy?*" *Political Science Quarterly* 75 (3): 457–60.

Niemeyer, Gerhart. 1961. "Review: *What Is Political Philosophy?*" *Review of Politics* 23 (1): 101–7.

Plutarch. n.d. *The Lives of the Noble Grecians and Romans.* Trans. John Dryden. Revised by Arthur Hugh Clough. New York: Modern Library.

Strauss, Leo. 1946. "On a New Interpretation of Plato's Political Philosophy." *Social Research* 13 (–3): 326–67.

———. 1952. *Persecution and the Art of Writing.* Glencoe, IL: Free Press.

———. 1953. *Natural Right and History.* Chicago: University of Chicago Press.

———. 1954. "Tyrannie et sagesse." In *De la tyrannie.* Paris: Gallimard.

———. 1958. *Thoughts on Machiavelli.* Chicago: University of Chicago Press.

———. 1959. *What Is Political Philosophy? and Other Studies.* New York: Free Press.

———. 1964. *The City and Man.* Chicago: Rand McNally.

———. 1983. *Studies in Platonic Political Philosophy.* Ed. Thomas Pangle. Chicago: University of Chicago Press.

———. 1991. *On Tyranny.* Ed. Victor Gourevitch and Michael S. Roth. New York: Free Press. Original edition, 1948.

———. 1995. *Philosophy and Law: Contributions to the Understanding of Maimonides and His Predecessors.* Trans. Eve Adler. Ed. Kenneth Hart Green. SUNY Series in the Jewish Writings of Leo Strauss. Albany: SUNY Press.

———. 2001. *Gesammelte Schriften,* vol. 3: *Hobbes' politische Wissenschaft und zugehorige Schriften—Briefe.* Ed. Heinrich Meier and Wiebke Meier. Stuttgart: J. B. Metzler.

———. 2011. *Hobbes's Critique of Religion and Related Writings.* Trans. Gabriel Bartlett and Svetozar Minkov. Chicago: University of Chicago Press.

Strauss, Leo, and Joseph Cropsey. 1987. *History of Political Philosophy.* 3rd ed. Chicago: University of Chicago Press.

Voegelin, Eric. 1949. "Review of *On Tyranny.*" *Review of Politics* 11: 241–44.

Wasserman, Louis. 1960. "Review: *What Is Political Philosophy?*" *Western Political Quarterly* 13 (3): 839–40.

Xenophon. 2001. *Cyropaedia.* Trans. Wayne Ambler. Ithaca, NY: Cornell University Press.

CHAPTER FIVE

How Strauss Read Farabi's *Summary of Plato's "Laws"*

Daniel Tanguay

Before we begin the difficult and unsettling examination of chapter 5 of *What Is Political Philosophy?*, a few general remarks on the work itself and on Strauss's philosophic style are useful. Strauss's writings can be classified in two broad categories: on the one hand are those he envisioned from the start as unified works reflecting a specific purpose; and on the other, those that are collections of texts and articles written without any clear or apparent intention to include them later in a unified single volume. Strauss's earliest works, some of the writings that assured his reputation in the United States, and most of his mature writing can be included in the first category.[1] In the second are various collections of articles that Strauss published in book form, ranging from *Persecution and the Art of Writing* (1952) to *The City and Man* (1964), and including *What Is Political Philosophy?* (1959). These two categories, however, are not airtight. We can, for example, question the precise place for *Natural Right and History* (1953), which began as a thoroughly revised collection of notes from six lectures given at the University of Chicago in 1949. In the same way, we could also demonstrate that it is difficult as well as somewhat artificial to apply the criterion of a unified intent to many of Strauss's monographs. Why should we assign a greater unified intention, for example, to *Thoughts on Machiavelli* (1958) than to such a carefully conceived and accomplished work as *Persecution and the Art of Writing*?

So we cannot be too dogmatic about the apparent division of Strauss's *œuvre*. It is useful only to the extent that it helps us to understand a problem that occurs with every author, particularly in the academic world, who considers publishing a volume of texts previously published separately over the years, possibly along with unpublished lecture notes or scientific papers. Authors find themselves wanting to give to their assembly of often disparate contributions an overall unity that was always not present when the original texts were written. It goes without saying that such a unity is usually more or less explicitly present and *a fortiori* in the case of a writer like Strauss who tries to create a body of work based on a tireless search for a deeper understanding of the answers to a few key questions. But this does not ease two difficult problems faced by Strauss when he put together *What Is Political Philosophy?*—what would be the book's unifying theme and how does the organization of the different parts throw light on this theme?

Such questions are treated in the introduction and in virtually every chapter of this volume. We would like to touch on them here only to the extent that they can help us understand the place that Strauss himself gave chapter 5 in his overall argument in the book. The obvious intention of the work is to answer the question indicated by its title: what is political philosophy? The very act of posing the question again implies that it has been forgotten for a host of reasons that Strauss intends to explore. So Strauss must find and recover its original meaning. He must return to the question as first formulated by Greek philosophy at the birth of political philosophy.

In the first four chapters of his work Strauss gives us the results of his efforts to overcome various obstacles to the rediscovery of political philosophy. In the two chapters at the center of his work, Strauss discusses the usefulness of certain medieval authors, particularly those belonging to Jewish or Muslim traditions, in showing us how to access the original question posed by the originators of political philosophy as well as informing us about the obstacles they too had to overcome. In chapters 7 and 8 Strauss returns to the modern authors who responded most strongly to and made the conscious attempt to overcome the classical solution to the essential problem of political philosophy. Chapter 9 permits us to understand how a certain skill in reading the ancient authors enables us to understand the true meaning of political philosophy. Chapter 10 seems to point toward the fundamental problem that is discreetly present throughout the work: the tension between political philosophy and philosophy itself and how to determine the true starting point to the philosophical quest. The sixteen book reviews assembled at the end form a sort of appendix to the work where the reader can delve into the information needed to clarify some of Strauss's propositions.[2]

Any reader familiar with Strauss knows how important he considered the plan of a work for its interpretation. Strauss also repeatedly drew the attention of his readers to the importance of the central chapters of a work for understanding the author's deepest intention. To the extent that we can suspect Strauss practiced a style corresponding to the art of writing that he claimed to have rediscovered, we can postulate that chapter 5 constitutes with chapter 6 the central pillars of the work, expressing Strauss's deepest thinking on its key question—what is political philosophy? Well, the reader who expected a clear and direct answer will be disappointed. He will not find in these chapters the powerful rhetoric and dialectic arguments used by Strauss in the earlier chapters to induce him or her to give political philosophy all its due.

The reader will no longer confront philosophical theses that carry to the same degree the personal seal of their author. He or she will not experience the same philosophical delight experienced in chapter 4 where Strauss responds with nobility and boldness to Alexandre Kojève and explains, perhaps better than anywhere else in his entire corpus, what is the ultimate task of political philosophy. Chapter 5, in contrast, gives the reader the impression of being an exercise in futile erudition devoted to an obscure text by a philosopher known today only to a limited number of specialists in medieval Arab thought.[3] After several pages, most will probably feel lost in a strange land and without a compass to guide them. Moreover, Strauss does nothing to ease the reader's task: he even appears to multiply obstacles so as to lead astray those readers who are not yet ready to "bear the toil of study and meditation." One would be sorely tempted to skip this chapter in search of other, more familiar territories easier of access.

It would be pretentious to affirm that we are among the sort of readers that Strauss addressed in such writings. We can perhaps console ourselves with the fact that such readers are rare indeed. We need to practice a specific art of reading over a long period of time to move easily and with sure judgment along the different levels of interpretation contained in a text like "How Fârâbî Read Plato's *Laws*." To get an idea of the difficulty of this task, one has only to consider Strauss's introductory remarks on Farabi's commentary on Plato's *Laws*.[4] The form of this commentary is surprising at first: it is not about the entire work known as the *Laws* of Plato (the subject of the commentary is restricted to only the first nine books). There is no discussion of all the elements found in the *Laws*, and there is some discussion of elements that cannot be found in it! In fact, the commentary often takes the form of a simple paraphrase of certain elements found in Plato's *Laws*. At first glance, then, the purpose of this commentary appears to be not to explain the whole book but instead to suggest to the reader the essential elements of what such an explanation should be. At least that's how Strauss describes Farabi's intention for us: "Fârâbî resolved to bring to light, or to extract, some of the thoughts to which Plato had alluded in his *Laws* or, as he also says, to bring to light, or to extract, some of the thoughts which Plato had intended to explain in his *Laws* (4,19–20; 43,6–9). For to allude to a thought means, not indeed to explain that thought, but to intend to explain it; whether or not the intention is consummated depends decisively, not on the author, but on the reader" (137; cf. 140–42).[5] If we follow the interpretive path proposed by Strauss, a question comes immediately to mind: what precisely is the status of Strauss's own interpretation? Does it consist solely in bringing to light some thoughts to which Farabi alluded concerning what Plato had already mentioned in the *Laws*? Or is Strauss using the allusions to guide the reader to his or her own conclusions about the philosophic questions at the heart of Farabi's commentary?

This illustrates some of the dangers faced by an interpreter of Strauss's thought. At any moment we risk losing ourselves in a labyrinth of suppositions, allusions, and the imperceptible slide of meanings, subtext, and half-veiled indices, never again to find our way out of this maze of references to texts, each one more obscure than the previous one. It goes without saying that Strauss left no trail of breadcrumbs behind for the reader. At best, we can offer a few indications that may aid the understanding of the philosophical questions that emerge from between the lines of the text and that resonate with the book's general theme. We do not offer a systematic analysis of Strauss's essay. And we certainly do not do a Strauss-type commentary on a commentary on a commentary. We propose instead to return to the text itself so as to provide a more general context that can help suggest a preliminary appreciation and perhaps even some encouragement to return to it.

Strauss's Farabi

Over the past twenty years or so, many works have shown the important influence of Muslim and Jewish philosophy on the thought of Strauss.[6] From the time of his first work on Spinoza, Strauss was concerned both with Maimonides and with questions about prophetology. His interest in Maimonides led him back to the Muslim philosophers—Avicenna, Averroes, and then Farabi. Strauss was one of the first to recognize the importance of Farabi for a general understanding of medieval Muslim and Jewish philosophy. In *What Is Political Philosophy?*, Strauss underlines the fact that Farabi was considered by Maimonides as second only to Aristotle as a philosophic authority (163). In his opinion, any serious study of medieval Muslim and Jewish philosophy should thus necessarily include an examination of the work of Farabi, who transmitted the teachings of Plato and adapted them to the context of Islam.[7] But this study faced a very serious obstacle. Farabi's work was known only in a fragmentary way, and the available editions of his writings were often not trustworthy.

Our understanding of Farabi has greatly increased since the pioneering work by Strauss and a few others in the 1930s.[8] But we are astounded by all that Strauss was able to draw from the fragmentary writings of Farabi available at the time. In fact it was during this period that Strauss first presented an overall interpretation of Farabi's work that scarcely changed over the years that followed. It was only enriched by the publication of texts by Farabi on Plato that had not been widely available previously, especially in the famous collection *Corpus Platonicum Medii Aevi. Plato Arabus*. It was volume 2 of this collection, titled *Alfarabius. De Platonis Philosophia* (1943), that paved the way for the most important text that Strauss wrote about Farabi, "Fârâbî's *Plato*";[9] and the publication of volume 3, *Alfarabius. Compendium Legum Platonis*, led Straus to write the interpretive essay contained in *What Is Political Philosophy?* It proved to be the last word Strauss wrote on Farabi.

The interpretations by Strauss of Farabi's work are specific, and Strauss did not deal in detail with all aspects of Farabi's works. In general, it can be said that Strauss neglects what many other interpreters of Farabi consider essential—the essays on metaphysics, cosmology, or epistemology. If Strauss has an interpretation of Farabi's total work, it is selective in that he emphasizes certain writings to the detriment of others and chooses to validate certain themes and questions that may appear secondary with respect to the whole corpus.

Strauss's basic interpretive choice is to favor those of Farabi's writings which comment on Plato's works as opposed to those in which he presents his doctrine in his own name. Strauss justifies this interpretive choice primarily by arguing that given the religious and political context of Farabi's time, he explained his unorthodox teachings in his "historical" rather than in his "philosophical" writings: "Fârâbî avails himself then of the specific immunity of the commentator, or of the historian, in order to speak his mind concerning grave matters in his 'historical' works rather than in the works setting forth what he presents as his own doctrine. This being the case, one has to lay down, and scrupulously to follow, this canon of interpretation: Apart from purely philologic and other preliminary considerations, one is not entitled to interpret the *Plato* or any part or passage of it, by having recourse to Fârâbî's other writings" (Strauss 1945, 375). Since Strauss has adopted such an interpretive canon, his interpretation clashes necessarily with other interpretations inspired by the modern historical method. Strauss presupposes that Farabi used a specific art of writing that requires of the reader the practice of an art of reading and interpreting that is just as specific.

So in Strauss's opinion, Farabi expresses his deepest thought in his commentaries on Plato. And Strauss further considers that the work by Farabi revealing the essential elements retained from Plato's teaching is *The Philosophy of Plato, Its Parts, the Ranks of Order of Its Parts, from the Beginning to the End.* At a crucial moment in "How Fârâbî Read Plato's *Laws*," Strauss mentions that to understand the underlying sense of the Farabi's *Summary of Plato's "Laws,"* attention must be paid to what is not said. The best way to understand what Farabi omits in the *Summary* is to compare what he says there with what he says in the *Philosophy of Plato* (138–39, 152–54). For example, Farabi does not mention in the *Summary* philosophy, the philosopher, or any expressions that can be linked to philosophy, although philosophy and the philosophic way of life are the themes of the *Philosophy of Plato.* So the *Summary* does not deal with the most elevated subjects of philosophic speculations and does not explicitly advance the idea that philosophy is a sufficient and necessary condition for human happiness or that it represents all that is best in humanity. The *Summary* deals with what the *Philosophy of Plato* omits: God, the gods, life after death, revealed law, or divine law. Strauss has a striking formula for the relationship that he sees between Farabi's two works: "The relation between the *Philosophy of Plato* and the *Summary* reflects the relation between philosophy and the divine law as between two entirely different worlds" (139).

The latter sentence is perhaps the key to the entire chapter. It returns us to the famous conflict between Athens and Jerusalem that is at the heart of Strauss's thought. This conflict surfaces here in a context—that of the political and social domination of a particular kind of law, the Islamic law—specific to Farabi. In the book's preceding chapter, Strauss tries to defend the idea of the independence of philosophers and their politics against Kojève's attempt to destroy philosophic alienation from the world by making philosophers the agents of real political power. Strauss maintains, to the contrary, that philosophers have always developed a political philosophy that assured their freedom of thought by convincing the city that they were good citizens: "This defense of philosophy before the tribunal of the city was achieved by Plato with a resounding success (Plutarch, *Nicias*, chap. 23). The effects have lasted down to the present throughout all ages except the darkest ones. What Plato did in the Greek city and for it was done in and for Rome by Cicero, whose political action on behalf of philosophy has nothing in common with his actions against Catiline and for Pompey, for example. It was done in and for the Islamic world by Fârâbî and in and for Judaism by Maimonides" (126–27).

In this passage, Strauss retraces an entire tradition of philosophy that goes back to Plato, a tradition that both defends philosophy and preserves the city. Philosophy has faced various political and religious challenges that have forced it to adapt its rhetoric before the court of the city, but at the same time, this rhetoric has never ignored what properly belonged to the city. The *Laws* of Plato are concerned with this rhetoric, and in a certain way Farabi's commentary represents an adaptation of this political rhetoric in favor of philosophy to a new situation.

If Farabi is truly a follower of Plato, it is in the specific sense that he too—as Strauss clearly indicates—tried to defend philosophy before the court of the city. One may even add that Strauss was led to understand the deepest meaning of Platonic political philosophy by reading Farabi. At least that is the impression we get from reading the final pages of chapter 5, where Strauss returns for the third and final time in the text to the relationship between the *Summary* and the *Philosophy of Plato*. Without getting into the subtleties of Strauss's interpretation, we can underline a fundamental distinction that our author finds in Farabi: a distinction between the Socratic and the Platonic paths of thought. The Socratic, that of philosophy in action, requires of the philosopher an open break with the opinions of the city. Socrates, who claims to be possessed by the *mania* for philosophy, appears unconcerned with the effect of his constant questioning of the dearest-held convictions of his fellow citizens on his own reputation. Plato would correct the direction taken by Socrates.[10] Plato certainly does not abandon his master's philosophic *mania*, but he wants to make it acceptable to the people. In this way, Plato combines Socrates's philosophical dialectic with Thrasymachus's rhetoric "which is appropriate for the philosopher's relations to the vulgar" (153). Thus Plato's path requires a certain conformity on the philosopher's part with commonly held opinions. In this respect, Plato's *Laws* can be seen as the most perfect expression in his philosophical writings of his correction to Socrates's course.

This latter suggestion can help us understand another of Strauss's essential claims about the relationship of the *Philosophy of Plato* to the *Summary*: "The *Philosophy of Plato* presents Plato's philosophy whereas the *Summary* presents his art of *kalâm*" (139). This is a surprising suggestion to the extent that the concept of *kalâm* refers to an entire current within Islamic thought that is aimed mainly at a rationalistic defense of the principles of law and religion against the opinions of the philosophers.[11] The exercise of *kalâm* presupposes then the acceptance of the revelation of the law by the Prophet. Thus the art of *kalâm* presented by Farabi can only be of a peculiar nature, because Plato in his *Laws* was incapable of defending a "revelation" that occurred long centuries after his death. So Plato's *kalâm* has a particular nature and can be called *kalâm* only as an analogy. It is a kind of *kalâm* specific to the defenders of philosophy and not to the defenders of religion.

Is Strauss trying to say that the *Laws* contains a teaching that could have the same function, in relation to Islam for example, as the Law itself? Such a teaching could claim to be true for all time. This sheds light on the opposition noted earlier between philosophy and the divine law. Platonic political philosophy did not just provide the *falâsifa* with a framework for the political-theological interpretation of divine law. It obliged Muslim believers to question the basic assumptions of the Law. So Strauss presents three possible responses by the "Muslim reader" to this challenge posed by Plato's *Laws*: "He could reject Plato's claim by contending that Plato lacked completely the guidance supplied by Revelation. He could use the Platonic standards for judging, or criticizing, specific Islamic institutions, if not for rejecting Islam altogether. He could contend that Islam, and Islam alone, lives up to the true standards set forth by Plato, and on this basis elaborate a purely rational justification of both the content and the origin of Islam" (144).

It is not easy to know the category of "Muslim reader" that Strauss associated with Farabi. And as Strauss is unclear on the subject, we are reduced to speculation on this important question. The first possibility is the least probable, since Farabi is not an orthodox defender of Islam who believes that Plato and Greek philosophy as a whole should be rejected because they ignore the Law as revealed by the Prophet. This position presupposes that the revealed Law contains everything needed for the happiness of all mankind and so it is unnecessary to add to it, while Farabi, as interpreted by Strauss, thinks that the "necessary and sufficient condition of happiness, or man's ultimate perfection, is philosophy" (138). Could another, more conciliating possibility reflect the posture that Farabi assumes before Islam? This implies that Plato's teaching is not purely and simply abandoned but adapted to the divine Law: Islam and only Islam creates the best city envisaged by Plato. On this basis, philosophy can justify itself before the Law by working toward a rational justification of its content and origin. In that case, in a totally different context and with other means, philosophy tends to become what it was in medieval Christian scholastic thought—an *ancilla theologiæ*. Strauss offers a few indications that suggest we can question whether this was Farabi's position. A complete and satisfactory response to this question requires that Strauss's analysis of prophetology in the Muslim and Jewish traditions be examined. We cannot offer such an examination here, but we can nevertheless summarize the basic question about Strauss's interpretation of Farabi in the following way: was Farabi truly engaged in the Platonic search for the best city governed by philosophers, or was that search rendered pointless by his acceptance of the revealed law of the Prophet?

The plausibility of the second possibility depends on the answer we give to this question. According to this second possibility, it is no longer the revealed law that establishes the standard for judgment but Platonic philosophy itself that becomes the judge of revealed religion. This in turn implies two more options—either the philosopher judges it possible for his own reasons to accommodate himself to the religion that dominates the political community without abandoning his capacity for critical judgment about the ultimate value of this legal code, or he rejects Islam because it does not conform to the philosophical requirements that he thinks are superior to all laws. We note that from the point of view of orthodoxy, or that of the revealed religion as it defines itself, the public declaration of either position would be tantamount to atheism, or at least to heresy, either of which must be fought with all possible vigor.

There is an overwhelming tendency for readers to see the rejection of Islam as the deepest meaning attributed by Strauss to Farabi. But we must avoid jumping to this conclusion too quickly. It can blind us and lead us to believe it before it is properly weighed and judged. That is why we must look more closely at the way that Strauss interprets the Platonic themes that Farabi repeated and sometimes modified.

Platonic Variations

Farabi's *Summary* is composed of an introduction and nine chapters that deal with the first nine books of Plato's *Laws*. There is some controversy about the reason that Farabi did not comment on all twelve books of Plato's work and about the extent of Farabi's possible knowledge of Plato's works. Strauss does not take part in these debates, which is not to say, of course, that he had no thoughts on the matter.[12] He begins with the premise that Farabi acquired an in-depth knowledge of Plato's thought and particularly of his political philosophy as illustrated in the *Republic* and in the *Laws* in ways that are largely unknown to us. In addition, Strauss believes that the oddities and incoherencies in the *Summary* cannot automatically be attributed to the poverty of Farabi's sources, or worse, to his philosophical incoherence. On the contrary, one must give full credit to Farabi's philosophical competence and thus follow the judgment of philosophers such as Maimonides who considered him a philosophic master. The inconsistencies, omissions, apparent contradictions, and even pure inventions should be considered intentional and to have hidden meanings that we must work out. This approach is all the more justified since it appears to be how Farabi himself approached the writings of Plato.

Strauss argues that Farabi's aim is not to explain the work or even to reproduce it in a totally faithful manner but rather to lead the reader by a series of suggestions and allusions to the philosophical questions found throughout Plato's *Laws*. That is why it is more difficult for us to establish what truly belongs to Plato and what can be attributed to Farabi in his *Summary* than it is to determine precisely what Farabi retains from the teachings of Plato. And as if that were not enough, Strauss chooses to practice an art of commentary not dissimilar from that of Farabi.[13] The reader runs then into the same kind of problems when he tries to understand Strauss's commentary on Farabi's commentary of Plato as Strauss experienced when he attempted to decipher Farabi.

Like musical variations, the Platonic themes can be so greatly modified that they are virtually unrecognizable. This leads us to a basic characteristic of Strauss's interpretation of Farabi and reveals a key aspect of the way that Strauss approaches the history of philosophy. In "Fârâbî's *Plato*," Strauss signals that Farabi's approach is not historical in the sense that Farabi is interested less in establishing the "historical" truth about Plato than in discovering what could be called (for want of a better term) the *philosophical intention* that guides Plato and any true philosopher: "He presents, not so much the historical Plato, as the typical philosopher who, as such, after having reached maturity of the mind, 'comme un homme qui marche seul et dans les ténèbres,' has to start afresh and to go his own way however much he may be assisted by the exertions of his teachers. His attitude to the historical Plato is comparable to the attitude of Plato himself to the historical Socrates, and to the attitude of the Platonic Socrates himself to, say, historical Egypt: 'With what ease dost thou, o Fârâbî, invent Platonic speeches.' By this very fact he reveals himself as a true Platonist. For Platonists are not concerned with the historical (accidental) truth, since they are exclusively interested in the philosophic (essential) truth" (Strauss 1945, 376–77).[14]

The true Platonism—or Socratic philosophy as expressed by Plato—described here distances itself from the current conception of Platonism that sees Plato mainly as a metaphysician. On the one hand, true Platonism is indissociable from a poetic rhetoric that tries to present the philosophic life in an attractive way, while presenting a justification of that life before the court of the city. In this sense, Plato's philosophy is not essentially metaphysical but political. On the other hand, true Platonism is not so much a mere body of well-defined philosophical doctrines as the incarnation of a philosophical attitude toward human life, an attitude that culminates in the solitary search for truth that the philosopher-apprentice has to undertake on his own without any guarantee of ultimate success. To return to the musical metaphor, true Platonism understood in this way is the underlying theme of all Farabi's and Strauss's variations.

One of these variations deals with the status of Platonic theology or the role attributed to the gods or to the divine by Plato or by his commentator Farabi. We know how important Platonic theology is for Neoplatonism in general and, by extension, for medieval philosophy. Historians of medieval thought have insisted on the fact that philosophers and theologians in this period were in touch with both Platonic and Aristotelian Greek philosophic traditions through a Neoplatonist synthesis. So for them Farabi's thinking can be understood only from this Neoplatonic viewpoint which presupposes that the truth of Plato is found in his metaphysics and his theology.[15]

Strauss rejects this conventional historical interpretation (Strauss 1945, 357–62).[16] That's why what he writes about the way Farabi treats Platonic theology and perhaps more importantly what he teaches us about this theology's function in the *Summary* must be closely examined. In fact it is in this text that Farabi deals with the concepts of God, the gods, and the divine laws, all subjects on which he is silent in the *Philosophy of Plato* (139, 147). In Strauss's view, the difference is significant: Farabi sees Platonic theology not primarily as a subject for metaphysical speculation on the substance of all beings but as an integral part of a political treatise dealing with the *Laws*. By emphasizing this different way of dealing with the subject, Strauss wants to make us aware that Farabi uses the *Summary* not to speculate on the metaphysical essence of beings but to reflect on the "'roots' of the laws" of the city. Does this reflection imply a sort of rational speculation on divine things? Strauss seems to reject this possibility, and he devotes a great deal of effort to show us that, in fact, even in the *Summary*, the relationship between Farabi and the gods and divine things is more problematic than it would appear at first sight. Could Farabi's reticence in dealing with the speculative discourse on the gods explain the curious fact that he does not comment on the tenth book of Plato's *Laws*, which happens to be where Plato deals most extensively with the gods in relation to the laws (134, 147–48)?

Strauss pushes even further his attempt to show that Farabi distances himself from any interpretation of divine matters that would be theological in the strictest sense. In an enigmatic passage, Strauss tries as much as possible to humanize the divine things. Such things do not belong to a world separate from the human world but in fact represent only a special quality of certain things in the human world: "The following divine things are mentioned in the *Summary*: divine virtues, divine pleasures, divine music, divine law, divine government, divine rulers, human occupations of a certain kind. In most of these cases 'divine' obviously designates a certain quality of human beings or of human achievements or of human pursuits, namely, their excellence. If one considers the fact that the divine laws are the work of a human legislator (8,18–20; 22,19; 29,15–17), there hardly remains a single example in which 'divine' has a meaning different from the one that we have indicated." (148–49) According to Strauss, the consequence of Farabi's argument would lead to the conclusion that divine things have nothing to do with the gods or separate substances, but are merely a natural quality belonging to humans (Strauss 1945, 391–92).

This suggestion, which is troubling enough in itself, is accompanied by another that is just as disturbing: divine laws are not of divine origin but are the work of human legislators. Earlier in the text, Strauss expressed the same idea but more indirectly (144–45): that while Farabi recognized the differences between Greek laws and Islamic law, he admitted that the

two legal systems shared things in common, or more precisely, that Plato
and Farabi had a common vision of the origins and limitations of the law.
It is harder to know when it is all summed up, however, whether Farabi
accepted Plato's natural explanation for laws and if he believed like the
Greek philosopher that divine law could perish like everything else created at a specific point in time. Could we say then that Plato himself had
questioned the divine origins of the Greek law (150–51)?

We must resist the temptation to draw conclusions too quickly on the
teachings of Plato from these variations by his two interpreters, Farabi
and Strauss. Strauss is very careful to state that "there is a great divergence between what Fârâbî explicitly says and what Plato explicitly says:
it is frequently impossible to say where Fârâbî's alleged report of Plato's
views ends and his own exposition begins; and Fârâbî does not often voice
assent to Plato's views" (143). Further on in the same paragraph, Strauss
affirms that Farabi "may have desired to ascribe his revised version of
Plato's teaching to the dead Plato in order to protect that version, or the
sciences generally speaking, especially by leaving open the question as to
whether he agreed with everything his Plato taught and by failing to draw
a precise line between his mere report and his independent exposition"
(144; Strauss 1945, 376–77). A true Platonist, which is to say a philosopher
true to the intentions of Plato's philosophy and not necessarily to all the
points of his philosophical doctrine, will adapt Platonic teaching to existing circumstances and thus propose a "revised version" of this teaching.
So the interpreter of Farabi, or any serious student of the philosophical
tradition, finds himself faced with a daunting task: to distinguish between
Plato's teaching and the revised version of this teaching, he must first dis-
engage what is Plato's authentic teaching from that of Farabi. This already
considerable effort—which requires the reader to bear "the toil of study
and of meditation" (137–38, 141)—is just the first step. If an interpreter
reads all the works of Plato and all the works of Farabi, he will then have
to decide the philosophical value of the doctrines they espouse. And then
he will have to judge whether they are true or false doctrines, and if they
offer a satisfactory description of reality.

What we just said about the interpretation of Plato and Farabi also applies to the interpretation of Strauss. Like Farabi, Strauss presented his
basic philosophical teachings in works and articles devoted to interpreting
the authors of the philosophical tradition and particularly the tradition
of political philosophy. He avails himself then of the specific immunity
of the commentator, or of the historian, in order to speak his mind con-

cerning the most fundamental questions of political philosophy. Now his remarks about the difficulties involved in understanding Farabi's philosophic teachings can also apply to his own work. The preliminary examination of Strauss's interpretation of Farabi offered here gives a foretaste of the problems involved: thanks in part to allusions that are often subtle and ambiguous, Strauss introduces us to an elusive teaching about Plato's *Laws*. Yet it is extremely difficult to ascertain the content and purpose of this teaching, and even more so to judge its value. It is easy to get lost in such a labyrinth and to finally forget why we entered it. This is both the charm and the great danger of Strauss's writings: they succeed in rendering the quest for truth again exciting and challenging, but at the same time they risk exhausting the mind in a new form of scholasticism that can be ultimately sterile. Strauss's art of reading can be either a tool for helping one to think for oneself or a subtle means to postpone this essential task indefinitely. All philosophy carries within it both remedy and poison. Strauss's thought is no exception.

Notes

1. Here in order are the most representative works for each period: for the first, *Die Religionskritik Spinozas als Grundlage seiner Bibelwissenschaft. Untersuchungen zu Spinozas Theologisch-politischem Traktat* (Strauss 1930); for the second, *Thoughts on Machiavelli* (Strauss 1958); for the third, *Xenophon's Socrates* (Strauss 1972).

2. So Strauss gives us an essential key to better understand his interpretation of Farabi in his critical notes on A. C. Pegis's edition of *Basic Writings of Saint Aquinas*: "In Thomas, as distinguished from the classical philosophers and certainly from their greatest follower in the Islamic world (Fârâbî), philosophy is divorced from the conviction that happiness can be achieved only by, or essentially consists in, philosophy" (Strauss 1959, 285).

3. The original version of the text was undeniably destined for such experts, because it appeared in *Mélanges* (see Strauss 1957) dedicated to the great French specialist on Islam, Louis Massignon (1883–1962).

4. Strauss's commentary is based on an edition of Farabi's text published in 1952 (see Gabrieli 1952). The critical history of this text is presented ten years later in a detailed way by Muhsin Mahdi, a student and then a colleague of Strauss (see Mahdi 1961) Strauss already knew the text in the 1930s. Paul Kraus (1904–44), the great orientalist and Strauss's friend and later brother-in-law, dictated to him in 1931–32 a German translation of Farabi's *Summary*. Mahdi indicates in his article that he had access to this translation (Mahdi 1961, 1 n. 1, 14–15). See also on this

subject Joel L. Kraemer (1999, 209). For a new critical edition of the *Summary* with an introduction on the history of the text, see Thérèse-Anne Druart (1998).

5. Numbers within parentheses refer to "How Fârâbî Read Plato's *Laws*" (Strauss 1959, 134–54).

6. This point has always been understood by serious readers of Strauss, the difference today being that with the publication of the first volumes of the *Gesammelte Schriften* including the works and correspondence of Strauss before his arrival in the United States, we have a better idea of his intellectual journey (Strauss 1997, 2001). The most important article to explore the extent to that his thinking was influenced by Muslim philosophy is still today that of Rémi Brague (1998). See also the very complete study of Georges Tamer (2001).

7. Strauss thought the Platonic teaching retained by Farabi was essentially political in nature, which is to say the true aim of Platonic thought is to guide us toward the perfect city. This suggestion by Strauss was assumed and deepened by an entire interpretive current of thought about Farabi. See on this subject Miriam Galston (1990, 11–12). For the point of view of someone who is very critical and unfavorable to Strauss and his school, see Dimitri Gutas (2002, 19–25).

8. In addition to the many references to Farabi that can be found in his great work of 1935 *Philosophie und Gesetz*, Strauss condensed the results of his research on Farabi and on Maimonides in a text published in 1936 (Strauss 1936a). In this article, Strauss gives capital importance to Farabi's role in the reception and diffusion of Plato's political philosophy in medieval Muslim and Jewish thought. Interest in Farabi was fed by Strauss's irresistible ability to dramatize the philosophical stakes inherent in Farabi's thought. Strauss spawned an entire school of Farabi interpreters, each of whom has their own way of seeking to better understand Farabi's thought from his writings on political philosophy.

9. Strauss (1945). Strauss never republished this text in its entirety. He did, however, reprint extracts in *Persecution and the Art of Writing* (Strauss 1952), and several passages in the chapter examined here are direct or indirect borrowings from this seminal essay. "Fârâbî's *Plato*" is a free commentary on a Farabi text that Muhsin Mahdi would translate under the title "The Philosophy of Plato, Its Parts, the Ranks of Order of Its Parts, from the Beginning to the End" (see Alfarabi 2001, 51–67). Many aspects of "How Fârâbî Read Plato's *Laws*" can be understood only in light of "Fârâbî's *Plato*." Finally we must note that from the 1930s Strauss knew Falaquera's Hebrew paraphrase of *The Philosophy of Plato*, as can be seen in his article "Eine vermißte Schrift Fârâbîs" (Strauss 1936b).

10. What motivated this correction is not mentioned here but is emphasized in "Fârâbî's *Plato*": the result of Socrates's audacity was his persecution, and then his death (Strauss 1945, 383).

11. This is the definition that Farabi gives of the *kalâm* in *The Enumeration of the Sciences*: "The art of dialectical theology (*kalâm*) is a positive disposition that enables man to argue in the defense of the specific opinions and actions stated

explicitly by the founder of the religion, and against everything that opposes these opinions and actions" (Lerner and Mahdi 1993, 27).

12. There is great debate among specialists as to whether Farabi had before him a complete translation of Plato's *Laws* or a partial one or even a mere summary of the text. Dimitri Gutas and Joshua Parens, for example, take opposing sides. For specific references and a measured and detailed discussion of the controversy, see Steven Harvey (2003, 51–68). This hypothesis that Farabi knew the *Laws* of Plato in their entirety is essential if one is to make sense of Strauss's interpretation. For him, what Farabi decided to keep silent about in his commentary is nearly as important as what he chose to comment on. One can presume that Strauss's thoughts on the matter were close to those of Muhsin Mahdi (see Mahdi 1961, 6–10). J. Parens decided to follow this line of interpretation to its ultimate conclusions in his detailed commentary on the *Summary*, which was written with the aim of presenting the intentions of Farabi's thought (see Parens 1995).

13. In his final works and with a constantly increasing freedom from the restraints and standards of modern academic writing, Strauss practiced a Farabi-style kind of commentary. It probably reached its peak in a work published posthumously dealing—likely not a coincidence—with the *Laws* of Plato: *The Argument and the Action of Plato's* Laws (Strauss 1975).

14. Note the repetition of the same formula at the end of "How Fârâbî Read Plato's *Laws*": "We admire the ease with which Fârâbî invented Platonic speeches" (154).

15. For a convincing contemporary defense of this traditional view, see Philippe Vallat (2004, 25–29, 33–83).

16. The reading that Strauss proposes of Farabi's Platonism and by extension Plato's own thought tends to subordinate metaphysics to political philosophy, perhaps indeed to make political philosophy the *prima philosophia*. For Strauss, the question of Being cannot be separated from the question about the best way of life, the political question par excellence. On this point, we refer the reader to our work (Tanguay 2007, 49–98). See also Susan Shell, chap. 10 below.

Works Cited

Alfarabi. 2001. *Philosophy of Plato and Aristotle*. Trans. Muhsin Mahdi. Rev. ed. Ithaca: Cornell University Press. Originally published 1962.

Brague, Rémi. 1998. "Athens, Jerusalem, Mecca : Leo Strauss's 'Muslim' Understanding of Greek Philosophy." *Poetics Today* 19 (2): 235–59.

Druart, Thérèse-Anne. 1998. "Le sommaire du livre des 'Lois' de Platon." *Bulletin d'études orientales* 50: 109–55.

Gabrieli, Franciscus. 1952. *Alfarabius. Compendium Legum Platonis*. London: Warburg Institute.

Galston, Miriam. 1990. *The Political Philosophy of Alfarabi*. Princeton: Princeton University Press.

Gutas, Dimitri. 2002. "The Study of Arabic Philosophy in the Twentieth Century: An Essay on the Historiography of Arabic Philosophy." *British Journal of Middle Eastern Studies* 29 (1): 5–25.

Harvey, Steven. 2003. "Did Alfarabi Read Plato's *Laws*?" *Medioevo* 28: 51–68.

Kraemer, Joel L. 1999. "The Death of an Orientalist: Paul Kraus from Prague to Cairo." In *The Jewish Discovery of Islam : Studies in Honor of Bernard Lewis*, ed. Martin Kramer, 181–223. Tel Aviv: Moshe Dayan Center for Middle Eastern and African Studies.

Lerner, Ralph, and Muhsin Mahdi, eds. 1993. *Medieval Political Philosophy*. Ithaca: Cornell University Press.

Mahdi, Muhsin. 1961. "The *Editio Princeps* of Farabi's *Compendium Legum Platonis*." *Journal of Near Eastern Studies* 20 (1): 1–24.

Parens, Joshua. 1995. *Metaphysics as Rhetoric. Alfarabi's "Summary of Plato's 'Laws.'"* Albany : SUNY Press.

Strauss, Leo. 1930. *Die Religionskritik Spinozas als Grundlage seiner Bibelwissenschaft. Untersuchungen zu Spinozas Theologisch-politischem Traktat*. Berlin: Akademie-Verlag. For a new edition, see Strauss 1996, 1–330. For the English translation, see Strauss 1965.

———. 1935. *Philosophie und Gesetz. Beiträge zum Verständnis Maimunis und seiner Vorläufer*. Berlin: Schocken Verlag. For a new edition, see Strauss 1997, 3–125. For the English translation, see Strauss 1995.

———. 1936a. "Quelques remarques sur la science politique de Maïmonide et de Fârâbî." *Revue des études juives* 100: 1–37. For a new edition, see Strauss 1997, 125–58. For the English translation, see Strauss 1990.

———. 1936b. "Eine vermißte Schrift Fârâbîs." *Monatsschrift für Geschichte und Wissenschaft des Judentums* 80 (1): 96–106. For a new edition, see Strauss 1997, 167–76.

———. 1945. "Fârâbî's *Plato*." In *Louis Ginzberg Jubilee Volume*, 357–93. New York: American Academy for Jewish Research.

———. 1952. *Persecution and the Art of Writing*. Chicago: University of Chicago Press.

———. 1957. "How Farabi Read Plato's *Laws*." In *Mélanges Louis Massignon*, ed. L'Institut d'études islamiques de l'Université de Paris and L'Institut français de Damas, 3 : 319–44. Damascus: Institut français de Damas.

———. 1958. *Thoughts on Machiavelli*. Chicago : University of Chicago Press.

———. 1959. *What Is Political Philosophy? And Other Studies*. New York: Free Press.

———. 1965. *Spinoza's Critique of Religion*. Trans. E. M. Sinclair. New York: Schocken Books.

———. 1972. *Xenophon's Socrates*. Ithaca: Cornell University Press.

————. 1975. *The Argument and the Action of Plato's* Laws. Chicago: University of Chicago Press.

————. 1990. "Some Remarks on the Political Science of Maimonides and Farabi." Trans. Robert Bartlett. *Interpretation. A Journal of Political Philosophy* 18 (1): 3–30.

————. 1995. *Philosophy and Law. Contribution to the Understanding of Maimonides and His Predecessors.* Trans. Eve Adler. Albany: SUNY Press.

————. 1996. *Gesammelte Schriften*, vol. 1: *Die Religionskritik Spinozas und zugehörige Schriften.* Ed. Heinrich Meier and Wiebke Meier. Stuttgart: J. B. Metzler.

————. 1997. *Gesammelte Schriften*, vol. 2: *Philosophie und Gesetz—Frühe Schriften.* Ed. Heinrich Meier and Wiebke Meier. Stuttgart: J. B. Metzler.

————. 2001. *Gesammelte Schriften*, vol. 3: *Hobbes' politische Wissenschaft und zugehörige Schriften—Briefe.* Ed. Heinrich Meier and Wiebke Meier. Stuttgart: J. B. Metzler.

Tamer, Georges. 2001. *Islamische Philosophie und die Krise der Moderne. Das Verhältnis von Leo Strauss zu Alfarabi, Avicenna und Averroes.* Leiden: Brill.

Tanguay, Daniel. 2007. *Leo Strauss: An Intellectual Biography.* Trans. Christopher Nadon. New Haven: Yale University Press.

Vallat, Philippe. 2004. *Farabi et l'École d'Alexandrie. Des prémisses de la connaissance à la philosophie politique.* Paris: Vrin.

CHAPTER SIX

Strauss on Maimonides's Secretive Political Science

Joshua Parens

Strauss's "Maimonides' Statement on Political Science" is among his shortest and strangest writings. Its shortness reflects the brevity of the work upon which it is based, Maimonides's *Treatise on the Art of Logic*, especially chapter 14, its final, brief chapter. The strangeness of Strauss's piece derives from three factors: First, the original Arabic of the *Logic* had not yet been found when Strauss wrote his article. It was based instead on Hebrew translations and Arabic fragments—leading inevitably to conjectural readings.[1] Second, Maimonides appears to argue that political science is not needed in his time! Third, Strauss's all too brief historical study seems initially to be out of place in a collection that includes such a substantive and provocative programmatic essay as "What Is Political Philosophy?," supplemented by somewhat less comprehensive though equally programmatic essays such as "Political Philosophy and History," "Classical Political Philosophy," and "Restatement on Xenophon's *Hiero*." In other words, the context in which Strauss chose to place the "Statement on Political Science" only intensifies the strangeness of the article itself.

Regarding the first source of strangeness, the problematic texts at Strauss's disposal: At least two articles have been written commenting on the limitations of Strauss's article, both of which appeared after the publication of Arabic versions of the *Logic* not available to Strauss.[2] When relevant, I will touch on those articles, but I will not focus, as they have, on Strauss's occasional faulty conjectures. After all, Strauss devotes an entire paragraph, the second paragraph of the piece, to underlining how conjectural his inquiry is (156).[3] Nevertheless, it is striking that Strauss would include in this collection a historical study filled with conjectures and some of his most "unscientific" speculations about numerology in the thought of Maimonides (see 165–68). A yawning chasm opens up between the kind of "data" considered in this historical study on Maimonides's political science and the kind considered in the contemporary, positivistic political science that Strauss discusses in "What Is Political Philosophy?" (17–26).

Why, the reader should wonder, does Strauss engage in such historical studies, which are foreign not only to contemporary social scientists but also to the very thinkers, such as Maimonides, whom Strauss interprets in these historical studies (also) on Alfarabi, Hobbes, and Locke (73–75)? According to Strauss, we live in an age in which "historicism" prevails. Historicism holds that the truth for our age must be different from that for other ages (71). Consequently, though it might embrace the study of former ages with an eye to clarifying our own present views, it rejects out of hand the possibility that insights acquired in another age could have permanent relevance. In addition, as denizens of the modern world we are the recipients of a modern history of political philosophy that, even before the advent of historicism, relied upon and criticized ideas about political things that it had received from premodern political philosophy (75, 79, 81). Consequently, contemporary political ideas and concepts often contain within them layers of sedimentation that impede our access to the original ideas, not to mention the original political phenomena (28, 74–75, 84). Strauss advocates historical studies of thinkers who themselves did not engage in such historical studies because in our contemporary situation we are able to gain access to the original phenomena only by peeling away the layers of sedimentation in our own ideas (75 n. 4) and because he has become convinced through his own study of political philosophy that political philosophy has more to offer than historicism (26).

Why does Strauss choose to write on two medieval political philosophers and two modern political philosophers, and why these two pairs: Alfarabi-Maimonides and Hobbes-Locke? The first question will be addressed shortly. For now, let us turn to the question why these particular pairs together. In each of these pairs, the reader is confronted by a less renowned but more outspoken political philosopher. Like that of Machiavelli before him, "Hobbes's teaching was still much too bold to be acceptable. It, too, was in need of mitigation. The mitigation was the work of Locke" (49). In the case of the pair Alfarabi-Maimonides, Strauss considers thinkers whose connection is less obvious than that of Hobbes and Locke.[4] Although Hobbes and Locke were divided over liberal *democracy*, it has been widely acknowledged for many decades if not for many centuries that Hobbes and Locke were central to the American founding. Strauss explains the affinity between Alfarabi and Maimonides in "Restatement on Xenophon's *Hiero*" as that of engaging in "philosophic politics," which despite the fact that Alfarabi engaged in such politics in the context of Islam and Maimonides in the context of Judaism proves to be a profound connection indeed (126–27). Is it possible that in spite of their different religious contexts, Maimonides did for Alfarabi what Locke did for Hobbes, that is, mitigate his teaching?

This preliminary consideration of Maimonides brings to mind an obvious and yet shocking similarity between Maimonides's situation and our own. Much as historicism seems to deny the need for (and the very possibility of) political philosophy (26, 57),[5] so many in Maimonides's time and place also denied the need for political philosophy—revelation, it seemed to them, made recourse to philosophy unnecessary. Much of Strauss's article is devoted to showing that Maimonides, though he appears at first to be denying the relevance of political philosophy to a revealed community, is in fact showing subtly and indirectly just how much his revealed community needs the guidance of political philosophy. Although as inheritors of the secularization of politics by the Enlightenment we would seem to have little or no need for the insights of Maimonides, it seems that the return of the gods under the auspices of historicism makes the untimely insights of Maimonides timely for us.

More broadly, why did Strauss choose to include these essays on two medieval and two modern authors? He seems to be drawing attention to the shift from medieval to modern with matching pairs of historical studies. In other words, "Maimonides' Statement on Political Science" is included in *What Is Political Philosophy?* to offer insights into that crucial turn in the history of political philosophy, the movement from premodern to modern, or as Strauss more often refers to it, the difference between ancient and modern. Heinrich Meier is likely correct that the central phenomenon with which Strauss is concerned is the theological-political problem and especially the opposition between philosophy and revelation, as we will see later in this chapter, but disagreement exists in Straussian circles about how important are the differences (or oppositions) between ancient or premodern and modern. The differences between medievals such as Alfarabi and Maimonides, on the one hand, and the moderns such as Hobbes and Locke, on the other, seem all too obvious. Yet Strauss shows again and again that the first modern, Machiavelli, has some odd connections with medievals, especially those whom the tradition has dubbed "Averroists." The reader is led to wonder, then, why Strauss connects such different thinkers as Machiavelli and Maimonides. Indeed, Strauss, though subtly and indirectly, insinuates that Maimonides is an "Averroist."[6] What could possibly link one of the most outspoken critics of Christianity with one of the strongest defenders of Judaism?

In both "What Is Political Philosophy?" (41) and "Restatement on Xenophon's *Hiero*" (102), Strauss notes an important connection between medieval political philosophy, especially medieval Islamic and Jewish political philosophy, and Machiavelli: This bold founder of modernity, whose boldness Strauss frequently highlights, is not as original as Strauss's accounts might lead us to believe initially. According to Strauss, Machiavelli is the inheritor of a "critique of religion" that dates back beyond the medievals to the classics (41).[7] The medieval bearers of that tradition belong to the "Averroistic tradition," about which contemporary scholars, such as Eric Voegelin, are pardonably ignorant (102). The "Statement" is part of an effort to replace that ignorance with knowledge. One wonders why it should be important to make scholars more aware of the Averroistic tradition if the classics are bearers of the same teaching. There must be other points of discontinuity between ancients and medievals that make the existence of the Averroistic tradition important to Strauss's overall account of the history of political philosophy. The obvious point of discontinuity is the most relevant one: The Averroistic tradition is the adaptation of the classical teaching to the setting of the monotheistic faiths (cf. 127).

In *What Is Political Philosophy?*, Strauss resists the suggestion by thinkers such as Alexandre Kojève that monotheism, any more than tyranny, is a wholly unprecedented phenomenon that transcends or eludes the framework of classical political philosophy. He argues this in the face of Kojève's insistence that the classics were limited to the view of the master, the honor-loving view, which stood in need of its biblical complement, the view of the slave (96, 108). Strauss insists that Platonic philosophy as embodied in the character of Socrates cannot be confused with the honor-loving view. Socrates is already the synthesis or transcendence that Kojève claims to find in Hegel's synthesis of the ancient and modern Christian "(Hobbian)" teaching (cf. 105 with 109–10). What could serve as better support for Strauss's view as expressed in "Restatement" than the evidence we will find in the "Statement on Political Science" that Maimonides testifies to the continued relevance of classical political philosophy under monotheistic conditions? Strauss's strange forays into medieval Islamic and Jewish political philosophy support what may be Strauss's most lasting contribution to political philosophy, namely, his insight that classical political philosophy, its *framework*, remains relevant to all political phenomena in every historical period. Students of political philosophy should never confuse the political "solution" of the classics (132; cf. 126–27), however, with the range of political phenomena their framework can make intelligible.[8]

Strauss describes Averroism elsewhere as the "secular alliance between philosophers and princes friendly to philosophy."[9] There, he also connects Machiavelli to his Averroist predecessors. According to Strauss, Alfarabi[10] departed from Plato in transforming the open alliance between philosophy and kings in the *Republic* into the "secret kingship of the philosopher."[11] The reader is led to wonder why that open alliance became secret. Once again, the reason proves to be monotheism. The unprecedented authority of monotheistic or revealed texts made it incumbent upon political philosophers to hide their philosophic activity—even more than had Socrates.[12] Maimonides's statement on political science in the *Logic* appears at first glance to deny the relevance of political science in the new revealed setting. The *Logic* does so because it needs to bow to the authority of revelation. Far from proving the irrelevance of classical political philosophy to the monotheistic setting, Maimonides's *Logic*, as long as one attends to its reasons for being secretive, reveals the continued relevance of the classics in the new setting.

Although Machiavelli's founding of modernity may emerge out of an Averroist critique of religion, I need hardly remind the reader of all of his radical departures from his predecessors, which seem to render our political experience so different from the premodern (see 41–43). Machiavelli's mode of expression of his critique of religion is part and parcel of that radical departure: Machiavelli is the "great master of blasphemy" (41), whose blasphemy is fueled by "anti-theological ire" (44). Although Machiavelli may continue the alliance of philosophers and princes, he chose to broadcast his critique of religion—using techniques that the founder of his own religion had first employed (45–46). In contrast, Maimonides's critique of religion could hardly be more secretive. In effect, the most salient difference between Machiavelli and Maimonides is the immoderation of the former and the moderation of the latter. Although Machiavelli may have links to the classical critique of religion by way of Averroism, his approach to the critique of religion gave rise to that secularization which led eventually to historicism. Perhaps moderation, a virtue that Strauss repeatedly associates with premodern philosophy, in such matters is the most important element in preserving political philosophy.

Strauss singles out three difficulties in the *Logic*: (1) Maimonides seems to repudiate "the philosophers on politics proper" as useless "'in these times,'"[13] (2) he "divides politics proper in an unusual manner," and (3) he distinguishes the subject matter of ethics from that of politics proper, "assign[ing] the understanding of happiness . . . to politics proper" (156–57). Strauss's discussion of these three difficulties is divided into six parts: (a) on whether and for whom the study of politics proper might be useless (157–59); (b) on the unusual divisions of politics proper (159–162); (c) on the rule of *nomoi*, living intelligence, and the "effects produced upon the character of laws by the change from paganism to revealed religion" (162–165); (d) on the overarching division of the sciences in the *Logic* (first look), including the relation between ethics, on the one hand, and politics proper and the issue of happiness, on the other (165–67); and (e) on the overarching division of the sciences (second look), which "leads directly into the center of the fundamental problem" (167–69). Part a takes up the problem set forth as difficulty 1. Part b takes up the problem set forth as difficulty 2. Part d addresses difficulty 3, although its significance must apparently be seen in light of parts c and e.

a. Is the Study of Politics Useless? (157–59)

It must be admitted that the Hebrew translations of the *Logic* that Strauss consulted led him more quickly than do the more accurate Arabic texts to the conclusion that, according to Maimonides's *Logic*, revelation repudiates the science of "politics proper." The question remains, however, whether that conclusion was not also implied by the more accurate Arabic. Strauss translates, based on what little he had, the following: "'But we have no need in these times for all this, viz. for [the commands], the laws, the *nomoi*, the governance [of] [these] human beings in divine things [for the laws and the *nomoi*; the governance of human beings is now through divine things]'" (156). In contrast, Muhsin Mahdi translates based on dependable Arabic texts the following: "In these times, all this—I mean the regimes and the nomoi—has been dispensed with, and men are being governed by divine commands" (Parens and Macfarland 2011, 182). The more restrained Arabic seems to leave open the possibility that aspects of the philosophic study of politics proper, other than the regimes and *nomoi* resulting from those studies, remain relevant. Although the latter translation based on the Arabic version is able to qualify "all this," further consideration of this qualified claim may lead, as Maimonides's *Logic* led Strauss, to the view that revelation repudiates the political science of the philosophers. In the preceding lines of chapter 14, among the regimes and *nomoi* given to the pagans, Maimonides singles out those given by philosophers. Those have been dispensed with. How do divine commands take their place? It would seem that God takes the place of philosophers in the giving of regimes and *nomoi*. If God can do this for man, it is unclear why human beings should feel any need to study "politics proper." Joel Kraemer objects that Strauss has made Maimonides's claim to dispense with philosophy in politics far too broad (Kraemer 1991, 99).[14] Although Strauss's translation may have lacked the precision of translations based on the Arabic, difficulty 1 proves to be precisely as he first stated it: Maimonides insinuates that revelation purports to make political science unnecessary—which is the very thing necessitating Maimonides's secretiveness about political science.

In addition to objecting that Strauss has been too hasty about Maimonides's (apparent) rejection of political science, Kraemer objects to Strauss's inference that "'the function of the Torah is emphatically political'" (157).[15] According to Kraemer, Strauss has inferred the political character of the Torah *because* of his misreading of Maimonides's repudiation of political science: if the Torah insinuates that revelation makes political science obsolete, then the Torah must be essentially political. Kraemer objects to Strauss's interpretation by claiming that there really is no comparison between pagan law and revealed law.[16] Initially, Kraemer seems to be on firm footing. At crucial moments in his *Guide*, Maimonides draws a clear distinction between *nomoi*, which are concerned merely with the well-being of the body, and truly divine Laws, which are concerned with the perfection both of the body and of the soul (*Guide* 2.40, 3.27–28). Furthermore, he appears to identify pagan laws with perfection of the body (*Guide* 2.39, end)—and to identify the Law of Moses with perfection of the soul.[17] If this simple portrait were accurate, we would be left with the strange implication that the philosophic study of politics proper was relevant for the pagans and remains relevant to the revealed religions because it treats merely the perfection of the body.[18] If this were the case, then why would Maimonides indicate that the teaching of the philosophers about the regimes and *nomoi* is obsolete (especially "in these times")? Furthermore, we would be left with the untenable suggestion that the philosophic study of politics proper concerns the well-being of the body only. Yet Maimonides states explicitly that in the *Logic* that study concerns happiness (cf. difficulty 3). Not even the adherents of the

"Averroistic tradition" held that happiness is merely a matter of the well-being of the body. Finally, in response to Kraemer's interpretation, Strauss might appeal to one of his favorite passages in the "Averroistic tradition," the passage he quotes from Avicenna's *On the Division of the Rational Sciences* as the epigraph to his final study of classical political philosophy, *The Argument and the Action of Plato's "Laws"*: "[T]he treatment of prophecy and the Law (*sharī'a*) is contained in [Plato's and Aristotle's] books on the laws."[19] It may serve the enlightened *kalām* of the *Guide* to denigrate pagan laws as Maimonides does in the penultimate paragraph of the *Logic* and the end of *Guide* 2.39;[20] however, even in the *Guide*, Maimonides hints to the attentive reader that a distinction should be drawn between traditional pagan laws and the laws of the philosophers. Although one might dispute whether the laws or the education of the soul in Plato's *Laws* in fact perfects the soul, it is obviously false to claim that Plato's *Laws* is not concerned with the soul's perfection.

Leaving aside Kraemer's objections to Strauss, it is worth pausing to attend to Strauss's careful consideration of the audience of the *Logic*, which necessarily has bearing on the question for whom might political science be said to be irrelevant.[21] Over the course of pages 157 through 159, Strauss carefully considers the "we" to whom the *Logic*, and thus the repudiation of political science, seem to be addressed. He shows that previous commentators on the *Logic* latched onto Maimonides's implied distinction between ethics and politics proper. Among them, Moses Mendelssohn voices an all-too-modern interpretation of Maimonides. According to Mendelssohn, so long as the Jewish people lack a homeland the political part of the Law is irrelevant.[22] In other words, Mendelssohn interprets Maimonides as dispensing with political philosophy owing to the Jewish lack of a homeland (157). He seems to imply that the ethical teaching of the Law might be separated from the political to be used separately. In doing so, Mendelssohn adopts the modern (especially late modern) view that happiness is the proper subject of ethics rather than of politics. In this subtle way, Strauss alludes to the radical difference between the premodern inclusion of ethics within politics and the modern separation of the two.

Strauss goes on to question the assumption of interpreters such as Mendelssohn that the "we" or the audience of the *Logic* is the Jewish people simply. After all, Maimonides refers to an audience that "in these times" has no need for these pagan philosophic works. Of course, "The Torah antedates philosophy, or Greek wisdom, by centuries. If it were the Torah which rendered superfluous the political books of the philosophers, those books would not have been needed by the Jewish people at any time" (157–58). Consequently, Strauss draws the important conclusion that the audience of the *Logic* is likely not as broad as "we Jews" but the far narrower grouping "we men of theory"—covering "the men who speculate about principles or roots."[23] Defenders of religion, in particular of monotheistic faiths, seem to be the target audience. Thus, Strauss expands his previous claim that "the function of *the Torah* is emphatically political" (157) to the broader claim "the function of *revealed religion* is emphatically political" (159). In addition, the identification of the target audience as persons above the vulgar, who are especially concerned to defend revealed religion, enables Strauss to refine the target of Maimonides's repudiation of political science. He separates "the most practical part of the political teaching of the philosophers" from "the theoretical understanding of revealed religion" and stresses that it is the former that Maimonides repudiates, not the latter (159).[24] How could the latter not be of interest to "the men who speculate about principles or roots"? We will see more of this aspect of the political teaching of the philosophers later.

b. The Divisions of Politics Proper (159–62)

Maimonides distinguishes, according to Strauss's accurate paraphrase, between the "governance of the city, and governance of the great [numerous] nation or of the nations" (155). Maimonides's possible sources for this striking division have already been discussed elsewhere.[25] Strauss notes that Alfarabi draws such distinctions primarily with reference to the size of the regimes ("city–nation–many [all] nations" [159]).[26] Maimonides seems to replace this "tri-partition" by size with a "bi-partition" involving religion (160, 165). It is not the overall bi-partition (city vs. great nation or the nations) that refers to religion so much as the second part of the bi-partition, which is itself subdivided (great nation or [vs.] the nations), that does so. Strauss, and before him Harry Austryn Wolfson,[27] ruminated over this odd subdivision at great length. According to Strauss,

> Wolfson has suggested that "the nations" stands for the ancient pagan nations, and "the great nation" stands for Israel, and therefore that Maimonides tacitly goes over from the distinction between political communities in regard to size to their distinction in regard to religion: the "city" stands for the "civil state,"

and the pagan nations and Israel stand for different forms of the "religious state." This suggestion necessarily implies that the governance, or guidance of Israel, i.e., the Torah, is a subject of political philosophy. (160)

Strauss agrees with the broad outlines of Wolfson's interpretation, especially the notion of a shift from size to religion (cf. 165) and with the inference that the Torah is a proper object of political philosophic study. Strauss goes on to argue that chapters such as *Guide* 2.40 that "deal with the difference between the Torah and the *nomoi* of the pagans would belong to political science." Furthermore, he notes that the political scientific character of 2.40, as the central chapter of the prophetology of the *Guide*, confirms that the "prophetology as a whole is a branch of political science" (160).[28] All of these observations run contrary to the initial impression that chapter 14 of the *Logic* leaves the reader with, namely, classical political science is irrelevant to the revealed setting. The apparent rejection of political science in the penultimate paragraph—the last impression Maimonides leaves the reader with—is intentionally misleading. It is part of his secretiveness about political science, not to mention the secret alliance of philosopher and prince.

Regarding the subdivision into governance of "the great nation" and "the nations," Strauss disagrees with Wolfson's conjecture that the "great nation" is Israel. After all, Israel is hardly "great"—as Amos 7:7 confirms (161). Rather, "the great nation" refers to any one of the monotheistic religions and "the nations" to the pagan nations (162).[29] Although the *Logic* is written in Arabic, it seems plausible that "the nations" (*al-umam*) should refer to the pagans—after all, the Torah frequently refers to the pagans as "the nations" (*ha-goyim*). Above all, the difference between the singular form of "the great nation" (*al-umma al-kabīra*) and the plural form of "the nations" provides the needed bridge from the focus on size to the focus on religion. The monotheistic faiths are "universalistic religion[s]" (162)—all of which claim to possess *the* truth. The pagan nations do not make the same type of universal claims. Furthermore, in monotheism, politics serves religion; in paganism, religion serves politics (164). It is hardly surprising then that Maimonides makes no reference to "the rule of living intelligence," a political option so relevant to Plato and Aristotle (163). The Law's claim to possess the final truth makes reference to the rule of a merely human living intelligence into a potential affront to the divine. Consequently, the penultimate paragraph of chapter 14 voices just the kind of deference revelation demands. Before that, however, in his distinction between "the great nation" and "the nations," Maimonides divides practical philosophy in such a way as to emphasize the continued relevance of (classical) political philosophy to the study of revealed law.

c. A Faulty Conjecture and the Unprecedented Challenge of Doctrine in the Monotheistic Setting (162–65)

As Strauss explains, "as a rule" Maimonides concludes each chapter of the *Logic* with an inventory of terms that he has explained above. At the conclusion of chapter 14, according to Strauss, he discusses only two terms relevant to politics proper (and economics or household rule), namely, " 'commands' and *nomoi*" (162–63). Strauss includes a footnote offering a conjecture regarding the Arabic equivalent to the various Hebrew terms by which translators rendered the original Arabic, which he renders "commands." Note 14 reads as follows: "Ibn Tibbon: *haḥuqqim* [the commands or statutes]; Vives: *haḥoq* [the command or statute]; Ahitub: *hahanhaga* [the regimen]. Could the original [Arabic] have read *ḥukm*?"[30] Strauss's conjecture about the Arabic equivalent of what he renders "command" is plausible though apparently incorrect. The two terms listed that refer to politics proper, which appear as the last two words of the whole treatise in the complete Arabic versions to which Strauss did not have access, are "regime" (*siyāsa*) and "*nomoi*."[31] Based on this faulty conjecture, Strauss goes on to discuss the relation between "command" and "*nomos*" as that between genus and species. *Nomoi* are laws set forth without regard to time or place, implying that there are other commands that change in accordance with time and place—not only time and place but from individual to individual.[32]

Over the course of the next page and a half (163–64), Strauss draws out this conjectured contrast between *nomos* as general command and more particular commands in relation to two other themes: On the one hand, Strauss discusses it in relation to another nonconjectural claim about the *Logic*. As mentioned previously, Maimonides is surprisingly silent about a key claim of his predecessors Plato and Alfarabi, namely, the rule of living intelligence (163–64). On the other hand, Strauss discusses the conjectured contrast in relation to the contrast between regimes ruled by *nomoi* (pagan regimes) in which religion serves politics and (regimes of) revealed law in which politics is made to serve religion (164). Even when Strauss overreaches in his interpretation of the *Logic*, he anchors his interpretation on solid ground in either the *Logic* or the *Guide*. Furthermore, the conclusion he draws from chapter 14 is a sound one. Maimonides intends here as in the much later *Guide* to focus the attention, at least of the thoughtful reader, on the "change from paganism to revealed religion" (165)—if only so that we might understand the new status and place of political science in the revealed setting. In addition to the problematic monotheistic expectation that politics should serve religion, Maimonides highlights related new problems on the horizon, ones that would become especially acute in Christendom: "The public discussion of 'the account of the creation' [that is, the account of the beginning], i.e., of physics, did not harm the pagans in the way in which it might harm the adherents of revealed laws. The divinely revealed laws also create dangers which did not exist among the Greeks: they open up a new source of disagreement among men" (164).[33] Although the pagan world saw philosophers put to death for proposing opinions that called the laws of the city into question, it was not until monotheism that cities and nations were themselves torn from within by intestinal conflicts over opinions. Alfarabi and Maimonides both sought, among other things, to protect their religious communities from succumbing to such conflict. Their communities' focus on laws and actions—not to mention the lack of political power of the Jewish nation—made their task far easier than it would prove to be for their Christian counterparts. In contrast, Christianity's emphasis on the spirit of the Law and thus on doctrine (as opposed to laws and actions) made the tendency toward such conflict over opinion inevitable and insupportable. In medieval Christendom, thinker after thinker attempted to overcome the consequences of such conflict for political life—until Machiavelli took his momentous turn to make the critique of religion so explicit that the political role of religious authorities might be permanently undercut. Yet Machiavelli's efforts at the secularization of politics did not prevent the eventual return of the gods.

d. The Initial Impression Left by Maimonides's Division of the Sciences (165–67)

After Strauss summarizes the results of all of his previous arguments (165, top), he turns to tackle the third problem (Maimonides's assignment of the problem of happiness to politics proper) through a consideration of Maimonides's division of the sciences, that is, his two different divisions

128   JOSHUA PARENS

of the sciences. Section d (165–67) gives an account of Maimonides's most
obvious division of the sciences into seven. Here, the reader is left with
the misleading initial impression that ethics has the central place among
the seven. This misleading impression provides Strauss the opportunity
to explore the disjunction between "common-sense morality" and "the
theoretical understanding of morality," which distinguishes between the
"requirements of society" and the "requirements of man's final perfection" (167). His main point is that ethics lacks centrality precisely because
it does not focus on "the study of man's end," since that is one of the jobs
of "politics proper" (166). A key implication: "politics proper" must not
be confused with what Strauss referred to on page 159 as "the most practical part of the political teaching of the philosophers." On the contrary,
"politics proper" is nothing if it is not, or at least does not include, the
"theoretical understanding of morality" (167).[34]

Maimonides's apparent division of science into seven sciences leads
one to other important problems—problems brought to the fore by
Maimonides's playful use of numerology. Although numerology is very
remote indeed from the methods considered acceptable by twentieth-
century positivistic political science, it is also evident that Maimonides
does indeed employ numerology, even if playfully, to set forth hints in his
Guide. Strauss need only inventory the number of chapters in the *Logic*
(7 x 2) and the number of terms explained in the work (7 x 25) to muster
evidence that the number seven—into which Maimonides has also divided
the sciences—plays some role in that work. Perhaps most interestingly of
all, Strauss goes on to show that this elaborate use of the number seven is
only part of the surface teaching regarding the division of the sciences. As
we will see, Maimonides's more profound division is in fact into eleven!
Before proceeding any further, however, it is worth highlighting one of
the most striking insights of Strauss's foray into numerology here. Ultimately in the deeper second division, Strauss will uncover Maimonides's
own critique of numerology. The latter will distance himself from serious
numerology, as practiced by ancient pre-Socratic philosophers, namely,
the Pythagoreans (168 n. 23)—and in doing so also call into question his
own link to the mysticism of the Talmudic sages (169). In the just-cited
substantive footnote, Strauss directs the attentive reader to not only a
radically new interpretation of Maimonides but also to what appears to be
a significant revision of Strauss's own way of reading medieval Jewish and
Islamic political philosophy.

Let us begin at the beginning, however (165–66). The number seven
stands for the pure (forms or) intelligences, among which are included

the traditional angels of Jewish lore as the subordinate unmoved movers of the Aristotelian tradition.[35] The number fourteen stands for man as the composite of matter and form, as Maimonides confirms when much later he discusses human procreation (among other crucial things about man) in *Guide* 1.7 and Adam as man in *Guide* 1.14. Strauss notes that the number fourteen recurs repeatedly in Maimonides's works, especially in his three different divisions of the Law. He follows up this connection between law and man in the number fourteen through a consideration of Maimonides's palace simile of *Guide* 3.51. Maimonides interprets the simile twice. In the first iteration, the fourth level of the palatial hierarchy is occupied by the practitioners of *fiqh* or the legalistic science of the Law; in the second iteration, the same level is occupied by students of logic.[36] Interestingly, Strauss does not mention that Maimonides includes in the latter group students of mathematics as well as logic—an omission that may be of interest when interpreting Strauss's key note on numerology mentioned above and discussed below. By the striking parallel between law and logic, Strauss is led to wonder whether Maimonides is inferring a proportion of the following sort: man's matter : man's form :: law : logic. This strange conjecture is confirmed by Maimonides's shocking contrast between the goods of the body and the goods of the soul in *Guide* 3.27–28. From seven and fourteen, Strauss turns eventually to the number seventeen (the number referring to nature; cf. *Guide* 1.17 on natural science)[37] and the observation that though the whole of the *Guide* is divided into seven sections, only one section consists of seven chapters: the Account of the Chariot in 3.1–7. Although that chapter is shrouded in mystery, it is surrounded by what are likely the two most important sections of the *Guide*, 2.32–48 (on prophetology) and 3.8–24 (on providence), both of which happen to consist of seventeen chapters.[38]

e. The Deeper Impression Left by Maimonides's Division of the Sciences (167–69)

According to Strauss, the more profound division of the sciences, the division into eleven sciences, "leads directly into the center of the fundamental problem." In this division, the central position is occupied not by ethics but by "God and the angels," leading us to "wonder whether 'the account of the chariot' is identical with the science of God and the angels" (168). This question of identity is the central conceit of Maimonides's *Guide*, that is, whether the two greatest mysteries of Judaism are identical with the

two most important theoretical sciences in ancient philosophy.[39] Strauss
goes on to raise the question whether the Talmudic sages were "men of
science or not" (169)—implying the same question that the central conceit of the *Guide* raises. Although Strauss gives many hints as to how to
resolve this central conceit, our clearest hint is contained in the obvious
connection between Maimonides's use of numerology and the traditional
mystical use of it. To address this central conceit, we return to the elusive
key footnote concerning numerology (168 n. 23).

In note 23, Strauss argues that in the second division of the sciences into
eleven, theoretical science itself was divided into seven parts with music in
the center (arithmetic, geometry, astronomy, music, physics, speech about
God and the angels, metaphysics). According to Strauss, placing music in
the center of the philosophical sciences is reminiscent of the "ancient" or
pre-Socratic or Pythagorean view of music as the center of theoretical science and theoretical science as the center of philosophy. Only when seen
in light of all eleven of the sciences (including the four practical sciences:
"ethics, economics, governance of the city, governance of the great nation
or of the nations" [167]) and the centrality of the problem of God and the
angels does the true center of philosophy come into view. That center is
the theologico-political problem. The older view, which privileges numbers or mathematics, is oddly dogged by the accusation of mysticism—as
Pythagoreanism came to be. Only at this most remote distance from what
Strauss elsewhere refers to as "the monistic positivism of the nineteenth
and twentieth centuries" (182) do we see that the opposites mathematics
and mysticism possess a peculiar affinity to one another. We are reminded
once again of the strange similarities between the hostility toward political science that Maimonides faced and the hostility Strauss faces in the
form of contemporary historicism—which, though it appears to be the
polar opposite of monistic positivism, is merely the other side of the coin
of contemporary philosophy.

Something even more curious than all of these affinities between pre-
Socratic, medieval, and late modern excesses is that Strauss diagnoses the
problem by means not only of Maimonides's *Logic* but also of Alfarabi's
Philosophy of Plato. The primary excess of Pythagoreanism was an over-
stated confidence not only in the centrality of music and number but
also in the view that "only the theoretical sciences are philosophic" (168
n. 23). Now Strauss himself in his much-discussed "Farabi's *Plato*" (1945)
came dangerously close to the view that only the theoretical sciences are
philosophic.[40] After all, in that article he insinuated that Alfarabi's view is

that political philosophy is little more than the exoteric face of theoretical philosophy. *What Is Political Philosophy?* as a whole is a crucial document in understanding the crisis in Strauss's thought, which he refers to as his "shipwreck" (1946).[41] Note 23, strange and off the beaten path though it is, seems to be one of the most telling confrontations with the central problem of philosophy. Following the shipwreck, Strauss seems to have come to appreciate more deeply the theoretical significance of political philosophy.

As I argued at the beginning of this chapter, the secretive alliance of philosophy and princes so central to the "Averroistic tradition," of which Maimonides is a part, is radically transformed in the hands of Machiavelli—especially by his blasphemous ire as expressed in propaganda (45–46). Yet the ambition for universal rule (exemplified in monotheism), which gave rise to this secrecy in the first place, has endured and at times only intensified throughout the history of Western political thought, even as, perhaps in part because, Machiavelli's antireligious propaganda heaped success upon success. For Maimonides, monotheism poses a novel challenge to political science: the former insinuates the latter is obsolete. Yet classical political philosophy has answers to monotheism's universal ambitions, as Strauss's humble "Statement on Political Science" begins to show.[42] If classical political philosophy possesses such resources, there is little reason to accept the argument of Kojève that the universalistic ambitions of his own brand of Hegelianism can be realized by means of the unprecedented resources of the biblical tradition. The "improbable" cities of the classics are in a sense more "possible"[43] than are the fantastic promises of Kojève's Hegelianism to provide "the actual satisfaction of all human beings" (131–32).

Notes

1. The "Statement on Political Science" originally appeared in the *Proceedings of the American Academy for Jewish Research*, a setting in which so conjectural a writing would not appear out of place.

2. Berman (1969, 106–11; Kraemer (1991, 77–104). For complete bibliographic information on the Arabic versions and the critical edition produced by Mubahat Türker, consult the first footnote of either of these articles. For an English translation more accurate than Strauss could produce, see the selected translation of chapter 14 by Muhsin Mahdi in Parens and Macfarland (2011, 180–82); also see the translation of the complete chapter 14 as well as selections from chapters 3 and 8 by Charles E. Butterworth in Weiss and Butterworth (1983, 158–63). Finally, the

interested reader should also compare Strauss's much later and far briefer piece on the *Logic*, entitled "Note on Maimonides' *Treatise on the Art of Logic*" (Strauss 1983, 208–9).

Herbert Davidson attempted to raise doubts about the authorship of the *Logic* (Davidson 2004, 318). He had expressed these objections in print prior to the publication of his book. Ahmad Hasnawi put these doubts to rest (Hasnawi 2004, 39–78). I thank Joel L. Kraemer for making me aware of this article.

3. All parenthetical citations in this chapter refer to page numbers in Strauss (1959), *What Is Political Philosophy? and Other Studies*.

4. Cf. Maimonides's praise of Alfarabi, especially his *Principles of the Beings* (viz., *Political Regime*), in one of his letters to Samuel Ibn Tibbon, cited in the biographical introduction to Charles E. Butterworth's translation of Alfarabi's *Political Regime* in Parens and Macfarland (2011, 36) and the related passage cited by Shlomo Pines in his translator's introduction to *Guide of the Perplexed* (Maimonides 1963, lx).

5. Also see Strauss's comment: "There is no room for political philosophy in Heidegger's work, and this may well be due to the fact that the room in question is occupied by gods or the gods," in "Philosophy as Rigorous Science and Political Philosophy" (Strauss 1983, 30).

6. Meier (2006). Regarding the connection between Machiavelli and the medievals, see especially the introduction to *Persecution and the Art of Writing* (Strauss 1988, 15). Regarding Maimonides's Averroism, see the introduction to "The Law of Reason in the *Kuzari*" (Strauss 1988, 95–98).

7. This characterization of the relation between premodern and modern critiques of religion should be contrasted with Strauss's characterization of that relation (Strauss 1995; 1997, 37–52).

8. Modern political philosophy eschews conventional slavery; however, classical political philosophy does not develop arguments to eliminate such slavery. This is an example of the difference in the political *solution* of ancients and moderns, but it does not preclude the possibility that classical political philosophy offers the resources to understand why one might wish to eliminate conventional slavery.

9. Strauss (1988, 15).

10. For evidence that Alfarabi is the medieval founder of what Strauss refers to as "Averroism" and evidence that Maimonides (though a contemporary of Averroes rather than a student of his thought) was as a follower of Alfarabi also an "Averroist," see Strauss (1988, introduction and 95–98).

11. Strauss (1988, 17).

12. See "Statement," 164–65 n. 19, citing *Guide* 1.31. Also cf. n. 33 below.

13. Strauss does not qualify this claim with "seems"; furthermore, he devotes significant attention to the question of "for whom" their teaching is useless. The Hebrew versions warrant the use of "we"; the Arabic versions are in the passive. Joel L. Kraemer takes Strauss to task at length for providing such a "fine example of how reliance on Hebrew translations of Arabic texts wreaks havoc with our

understanding" (Kraemer 1991, 98–101). Strauss, however, offers the equivalence of the Hebrew "we" to "we Jews" as a questionable interpretation, which he entertains among other possibilities. Kraemer insists that Maimonides states clearly what is and is not relevant about classical political philosophy in this penultimate paragraph of the *Logic*, at least in the Arabic versions. Below, I will try to show that the relevant passage does insinuate a rejection of political science, as broad as Strauss claims.

14. Strauss is addressing the mere *appearance* that Maimonides is dispensing with political science. Kraemer attempts to argue that Maimonides does not claim to dispense with so much. Ultimately, Strauss agrees that political science remains relevant.

15. Cf. Kraemer (1991, 99).

16. Kraemer (1991, 99–101).

17. Cf. Strauss's reference to these chapters of the *Guide* at 164 n. 17.

18. Cf. Kraemer (1991, 100–103).

19. See Mahdi's translation in Parens and Macfarland (2011, 75). Note that Strauss himself refers to this passage in the "Statement on Political Science" while confirming that the *Guide*'s prophetology is a branch of political science (161).

20. For the difference between enlightened *kalām* (dialectical theology or apologetics) and traditional *kalām*, see "The Literary Character of the *Guide for the Perplexed*" (Strauss 1988, esp. 40–41). For accounts of traditional *kalām*, see Charles E. Butterworth's translation of Alfarabi's *Enumeration of the Sciences*, chap. 5, either in Parens and Macfarland (2011, 18–23) or in Butterworth (2001, 76–84), and see *Guide* 1.71.

21. See n. 13 above for the acknowledgment that the Hebrew versions use "we" but the Arabic are in the passive.

22. See Green (forthcoming, n. 2) for full citations of the relevant commentaries and a translation of the relevant passage from Mendelssohn. Mendelssohn's interpretation follows the lead of Spinoza's *Theologico-Political Treatise*—despite his well-known preference for Leibniz—in claiming that with the loss of the Jewish homeland Jewish Law becomes irrelevant.

23. It is well worth comparing this determination of the audience of the *Logic* with the opening lines of Strauss's later piece on the same work: "Maimonides' *Treatise on the Art of Logic* is not a Jewish book. He wrote it in his capacity as a student of the art of logic at the request of a master of the legal (religious) sciences, as a man of high education in the Arabic tongue who wished to have explained to him as briefly as possible the meaning of the terms frequently occurring in the art of logic" (Strauss 1983, 208). The reference to the "master of the legal (religious) sciences" echoes his reference in "Statement" to "the men who speculate about the principles or roots." Furthermore, the opening sentence from the later work was already anticipated in "Statement" (162).

24. One thing is certain: one must be very careful not to confuse "the most practical part of the political teaching of the philosophers" with what was previously

referred to as "politics proper." It would be more accurate to say that that practical part is more or less the same thing as what I referred to above as the "political solution." Indeed, "politics proper" in the "Statement" is more or less equivalent to the "theoretical understanding of revealed religion" or what I called the "framework" of classical political philosophy.

25. Kraemer offers an exhaustive exploration of parallel passages in Maimonides's immediate antecedent, Alfarabi (Kraemer 1991, 90–94), as well as the possible ultimate antecedent, Aristotle, and in particular a conjectured paraphrase of Aristotle's *Politics* (Kraemer 1991, 94–95). In conjecturing such an ultimate antecedent Kraemer relies upon Pines (1975, 156–59).

26. In 159 n. 9, *Siyāsāt* = *Political Regime* and *Al-madīna al-fādila* = *Virtuous City*. For the former, see Charles E. Butterworth's translation in Parens and Macfarland (2011, 36–55) or forthcoming in *Alfarabi: The Political Writings* series for Cornell University Press; for the latter, see Walzer (1985).

27. Strauss's citations on 159–60 nn. 7 and 10 refer to Harry Austryn Wolfson, "Note on Maimonides' Classification of the Sciences" (Wolfson 1935–36, 369–77); Strauss mistakenly added the letter "s" to "Note" making it "Notes."

28. Cf. Strauss's interpretation of the prophetology and the *Guide* with Kraemer (1991, 101–4). Although Kraemer argues here with great delicacy against Strauss, I think that his conclusion that the *Guide* is a dialectical, philosophic book (1991, 101–2) and a "book of political governance (just as the Torah is a book of political governance)" (1991, 103) is not an advance over Strauss's claim that it is, in the first instance, a work of enlightened *kalām* and, in the second instance and at a much deeper level, a work of political philosophy, especially in the prophetology section (*Guide* 2.32–48) and in its mate the section on providence (3.8–24). (Cf. Kraemer 1991, 99; "Statement," 166; and Strauss 2004, 537–49.) Kraemer's account gives a far more harmonious portrait of the *Guide* than Strauss's.

29. Kraemer objects to this interpretation based on similarity between this passage in the *Logic* and one in Alfarabi's *Book of Religion* (Kraemer 1991, 93). For reasons I lack space to treat here, I think that he overstates the similarity—though such a similarity would not undermine the essential point, which is that these terms are references to differences not in size but in religion.

30. I have added diacritical marks (as well as English translations of the Hebrew), which were missing from Strauss's original version due to printing limitations of the time.

31. See Butterworth's translation for this rendering (Weiss and Butterworth 1983, 161). The list of terms is omitted from Mahdi's translation. It should also be underlined that the term "command" or "commands" (though not *hukm*) appears in the *Logic*. Indeed, the phrase "divine commands" (*al-awāmir al-ilāhiyya*) is the concluding phrase of the body text (as opposed to the concluding list of terms) in chapter 14. See both Mahdi's and Butterworth's translations. Strauss's translation based on the Hebrew has "things" for "commands"—though "things" is also a plausible rendering of *awāmir* (156).

32. Strauss (163 n. 15) is correct that Maimonides contrasts individual and law in a radical, even shocking, way in the chapters of the *Guide* that Strauss then cites (3.34 and 2.40). Nevertheless, Strauss's conjecture about " 'commands' and *nomoi*" lacks textual support in the original Arabic of the *Logic* to which he did not have access.

33. Strauss (165 n. 19) directs the interested reader to *Guide* 1.17, 1.31, 3.29, and other passages. See esp. 1.31.

34. Compare the preceding two sentences with n. 24, above.

35. Cf. Ralph Lerner's translation of the opening four chapters of Maimonides's *Mishneh Torah*, in which Maimonides summarizes the Account of the Chariot (chaps. 1 and 2) and the Account of the Beginning (chaps. 3 and 4) (Lerner 2000, 141–53, esp. 145). Also see *Guide* 2.3–12 and 3.1–7.

36. See Maimonides (1963, 619, ¶¶4 and 6 respectively).

37. Also see Nasser Behnegar's observation in chap. 1 n. 5 above, that Strauss traces the source of the numerological significance of the number seventeen to the existence of seventeen consonants in Greek. We are not surprised that Maimonides would rely on a Greek tradition here once we remember that the Hebrew Bible does not have any word for "nature."

38. See n. 28 above.

39. Pines (1963, 6).

40. Strauss (1945, 357–93).

41. Strauss (2001, 660); also see Meier (2006, 29 n. 1).

42. Cf. Kraemer (1991, 93 n. 46); his citation in Kraemer (1984, 141 n. 46); and Kraemer (1987, 288–324); with Parens (2006, chap. 4, esp. 60–76).

43. Cf. Parens (2006, chap. 2).

Works Cited

Berman, Lawrence V. 1969. "A Reexamination of Maimonides' 'Statement on Political Science.' " *Journal of the American Oriental Society* 89: 106–11.

Butterworth, Charles E., trans. 2001. *Alfarabi: The Political Writings; "Selected Aphorisms" and Other Texts*. Ithaca: Cornell University Press.

Davidson, Herbert. 2004. *Moses Maimonides: The Man and His Work*. New York: Oxford University Press.

Green, Kenneth H. Forthcoming. *Leo Strauss on Maimonides: The Complete Writings*. Chicago: University of Chicago Press.

Hasnawi, Ahmad. 2004. "Réflexions sur la terminologie logique de Maïmonide et son contexte farabien: le *Guide des perplexes* et la Traité de logique." In *Maïmonide: Philosophe et savant*, ed. Tony Lévy and Roshdi Rashed, 39–78. Leuven: Peeters.

Kraemer, Joel L. 1984. "On Maimonides' Messianic Posture." In *Studies in Medieval and Jewish History and Literature*, vol. 2, ed. Isadore Twersky, 109–42. Cambridge: Harvard University Press for the Littman Library.

———. 1987. "The *Jihād* of the *Falāsifa*." *Jerusalem Studies in Arabic and Islam* 10: 288–324.

———. 1991. "Maimonides on the Philosophic Sciences in His *Treatise on the Art of Logic*." In *Perspectives on Maimonides*, ed. Joel L. Kraemer, 77–104. Oxford: Oxford University Press for the Littman Library.

Lerner, Ralph. 2000. *Maimonides' Empire of Light*. Chicago: University of Chicago Press.

Maimonides, Moses. 1963. *Guide of the Perplexed*. Trans. Shlomo Pines. Chicago: University of Chicago Press.

Meier, Heinrich. 2006. *Leo Strauss and the Theologio-Political Problem*. New York: Cambridge University Press.

Parens, Joshua. 2006. *An Islamic Philosophy of Virtuous Religions: Introducing Alfarabi*. Albany: SUNY Press.

Parens, Joshua, and Joseph C. Macfarland, eds. 2011. *Medieval Political Philosophy: A Sourcebook*. 2nd ed. Ithaca: Cornell University Press.

Pines, Shlomo. 1975. "Aristotle's *Politics* in Arabic Philosophy." *Israel Oriental Studies* 5: 150–60.

Strauss, Leo. 1945. "Farabi's *Plato*." In *Louis Ginzberg Jubilee Volume*, ed. A. Marx, S. Lieberman, S. Spiegel, and S. Zeitlin, 357–93. New York: American Academy of Jewish Research.

———. 1959. *What Is Political Philosophy? and Other Studies*. New York: Free Press.

———. 1983. *Studies in Platonic Political Philosophy*. Chicago: University of Chicago Press.

———. 1988. *Persecution and the Art of Writing*. Chicago: University of Chicago Press.

———. 1995. *Philosophy and Law*. Trans. Eve Adler. Albany: SUNY Press.

———. 1997. *Spinoza's Critique of Religion*. Trans. E. M. Sinclair. New York: Schocken, 1965; rpt., Chicago: University of Chicago Press.

———. 2001. *Gesammelte Schriften*, vol. 3: *Hobbes' politische Wissenschaft und zugehörige Schriften—Briefe*. Ed. Heinrich Meier and Wiebke Meier. Stuttgart: J. B. Metzler.

———. 2004. "The Place of the Doctrine of Providence According to Maimonides." *Review of Metaphysics* 57: 537–49.

Walzer, Richard. 1985. *Al-Farabi on the Perfect State*. Oxford: Clarendon Press.

Weiss, Raymond L., and Charles E. Butterworth, eds. 1983. *Ethical Writings of Maimonides*. New York: New York University Press, 1975; rpt., New York: Dover.

Wolfson, Harry Austryn. 1935–36. "Note on Maimonides' Classification of the Sciences." *Jewish Quarterly Review* 26: 369–77.

CHAPTER SEVEN

Leo Strauss's "On the Basis of Hobbes's Political Philosophy"

Devin Stauffer

hapter 7 of *What Is Political Philosophy?*, "On the Basis of Hobbes's Political Philosophy," is preceded by four chapters on premodern political philosophy and followed by a chapter on Locke.[1] If the central theme of *What Is Political Philosophy?* is the quarrel between the ancients and the moderns, or the contest between "the classical solution" and "the modern solutions" (see 27–55),[2] then the chapter on Hobbes is the crucial pivot point from the premodern to the modern section of the book. Indeed, Strauss indicates that his interest in Hobbes stems, above all, from his concern with the quarrel between the ancients and the moderns (172–73). Now, between his first published work on Hobbes, *The Political Philosophy of Hobbes*, and the chapter on Hobbes in *What Is Political Philosophy?*, Strauss revised his view that Hobbes was the originator of modernity. That title, in Strauss's revised view, belongs to Machiavelli. As he put it in another statement on Hobbes, which he wrote well after *The Political Philosophy of Hobbes* but shortly before our present chapter, "it was Machiavelli, that greater Columbus, who had discovered the continent on which Hobbes could erect his structure."[3] Yet, as that formulation indicates, Hobbes, while following the route discovered by Machiavelli, was modernity's first great architect and builder. Thus, both for understanding ourselves as moderns and for reexamining the quarrel between the ancients and the moderns, the study of Hobbes is essential. This is especially so, according to Strauss, since modernity has not simply moved beyond Hobbes but rather "has progressed to the point where it has visibly become a problem" (172; cf. Strauss 2006, 122–25).

I

Strauss's chapter begins as a response to an interpretation of Hobbes by the French scholar Raymond Polin.[4] Strauss has considerable praise for Polin's interpretation of Hobbes (see, e.g., 174–75, 195–96).[5] More important than his praise, however, is his criticism of Polin. Polin's interpretation of Hobbes focused on Hobbes's transformation of the traditional understanding of man, and in particular on Hobbes's novel view that man, through his invention of speech, creates the categories by which his reason operates and thus in a sense creates his own world and even himself. Man, according to Polin's Hobbes, is the natural being who revolts against nature by creating a world of artificial human constructs (174–76; see Polin 1953, xviii, 5–13, 99–100). Yet, to be consistent with Hobbes's materialism and determinism, must not the very revolt against nature be driven by a natural necessity? Polin's Hobbes seems to have wavered over the question of whether human beings, through their creations, break free from nature or whether they are compelled, even in constructing their artificial works, by a natural necessity. This unresolved dilemma bears on Hobbes's political philosophy or political science: "Polin may be said to come close to what Hobbes suggests by contending that there is both a discontinuity and an unbroken continuity between the natural mechanism and the social mechanism, or that man both escapes and does not escape the natural mechanism" (177; see, e.g., Polin 1953, 23, 51–55, 61–66, 149–50). Strauss does not entirely blame Polin for this wavering, because it captures or reproduces a wavering or ambiguity in Hobbes's own teaching. Polin, however, did not face squarely enough "the fundamental ambiguity of Hobbes's teaching." Had he done so, according to Strauss, he would have had to confront the "necessity of choosing one of two alternative interpretations of Hobbes's political science and of acting on this choice in a consistent manner" (177).

   The two alternative interpretations of Hobbes's political science "may loosely be called," Strauss says, "the naturalistic and the humanistic interpretations" (177). Strauss then revises: "It is better to say that the student of Hobbes must make up his mind whether he is going to understand Hobbes's political science by itself or whether he is going to understand it in the light of Hobbes's natural science" (177). Now, in his own earlier interpretation of Hobbes in *The Political Philosophy of Hobbes*, Strauss chose the former of these two alternatives. The thesis of that book was that Hobbes's political philosophy rested on a moral foundation or a "specific moral attitude" that was independent of and prior to Hobbes's natural science (see Strauss 1963, ix–xi, 1–29). That view, in its essentials, seems to have remained unchanged for Strauss throughout his study of Hobbes. He repeats a version of it here. And he offers several reasons for interpreting Hobbes's political science on its own terms: if one interprets Hobbes's political science through the lens of his natural science, it loses its "native hue" and one cannot "do justice to the life that vibrates in Hobbes's political teaching" (178); Hobbes himself indicates that his political science is based on principles of its own, derived from experience, and does not depend on his natural science (179); and the moral judgment at the core of Hobbes's political science is obscured if his political science is seen as derivative from his natural science (192). Although these points indicate that Strauss did not change his mind on the key issue, his present statement is not simply a repetition in briefer form of the main points of his earlier work. For, as much as he continues to interpret Hobbes's political science on its own, Strauss now insists, more emphatically than he did in his earlier work, that there *is* a relationship between Hobbes's political science and his natural science: "While Hobbes's political science cannot be understood in the light of his natural science, it can also not be understood as simply independent of his natural science or as simply preceding it" (180). The relationship between Hobbes's political science and his natural science — or better, the question of that relationship — is the central theme also of Strauss's discussion of Hobbes in *Natural Right and History*. There, Strauss posed this crucial question without providing a clear or direct answer to it.[6] In the present discussion, he takes a similar approach. There *is* an important relationship, he insists, between Hobbes's political science and his natural science. But what is it?

II

Strauss's basic suggestion, to repeat, is that Hobbes's political science should not be understood as derivative from his natural science, but neither should it be understood as simply independent of his natural science or as simply preceding it. Strauss elaborates by claiming that although there are good reasons to accept the assertion that Hobbes's political science "stands on its own feet" and was "conceived in an *esprit de finesse* rather than in an *esprit de géométrie*," "this does not mean the substance of his political science is completely unrelated to his natural science" (180). As for what the relationship is, Strauss gives this answer: "The relation between his political science and his natural science may provisionally be compared with that between theological dogmatics and theological apologetics. What Hobbes discovered about human things by reasoning from his experience of man, is put forth as indubitably true; but it must be defended against misconceptions of man which arise from vain opinions about the whole" (180).

This answer, however, is merely provisional. Strauss almost immediately modifies it by suggesting that Hobbes's "view of man" was informed by a "view of the whole" (181). According to Strauss's modified suggestion, Hobbes's "view of man" expresses the humanly relevant implications of "the new view of the whole." This can be seen nowhere more clearly than in the emphasis Hobbes placed on fear: "the mood generated by the truth, the true mood, is fear, the fear experienced by a being exposed to a universe which does not care for it by properly equipping it or by guiding it" (181). The fear on which Hobbes builds is to be distinguished from the abject fear that grips men by nature. Natural fear, despite or even because of its abject character, goes together with a certain kind of presumption or pride, for it leads men to hope and pray for the providential care of "spirits invisible." In contrast to such fear and pride, Hobbesian fear, the "true mood" generated by the "true view," arises not from man's initial blindness but from his realization of his true situation; it can therefore arise "only after man has made a considerable effort" (181). It differs from natural fear also in directing men, not to hope or prayer, but to human enterprise in order to secure themselves against the harsh and uncaring natural world. Hobbes's political science, then, would seem to depend on a mood that can arise only with the acceptance of the new view of the whole, which presumably is the view of the new natural science of which Hobbes was a proponent (see 180). Yet, for Hobbes's political science to succeed, the new view of the whole must be accepted not only by Hobbes himself but also by his readers and even by the public as a whole. The new view, in other words, must become the dominant view by overcoming the traditional views that oppose it in the minds of most men. Thus Hobbes's natural science must play a role that extends beyond the "apologetic" role of defending the assertions of his political science from attack (or counterattack); it must also help to supply the premises whose widespread acceptance is essential if his political science is to be truly compelling or convincing. In sum, if Hobbes's political project is to succeed, men must be brought to accept the new view of the whole, and that would seem to require, if not the widespread education of men in the principles of the new natural science, at least the popularization of the key conclusions of that science as they bear on the situation of man in the whole (180–81; cf. Strauss 1953, 198–99).

This suggestion would seem to provide a clear answer to the question of the relationship between Hobbes's political science and his natural science. Yet, after sketching it out, Strauss surprisingly downplays its adequacy: "This suggestion is by no means sufficient for removing the fundamental obscurities of Hobbes's teaching" (181–82). Now, given that pronouncement, one would expect Strauss at this point to supply a further explanation of the relationship of Hobbes's political science and his natural science. But that is not what he offers, at least not immediately. He will return to the question of the "link" between Hobbes's political science and his natural science (190). In the meantime, and thus in what would seem to be a digression from his main theme, Strauss turns in another direction. Perhaps, however, the themes that he takes up in this apparent digression bear in some way on his central question and point to a more adequate answer to that question. To see how that might be the case, let us consider the two main themes of Strauss's apparent digression. They are, first, the obscurities and wavering of Hobbes's teaching on certain essential questions that bear on his understanding of the objects of his natural science and, second, Hobbes's atheism. What is the connection between these two themes? And how might they bear on the question from which Strauss appears to digress?

III

In his consideration of the obscurities and wavering in Hobbes's teaching, Strauss returns to the question of whether Hobbes's emphasis on the importance of human making can be squared with his corporealism and determinism. How is the world of artificial human constructs related to the natural world of which man is a part? This question arises, or at any rate Hobbes's answer to it becomes ambiguous, when Hobbes's assumption of "a fundamental bipartition of things" into the natural and the artificial is extended to the principles of understanding. Are the principles of understanding artificial human constructs that are "not only irreducible to the natural but even primary," or, insofar as all human works are products of universal motion, do they remain determined by the natural (182; cf. 175–76)?

According to Strauss, Hobbes never reached a clear and final answer to this question: "Hobbes wavers not only between corporealism and what we may call constructionism; he is also uncertain whether the non-corporealist beginning has the character of arbitrary construction or of 'data of consciousness'" (182). In his earlier discussion of Polin's interpretation of Hobbes, Strauss already indicated a "fundamental difficulty" that besets Hobbes's view of speech as an artificial human invention and his constructivist understanding of reason: "If, as [Hobbes] contends, the bases of all reasoning are arbitrary definitions, it is hard to see how reasoning can disclose to us the true character of reality" (174). According to a suggestion Strauss makes elsewhere, Hobbes would have liked to avoid this difficulty simply by affirming his corporealism: "Hobbes had the earnest desire to be a 'metaphysical' materialist" (Strauss 1953, 174). But Hobbes—whether because he regarded such materialism as indemonstrable or because he thought that it rendered the universe unintelligible, or for both reasons—was forced to retreat from that aim and to turn instead to the constructivist view according to which we understand only what we make.[7] Yet to turn in that direction has the result that at least in its attempts to use human constructions to draw conclusions about the true character of the natural world, "natural science is and will always remain fundamentally hypothetical" (Strauss 1953, 174, 201; see also Hobbes, *De homine*, chap. 10). A constructivist natural science can promise the human conquest of nature, but only at the expense of affirming that nature itself is ultimately unintelligible or that "the universe will always remain wholly enigmatic" (Strauss 1953, 174). Thus we can understand why Hobbes wavered between incompatible positions, unable to rest satisfied with any of them. Yet if such fundamental questions about the very objects and method of his natural science are left unresolved by Hobbes, can that science truly vindicate the new view of the whole to which Strauss has referred? Or, to put the matter more directly, can Hobbes's natural science, with its obscurities and wavering, vindicate his atheism?

Hobbes was indeed an atheist, according to Strauss. Strauss now tells us that "the most important element of Hobbes's view of the whole is his view of the deity"—and Strauss leaves no mystery about what that view is (182–89). But to repeat the question: Can Hobbes's natural science have supplied an adequate basis for his atheism? By putting his most direct declaration of Hobbes's atheism immediately after his statement on the wavering and obscurities at the foundations of Hobbes's natural science, Strauss may intend to provoke that question. At any rate, he chooses this moment to try to dispel any doubts about whether Hobbes was an atheist.

He does so by laying out a series of arguments that would seem to belong, not exactly to Hobbes's political science or to his natural science, but to his critique of religion.

Hobbes's critique of religion, as Strauss summarizes it, runs along two main lines. The first is Hobbes's "natural theology," the true purpose of which, Strauss argues, is to show that "natural reason knows nothing of God," that is, to demonstrate that reason operating on its own does not lead to belief in God's existence (183–84). Strauss is well aware, of course, of Hobbes's claim that natural reason can come to know, if not God's attributes, at least God's existence. Hobbes's God, the God of Hobbes's "natural theology," is the first mover, the mysterious x at the beginning of the chain of causes, whose existence was acknowledged "even by the heathen philosophers" (183–84; see Hobbes, *Leviathan* 11.25, 12.6, *Elements of Law* 11.2). Yet, since Hobbes contends that it is impossible to form a meaningful image or conception of this God, Hobbes's doctrine of "God," in Strauss's interpretation, has as its ultimate purpose, not to honor or illuminate the deity, but to show the limits of human knowledge and the groundlessness of human claims about God's power, goodness, and providence. Such claims rest on mere belief or opinion, not on knowledge (183–84; see Hobbes, *Leviathan* 3.12, 12.7, 31.28, 31.33; Hobbes, *Elements of Law* 11.2–4; Hobbes [1839–45] 1966, 4: 296–97). Strauss goes a step further. For it could seem that the one thing Hobbes thinks human reason can know of God is His existence as the first mover. But reason inquiring after causes, according to the genuine view of Strauss's Hobbes, does not really know of an unmoved mover. And if God is a moved mover and therefore, as Hobbes contends, a body that is a part of the universe, it is not clear why the name "God" should continue to be used for such a conception, especially since Hobbes's "theology" proves to be identical to a philosophic view he himself identifies as atheistic. Perhaps the name "God" remains meaningful insofar as Hobbes points to the creation of the world as an argument for regarding the moved mover in question as a deity. But reason, Hobbes indicates, does not truly support the view that the world was created.[8]

If reason cannot establish God's existence in Hobbes's view, neither can Scripture. In his summary of the second dimension of Hobbes's critique of religion, Strauss argues that despite some appearances to the contrary, Hobbes does not turn from natural reason to a reliance on the Bible. Hobbes's "revealed theology," as Strauss interprets it, cannot be understood as a good faith effort to discern the true meaning of the Biblical text. Rather, Hobbes uses that "theology" to sow seeds of doubt about the revealed character of the Bible (185–88). Strauss points in this connection to some of the more outlandish conclusions of Hobbes's "interpretation" of the Bible, such as his suggestion that there are corporeal angels but no devils and his claim that after the Second Coming the dead will be resurrected to a new life on earth in which the fate of the reprobate is not clearly worse than that of the elect (185). More important than such points of "interpretation" are Hobbes's arguments meant to show that there is no noncircular reason, that is, no reason that does not depend on a prior belief in the authority of the Bible, to accept the claim that the Bible is genuine revelation. Hobbes denied that the revealed character of the Bible could be established by the antiquity of the Bible or by arguments that begin from miracles (185). And he sought to awaken and justify doubts by arguing that the thinking mind cannot simply will itself to believe in an uncertain proposition and thus it must doubt, in particular, the unverifiable claim that the Bible is the true word of God (186–87). In his critique of this claim, Hobbes attempts to show, not only that reason cannot establish the actuality of revelation, but that the content of the Bible is "against reason" (187). Strauss limits his sketch of this last line of argument to Hobbes's moral and political critique of the Bible: the extreme demands of the moral teaching of the Bible encourage a fanatical zeal that is at odds with good citizenship in "large societies," and the Bible's political teaching lays the foundation of the dualism of temporal and spiritual power that is so destructive of peace, "the demand *par excellence* of reason" (187–88).

Now, in the long section in which he treats Hobbes's atheism, Strauss is concerned not merely to establish that Hobbes was an atheist. He is also sketching Hobbes's effort to refute revealed religion (see 187). More than that, Strauss suggests that Hobbes contemplated the very destruction of Christianity: "Certainly the study of 'the causes of change in religion' leads to the conclusion that Christianity can as well be abolished as paganism was before" (186). But why— Strauss prompts us to wonder—would Hobbes be interested in such a thing? Strauss prompts us to ask that question by posing this one: "But why should a sovereign in Christendom think of such an extreme policy, seeing that the Bible is susceptible of an interpretation, namely the Hobbesian interpretation, which makes it an excellent vehicle of any government, especially if care is taken that all Christian sects which are not seditious are fully tolerated?" (186). That Hobbes himself *did* think of such an extreme policy indicates that his interests extended beyond the needs of stable politics. Yet to say that political considerations alone do not suffice to explain Hobbes's interest in this "extreme policy" is not to say that his political project may not have contributed to the effort to achieve such a far-reaching end by promoting an outlook that would contribute to the withering of belief in revelation (cf. Strauss 1953, 169, 175, 198). Might Strauss be pointing us here to another and deeper relationship between Hobbes's political science and his natural science, this time with his political science in the role of the handmaid? In this connection, it is noteworthy that Strauss treats Hobbes's contemplation of the destruction of Christianity—after which there would be "no necessity" of another "formed religion" arising in its place—as part of Hobbes's effort to refute revealed religion (consider 185–87). Might Hobbes have regarded the abolition of Christianity and the emergence of a successful "a-religious or atheistic society" (Strauss 1953, 198) as supplying a kind of refutation that his natural science could not supply (cf. Strauss 1953, 175, 201; 1995, 31–32; 1997, 28–29)?

If Strauss does mean to point us to this last suggestion, he does not make it explicit or spell it out. Instead, after his brief statement on Hobbes's interest in the destruction of Christianity, he returns to the more evident aspects of Hobbes's critique of religion. He discusses Hobbes's political critique of the Bible as destructive of peace, and then he sketches Hobbes's attempt at a natural explanation of Biblical religion. According to Hobbes's indicated explanation, Biblical religion arose out of an excessive hatred of human government, bred by the experience of slavery in Egypt, which then led to so defective a government that hopes eventually emerged for a new human king; these Messianic hopes, in turn, were the source of a political movement whose initial failure required that it be drastically reinterpreted in order to salvage Jesus' claim to be the Messiah (188–89). Strauss's summary of this last line of argument allows him to conclude his consideration of Hobbes's critique of religion with a harsh dismissal of that critique: "But enough of Hobbes's shocking oversimplifications, not to say absurdities, which the most charitable man could not describe more aptly than by applying to Hobbes, with the necessary modifications, a remark which he himself makes about Lucian: *Homo blasphemus, licet sit author quamvis bonus linguae Anglicae*" (189).

IV

In the wake of this remark, which leaves the impression that he is turning away in contempt from Hobbes's critique of religion, Strauss returns explicitly to the question of the relationship between Hobbes's political science and his natural science. He now offers what would seem to be a nonprovisional and direct answer to that question:

> Hobbes's unbelief is the necessary premise of his teaching about the state of
> nature. That teaching is the authentic link between his natural science and his
> political science: it defines the problem which political science has to solve by
> inferring from the preceding exposition of the nature of man, and especially of
> the human passions, the condition concerning felicity and misery in which man
> has been placed by nature. More specifically, the teaching about the state of na-
> ture is meant to clarify what the status of justice is prior to, and independently
> of, human institution, or to answer the question of whether, and to what extent,
> justice has extra-human and especially divine support. (189–90)

With this statement, Strauss seems finally to have given us the answer we
have been looking for. But how clear and complete is this statement?

There would seem to be the following puzzle in Strauss's statement.
Strauss begins by saying that Hobbes's unbelief is the "necessary premise"
of his teaching about the state of nature, and that Hobbes's political science sets out to solve a problem whose parameters are inferred from his
preceding exposition of the nature of man and especially of the human
passions. The initial impression conveyed by these remarks, especially as
they speak to "the authentic link between [Hobbes's] natural science and
his political science," is that Hobbes's natural science provides the basis
upon which his political science rests: Hobbes's political science, it would
seem, is derivative from his natural science, both in the sense that it depends on a prior account of human nature and in the sense that it begins
from an atheistic premise it does not supply. Yet hasn't Strauss already
given us reason to doubt, not only that Hobbes's political science is in fact
derivative from his natural science, but also that Hobbes's natural science
can adequately establish the premise in question? Is that why Strauss, in
speaking here of "the problem which political science has to solve" and
of the role of Hobbes's state of nature teaching in answering the question
of whether justice has "extra-human and especially divine support," uses
formulations that may point to a more fundamental role for Hobbes's political science than first meets the eye? Does Strauss mean to suggest that
Hobbes's state of nature teaching, as the crucial first step in his political
science, aims at the vindication of its own premises by giving an account
of our natural condition that can provide the basis for a new understanding of justice and for a political order that can solve the human problem
without the need for "divine support"? Does the "link" to which Strauss
refers, in other words, work in both directions?[9]

Whether or not that is what Strauss means to indicate, he goes on to give us further reason not to take his statement in the most straightforward way, that is, as suggesting that Hobbes's state of nature teaching simply spells out the implications for the human condition and for justice of a view of the nature of man that rests on the foundation of Hobbes's natural science. For Strauss indicates that there is a moral judgment at the heart of Hobbes's state of nature teaching, a distinction between the legitimate motive of the fear-driven desire for self-preservation and the illegitimate motive of the vanity-driven desire for glory. That distinction, according to Strauss, rests on a "common sense" opinion about justice rather than on a "'scientific' conception of necessity" (192; cf. 48; Strauss 1953, 173 n. 9, 180 n. 16; cf. Polin 1953, 184–86). Moreover, if Hobbes's state of nature teaching simply spelled out the implications of a view taught by natural science, one would expect that teaching to be merely descriptive. But Strauss indicates that, from the start, Hobbes's description of the state of nature is guided by a prescriptive intention or by a vision of a certain kind of civil society. Hobbes's state of nature, as Rousseau pointed out, is surreptitiously teleological; it is "characterized by the existence of natural rights or natural duties in such a manner as to point towards civil society as the home of justice" (190–91; see Strauss 1953, 184–85, 189–90). These two points—the moral claim at the heart of Hobbes's doctrine of natural right and his prescriptive vision of civil society—go together, as one can see from the fact that Hobbes draws a distinction, even in the state of nature, between the just intention and the unjust intention: "there is this decisive difference between the just man and the unjust man in the state of nature: the just man in the state of nature is already the potential citizen, i.e., he is already animated by the principles animating the citizen although he cannot yet act on those principles, while the opposite is true of the unjust man in the state of nature. Furthermore the fundamental natural rights persist within civil society" (192–93). The moral judgment in Hobbes's view of natural right is thus shaped by a vision of the legitimate motives of would-be citizens of "the reasonable state" (194). By the same token, Hobbes's vision of the reasonable state is shaped by his understanding of natural right (cf. Strauss 1953, 184–92; 1983, 142–43).

V

In pointing to the moral judgment and the prescriptive vision at the core of Hobbes's political science, Strauss does not fault Hobbes for failing to

stick rigorously to a scientific conception of necessity. After all, it is unlikely that Strauss thought that an attempt to deduce natural right from
such a conception could succeed.[10] In this respect, Strauss must have regarded it as an advantage of Hobbes's approach that it stays in touch with
"common sense" in a way that, for example, Spinoza's approach to natural
right does not (see 192; cf. Strauss 1963, 28–29). That is not to say, however, that Strauss is not critical of the path Hobbes followed. Although
his criticisms of Hobbes are muted in "On the Basis of Hobbes's Political
Philosophy," Strauss does indicate the initial tracks of a critique. Regarding that aspect of Strauss's analysis, let me highlight two points by way of
conclusion.

First, as he is bringing out Hobbes's moral judgment and the prescriptive
political vision with which it travels, Strauss calls into question Hobbes's
denial of natural sociality. Hobbes emphatically denies that human beings
are naturally social (see, e.g., *De cive* 1.2; *Leviathan* 17.6–12). Indeed, in a
now famous footnote, whose importance he would later highlight, Strauss
suggested that Hobbes's very abandonment of the traditional definition of
man as the rational animal in favor of the definition of man as the animal
that can imagine the possible effects of potential causes was guided by
the necessity, for Hobbes, of rejecting the implication of the traditional
definition that man is a social animal.[11] Only by rejecting the traditional
definition and its implication could Hobbes develop "his characteristic
doctrine of man" as naturally concerned, not with the common good or
the moral law, but with his own power (see 176–77 n. 2). But Strauss leads
us to ask whether Hobbes does not acknowledge, despite himself, that
human beings are directed toward society. Can Hobbes consistently claim
that nature dissociates men while also acknowledging, not only that men
in the state of nature already possess speech and that even savages already
have government, but also that some motives are legitimate and others
illegitimate (consider 190–93)? Doesn't that distinction suggest that there
is a moral law limiting human beings prior to the establishment of a sovereign authority, even if that law requires such authority in order to become
fully effective and binding? If Hobbes's position implicitly affirms in this
way that men have natural duties toward one another, it also obscures
the meaning of such duties by asserting the primacy of the right of the
isolated individual. The "enlightenment" promised by Hobbes's natural
right teaching thus proves to be the source of a new form of confusion
or of a distinctively modern obstacle to self-knowledge and philosophy
(compare Strauss 1953, 186–92; see also 1965, 344–45; 1995, 135–36 n. 2;
1958, 290–95).

Second, Strauss suggests that it was extremely important to Hobbes—far more so than it was, for instance, to Plato—that his vision of the reasonable state be actualized in the world (194–95, cf. Strauss 1953, 182–83, 191–200). Against the impression that Hobbes was simply urging obedience to the given state, an impression that shaped Polin's "statist" interpretation of Hobbes, Strauss argues that Hobbes drew a distinction "between the state simply and the reasonable state" (194; compare Polin 1953, 148–50, 247–49). Strauss's Hobbes, in other words, was not so much a defender of authority as such or of the status quo as the architect of a new social and political order whose construction he was anticipating. More than that, he was concerned, as Strauss puts it elsewhere, with "a human guaranty for the actualization of the right social order" (Strauss 1953, 182; see also 175–77, 188–91). Hobbes was unable, however, to guarantee the actualization of his ideal state: "The actualization of Hobbes's reasonable state is almost as little necessary as the actualization of Plato's reasonable state" (194; see also 45–51; Strauss 1953, 175, 179, 199–201). This difficulty is particularly problematic if it is true that Hobbes intended his political science to play a role in helping to resolve a question that his natural science was unable to resolve.

As for whether that earlier suggestion was on the right track—first as to Strauss's indications, and then as to Hobbes's intentions—that must remain an open question. For Strauss does not provide us with a clear or conclusive answer. His restraint is intentional, as he indicates by the way he concludes. Returning to Polin to give his final verdict, Strauss writes: "It seems to us that Polin has not succeeded in laying bare the unity of Hobbes's thought, or that single fundamental problem whose complexity explains why he expressed himself with such ambiguity and contradiction on some most important subjects" (196). Strauss does not claim that he himself has done what Polin failed to do. Rather, he suggests that only the foundation has been laid for "the adequate interpretation of Hobbes's political philosophy," which remains a task for the future (196).

Notes

1. For comments on this essay that were helpful as I made revisions, I would like to thank Christopher Bruell, Heinrich Meier, Rafe Major, Nasser Behnegar, and Dana Stauffer.

2. Unless otherwise noted, all citations in parentheses in the text and notes are to Leo Strauss, *What Is Political Philosophy?* (Strauss 1959).

3. Strauss (1953, 177). See also Strauss (1963, xv–xvi; 1959, 40–49). Strauss first

published *The Political Philosophy of Hobbes* in English translation in 1936; the U.S. edition was published in 1952, with a paperback edition in 1963. The U.S. edition includes a new preface, in which Strauss expresses his revised judgment of Hobbes and Machiavelli. *Natural Right and History* was first published in 1953; the chapter on Hobbes in that work is based on an article, "On the Spirit of Hobbes's Political Philosophy," which Strauss published in the *Revue Internationale de Philosophie* in 1950. The chapter on Hobbes in *What Is Political Philosophy?*, "On the Basis of Hobbes's Political Philosophy," first appeared in French translation in *Critique* in 1954.

4. *Politique et philosophie chez Thomas Hobbes* (Polin 1953). I would like to thank Laura Field for her help in translating Polin's text.

5. Near the end of his essay, Strauss will even concede that there is some legitimacy to Polin's critique of Strauss's own "developmental" interpretation of Hobbes in his earlier work *The Political Philosophy of Hobbes* (see 195–96).

6. Consider especially the section of the chapter on Hobbes in *Natural Right in History* (Strauss 1953, 169–77). After pointing to the connection between Hobbes's founding of political hedonism and his founding of political atheism, Strauss begins the section in question with the remark: "For in trying to understand Hobbes's political philosophy, we must not lose sight of his natural philosophy" (Strauss 1953, 169). The bearing of that remark, however, is obscure. And that obscurity is surely intentional, since, in the section that the remark introduces, Strauss does not provide a clear or complete explanation of the connection between Hobbes's political philosophy and his natural philosophy. That is not to deny that he may provide some important hints and indications. See especially Strauss 1953, 174–77; see also 199–201.

7. See Strauss 1953, 169–75, 201. Consider also Strauss 1959, 178: "the real is the natural, i.e., the bodily. But are even bodies real? Is Hobbes not eventually forced into 'phenomenalism'?"

8. In laying out the line of argument I have just sketched, Strauss puts together scattered statements of Hobbes. See especially 184 n. 13. The most important passages to which Strauss points for Hobbes's thoughts on the question of the creation of the world are *De corpore* 26.1 and 26.5 and Hobbes [1839–45] 1966, 4: 349 and 427–28 (see also *De corpore* 8.20). Concerning the question of Hobbes's atheism, Strauss asks his readers in *Natural Right and History* (see Strauss 1953, 198–99 n. 43), to compare *De cive* 15.14 with Hobbes [1839–45] 1966, 4: 349. In the former passage, Hobbes says that those philosophers who maintain that God is the world or a part of the world "attribute nothing to him, but wholly deny his being"; in the latter passage, Hobbes presents the same position as his own. See also *Leviathan* 46.15.

9. Consider the formulation on pages 180–81: "Hobbes's natural science is more than a postulate or projection of his political reason." See the equally enigmatic statement on page 193: "It is perhaps not superfluous to recall here the connection

between the assertion that only the rights of the individual are primary and inde-
feasible and the assertion that only natural bodies are real." See also *Natural Right
and History*, where Strauss speaks of the "antitheological implication of the 'state
of nature'": "[Hobbes] denied, if not the fact, at any rate the importance of the
Fall and accordingly asserted that what is needed for remedying the deficiencies
or the 'inconveniences' of the state of nature is, not divine grace, but the right kind
of human government" (Strauss 1953, 184). Consider also Strauss 1953, 199–200,
especially regarding the basis of "Hobbes's rationalism."

   10. See Strauss 1953, 145: "Can natural right be deduced from man's natural
end? Can it be deduced from anything?"

   11. The note in question is note 2 on pages 176–77. In the preface to the seventh
impression of *Natural Right and History*, which was added in 1971, Strauss points
to this note as indicating "the nerve of Hobbes's argument." In reference to the
same note, Strauss wrote in the 1964 preface to the German original of *Hobbes'
politische Wissenschaft* of his success in uncovering "the simple leading thought of
Hobbes's doctrine of man." This preface and the work it introduces can be found
in volume 3 of Strauss's *Gesammelte Schriften* (Strauss 2001, 8). I am indebted to
Heinrich Meier for the translation of the line from the preface and for calling my
attention to it in the first place. See Meier (2011, 13–14 n. 37). Meier also alerted
me to the fact that the key section of the note under consideration did not appear in
the 1954 French version of "On the Basis of Hobbes's Political Philosophy" but was
added to the English version that appears in *What Is Political Philosophy?* It dates,
then, to 1959, not to 1954. The key section of the note reads as follows:

> According to Hobbes, the only peculiarity of man's mind which
> precedes the invention of speech, i.e., the only natural peculiarity
> of man's mind, is the faculty of considering phenomena as causes
> of possible effects, as distinguished from the faculty of seeking
> the causes or means that produce "an effect imagined," the lat-
> ter faculty being "common to man and beast": not "teleological"
> but "causal" thinking is peculiar to man. The reason why Hobbes
> transformed the traditional definition of man as the rational ani-
> mal into the definition of man as the animal which can "inquire
> consequences" and hence which is capable of science, i.e., "knowl-
> edge of consequences," is that the traditional definition implies
> that man is by nature a social animal, and Hobbes must reject this
> implication (*De cive*, I, 2). As a consequence, the relation between
> man's natural peculiarity and speech becomes obscure. On the
> other hand, Hobbes is able to deduce from his definition of man
> his characteristic doctrine of man: man alone can consider himself
> as a cause of possible effects, i.e., man can be aware of his power;
> he can be concerned with power; he can desire to possess power;
> he can seek confirmation for his wish to be powerful by having his

power recognized by others, i.e., he can be vain or proud; he can
be hungry with future hunger, he can anticipate future dangers, he
can be haunted by long-range fear. Cf. *Leviathan*, chs. 3 (15), 5 (27,
29), 6 (33–36), 11 (64), and *De homine* X, 3.

The page numbers of the *Leviathan* at the end of this note refer to the Blackwell's
Political Texts edition.

Works Cited

Hobbes, Thomas. [1839–45] 1966. *The English Works of Thomas Hobbes of
Malmesbury*. Ed. Sir William Molesworth. 11 vols. Darmstadt, Germany:
Scientia Verlag Allen.

Meier, Heinrich. 2011. "The History of Strauss's Hobbes Studies in the 1930s." In
Hobbes's Critique of Religion and Related Writings, by Leo Strauss, trans. and
ed. Gabriel Bartlett and Svetozar Minkov, 1–19. Chicago: University of Chicago
Press.

Polin, Raymond. 1953. *Politique et philosophie chez Thomas Hobbes*. Paris: Presses
Universitaires de France.

Strauss, Leo. 1953. *Natural Right and History*. Chicago: University of Chicago
Press.

———. 1958. *Thoughts on Machiavelli*. Chicago: University of Chicago Press.

———. 1959. *What Is Political Philosophy? And Other Studies*. New York: Free
Press.

———. 1963. *The Political Philosophy of Hobbes: Its Basis and Its Genesis*. Trans.
Elsa M. Sinclair. Chicago: University of Chicago Press.

———. 1965. "Comments on Carl Schmitt's *Der Begriff des Politischen*." In *Spinoza's Critique of Religion*. Trans. Elsa M. Sinclair, 331–51. New York: Schocken
Books.

———. 1983. "On Natural Law." In *Studies in Platonic Political Philosophy*. Ed.
Thomas L. Pangle, 137–46. Chicago: University of Chicago Press.

———. 1995. *Philosophy and Law: Contributions to the Understanding of Maimonides and His Predecessors*. Trans. Eve Adler. Albany: SUNY Press.

———. 1997. *Spinoza's Critique of Religion*. Trans. Elsa M. Sinclair. Chicago: University of Chicago Press.

———. 2001. *Gesammelte Schriften*. Ed. Heinrich Meier and Wiebke Meier. Vol. 3.
Stuttgart: J. B. Metzler.

———. 2006. "Living Issues in German Postwar Philosophy." In *Leo Strauss and
the Theologico-Political Problem*, by Heinrich Meier, 115–39. New York: Cambridge University Press.

CHAPTER EIGHT

Strauss on Locke and the Law of Nature

Michael Zuckert

In a letter to Willmoore Kendall, Strauss commented that of all the unorthodox readings of canonical political philosophers he had produced, none had caused as much controversy and raised as much ire as his interpretation of Locke in *Natural Right and History* (*NRH*). The essay on Locke in *What Is Political Philosophy?* (*WIPP*) needs to be seen in the context of that controversy, for the original *NRH* chapter had been written prior to the 1954 public appearance of the text on the law of nature that had been found in Locke's papers. The new text, published a year after *NRH,* was relevant because in *NRH* Strauss had argued that, first impressions to the contrary notwithstanding, Locke was not an adherent of traditional natural law but held a doctrine much closer to that of the modern and very antitraditional Thomas Hobbes. As the editor of the recent Norton Critical Edition of Locke's political writings put it, "Strauss's case was challenged in 1954 . . . when Locke's early *Essays on the Law of Nature* were translated and published." These essays "described a theologically based natural law theory that rejected Hobbesian self-interest as the basis of moral obligation" (Sigmund 2005, xxvii). That is to say, *Essays on the Law of Nature* (*ELN*) was seen as a definitive rebuttal to Strauss's version of Locke.[1]

I. Vindication

Strauss published his Locke essay in the *American Political Science Review* (*APSR*) in June of 1958 (Strauss 1958a); it was the most recent of all the essays reprinted in *WIPP*. In connection with writing that essay Strauss had offered a seminar on Locke in the winter quarter of 1958. It is clear from the transcript of that course that Strauss was just then working through the *ELN*, and no doubt writing his essay then or soon thereafter.

In neither his seminar nor his essay does Strauss show any signs of realizing that *ELN* would be taken by many to be the definitive refutation of his very unorthodox Locke, but whether aware of that or not, Strauss nonetheless oriented his treatment of *ELN* around the issue as it would emerge in the literature. His main theses were in effect a response in advance to the critics who would rely on *ELN*. That text, Strauss maintained, appeared to present a version of traditional natural law doctrine reminiscent in many places of Thomas Aquinas and Richard Hooker (198).[2] Locke's text also, however, "deviates from the tradition" in a number of ways (198). Strauss was also impressed with the number of outright and elementary contradictions that were to be found in it (204). In line with his general approach to reading he concluded that such contradictions were "deliberate" and intended "to indicate [Locke's] thought rather than to reveal it" (206). Strauss concluded that Locke "indicated" not an endorsement of traditional natural law but a subtle critique, or at least a raising of serious questions and reservations about it (206–14). In place of the traditional doctrine, Locke pointed toward an alternative—much more Hobbesian—natural law doctrine (214–20). So, completely contrary to the critics who saw *ELN* as the refutation of Strauss's chapter on Locke, Strauss himself saw it as the decisive confirmation. Indeed, Strauss thought his reading so compelling that he put forward a theory on why Locke failed to publish these essays: "he rightly did not publish [them], because here the self-contradictions, and the other shocking things are so obvious" that they would be readily spotted and would prevent the work from having "the tremendous success which the *Treatises* [on government] had."[3] Strauss believed, in other words, that *ELN* was too crude, too obvious to serve Locke's purpose of moving his readers subtly away from traditional and toward modern natural law.

If Strauss's main concern was to vindicate his *NRH* reading of Locke, then his treatment of the last of Locke's *Essays* should have sufficed, for this essay was taken, as Strauss seems to have anticipated it would be, as the decisive proof that Locke was not the kind of thinker Strauss had claimed him to be. Thus Paul Sigmund refers to the last essay as the place where Locke "rejected Hobbesean self-interest as the basis of moral obligation" (Sigmund 2005, xxvii). That essay would seem to do what Sigmund says; it is addressed to the question: "Is the private interest of each the basis of the law of nature?" to which Locke answers "No." Since Hobbesian natural law is a series of moral rules derived by reason conducive to the preservation (or more broadly the interest) of each, it certainly appears that Locke's essay repudiates Hobbesian natural law.

But Strauss shows that such a conclusion would be hasty and based on a careless reading of Locke's text. Strauss traces Locke's step-by-step definition and redefinition of the question he is addressing in this text, until, it turns out, Locke is refuting a claim that is not at all the Hobbesian position. Locke begins with the Carneadean challenge to natural law (or right): "there is no natural law [or right—*jus naturale*], for all, both men and animals, are driven to their own interest [*utilitas*] by nature's guidance" (Locke 1954, 204).[4] Nature prompts men not to right but to their own interest. Locke is very praising of Carneades, so much so that he does not dwell on Carneades himself but on some very zealous followers of his. The followers lack Carneades's "virtues" and "gifts of mind." For reasons related to their inferiority and resentment, they reformulate Carneades's maxim about natural law: "every right and equity [should be] determined not by an extraneous law but by each person's own self-interest" (Locke 1954, 205). As Strauss points out, "Locke does not even attempt to refute Carneades' assertion that each man is by nature driven to seek his own interest and not to act justly" (216); what he does attempt to refute is a particular interpretation of the position of Carneades's inferior followers. That interpretation proves to be both easy to refute and largely irrelevant to Hobbesian law of nature.

In a remarkable sleight of hand, Strauss points out, Locke identifies "the *basis* of natural law with the *basic* natural law" (216, emphasis added). Locke's translation of the Hobbesian thesis is almost comical. He transfers what in Hobbes is a right (a liberty) into a duty (an obligation); that is, Hobbes says: in a state of nature it is morally permissible to do what, in your judgment, it takes to secure your preservation (your interest). This right, however, is shown by Hobbes to lead to the famous state of war, which men find to be an unacceptable state. Thus in two stages he derives an escape from the state of war. The first stage is the generation of so-called laws of nature from the Hobbesian right of nature. These are rules that, if followed, lead to peaceful relations among men. Without government to enforce the rules, however, they cannot be maintained; therefore the laws of nature themselves point toward the second stage, the social contract creating the sovereign. Both the "laws of nature" and the contract depend on men's renouncing the original right of nature that grants them the liberty that produces the state of war. They must instead agree to obey a sovereign and his laws. The "basis" of the Hobbesian laws of nature is indeed the "private interest of each," for the laws are the rules that specify how to achieve what each most seeks—peace and the preservation to which peace conduces (cf. 200).

According to Locke's transformation, the Hobbesian escape from the state of nature would be impossible, indeed prohibited. To turn the claim that private interest is the *basis* of the law of nature into the *basic* law of nature commanding or requiring that each pursue what Hobbes said men have only a right or liberty to do means it is unlawful for men to renounce their rights to everything (their "private interest") and adhere to the rational rules that make for peace by obeying the sovereign. The numerous scholars who believe that *Essays on the Law of Nature*, especially the last essay, somehow refute the Straussian Locke are thus quite mistaken.

It might appear that Strauss's aim in his essay is to reaffirm his Hobbesian reading of Locke, but that turns out to be only partly the case. He reaffirms his earlier view that Locke does not accept "the traditional natural law teaching" (214), but he also attempts to show that Locke does not precisely accept the thesis that "private interest is the basis of the law of nature." In the last essay in *ELN*, Strauss's Locke modifies the Hobbesian formulation because the "fundamental harmony between private interest and the law of nature . . . does not mean that that harmony is complete" (218). Strauss cites, as an instance, the Lockean doctrine of revolution. It protects against governmental misdeeds that arouse "the great body of the people," but it does not protect each and every individual, for some tyrannical acts affect only a few and do not arouse the opposition of the "great body of the people." Thus Strauss reformulates the Lockean position: "For all practical purposes it may therefore be better to say that the basis or end of society is not the private interest of each but the public interest, i.e., the interest of the large majority" (218). That reformulation allows Strauss to account for the motto Locke appended to the *Two Treatises*—"*Salus Populi surprema lex esto*"—but the limits of his reformulation are indicated by his reaffirmation that the "root of the public interest is the private interest of each" (218).

Strauss identifies another significant shift away from Hobbes in Locke's presentation of the natural law. Hobbes, Strauss pointed out in an earlier essay, refused "to speak of laws ordering non-human beings" (175).

Locke, however, "speaks of a natural law which cannot be transgressed" (203, 204) and which applies to nonhuman as well as human beings. Indeed, the law that cannot be transgressed and that governs much beside man is one of Strauss's great concerns in this essay.

Strauss thus uses the occasion of his essay to modify his position on Locke. Just as his essay on Hobbes in *WIPP* is the locus for adjustment to his earlier reading of Hobbes, so he has revised his position on Locke. Perhaps the key to *WIPP* as a book is not so much the title essay as the "Restatement or Xenophon's *Hiero*"—the collection is held together by its revisionist character. That in turn coheres with the title essay, for in that essay Strauss emphasizes the Socratic, i.e., necessarily incomplete, character of philosophy: it is not the possession of the whole truth and nothing but the truth but a quest, necessarily incomplete and hence always open to revision (11).

The original *APSR* version of the essay is quite helpful in capturing Strauss's chief strategy in dealing with Locke's *ELN*. The *APSR* version is nearly identical to the *WIPP* version, but with differences of three sorts. First, Strauss modified the paragraphing of the essay from 28 in the original to 17 in the reprinted version. Second, Strauss has edited the text slightly, so far as I can tell for style and readability. I have not found any of these slight modifications to affect the meaning of the text in any significant way. Third, and most important, the *APSR* version had section titles. The essay was divided into five parts, titled respectively: I. Description of Locke's early essays on Natural Law (¶¶1–4 of *WIPP* version); II. A Natural Law which cannot be transgressed (¶¶5–8); III. Is the Natural Law based on speculative principles? (¶¶9–11); IV. Is Natural Law duly promulgated? (¶¶12–13); V. An Alternative to the traditional Natural Law teaching (¶¶14–17).

The section headings identify three different forms of what might be called natural law in Locke's text—the natural law that cannot be transgressed, i.e., laws like the law of gravity; the traditional "natural law proper, i.e., . . . a natural law which man can transgress"; and finally the quasi-Hobbesian sort of "law" we have already had occasion to discuss. Strauss makes sense of the "confusions" in Locke's text by claiming that he is speaking of these three different kinds of natural law without being explicit that that is what he is doing and without sorting out for the reader which claims belong to which law. The nontransgressible natural law allows Locke to speak of natural law in a much more extended—and confusing—sense than Hobbes had done.

II. History of Political Philosophy

Strauss believes that the editor of *ELN*, Wolfgang von Leyden, falls short as an editor, translator, and interpreter of Locke's text because von Leyden is convinced before confronting the text that it deals with "a topic now regarded by many"—which seems to include himself—"as obsolete" (Locke 1954, v). "As a consequence of his dogmatism," Strauss observes, "the editor's interest in Locke's teaching cannot but be purely antiquarian or must lack that philosophic concern without which the adequate understanding of philosophic teachings is impossible" (201). Strauss's complaints against von Leyden are instances of his more general concerns about historicism as developed in the essay "Political Philosophy and History," also reprinted in *WIPP*. As he says in that essay, "our understanding of the thought of the past is liable to be the more adequate, the less the historian is convinced of the superiority of his own point of view, or the more he is prepared to admit the possibility that he may have to learn something, not merely about the thinkers of the past, but from them" (68).

Historical studies inspired by historicist assumptions cannot produce good historical, much less philosophical, understanding. Historicists assume that the thinker reflects his age, an assumption that can lead to one of two apparently opposite defects (cf. 63). On the one side, readers like the editor of *ELN* think that philosophical questions are settled by history and can thus become obsolete, like last year's model iPhone. On the other side, readers like the editor of the Norton edition of Locke's writings believe that thinkers fit so simply into their times that they are unlikely—or even unable—to disagree with dominant opinions of their day. Historicists do not take seriously enough the possibility that a given thinker may indeed differ from the reigning consensus in his society, but may think himself able to convey that disagreement only subtly, between the lines, so to speak.

Such is Strauss's view of Locke's position regarding the law of nature. Locke appears to endorse the "traditional view" that is intellectually dominant in his time, but by his "contradictions" and other quiet indications tells readers that he is greatly "doubtful of the traditional natural law teaching" (218). Locke pays more than obeisance to those traditional views, but Strauss insists that a proper historical grasp of a past thinker requires that one not merely take at face value their professions of faith, especially when these fit snugly into reigning accepted views, the denial of which would be problematical in one way or another for the thinker. One must not merely pay attention to what a writer like Locke says he is saying, but take seriously what he actually says or clearly implies. This means that the historian must engage in philosophic activity. That is, as Strauss puts it, "the philosophic effort and the historical effort have become completely fused" (23). To be a political philosopher one must for now be a historian, but the reverse holds true as well.

Paradoxically, Strauss holds that "the philosophic questions of the nature of political things and of the best, or the just, political order are fundamentally different from historical questions. . . . The question of the nature of political things," i.e., the philosophic question, "and the answer to it cannot possibly be mistaken for the question of how this or that philosopher or all philosophers have approached, discussed, or answered the philosophic question mentioned" (56). One may not require the answer to the philosophic question in order to do history of philosophy but one must engage in the philosophic activity of subjecting "the doctrines concerned to a philosophic critique concerned exclusively with their truth or falsehood" (66).

At times Strauss speaks as if history of political philosophy can precede political philosophy proper, as if one first ascertains the historical doctrines and then subjects them to "critique concerned exclusively with their truth or falsehood." That is a mistaken view, for the relation between historical and philosophic inquiry is much more intimate and dialectical than that description suggests, even if at the end of the day the two activities remain in principle somewhat separable. To be more concrete: in the case of Locke, many scholars have noticed Locke's affirmations of the traditional doctrine, but they have failed to note or to take seriously the many ways in which Locke differs from and even rejects the traditional view. The traditional view as Strauss identifies its elements "derives man's duties from man's natural constitution or his natural inclinations; it assumes that each man is by nature ordered toward virtue; it also presupposes that each man and each nation is ruled by divine providence, that men's souls are immortal, and that the natural law is sufficiently promulgated in and to the conscience of all men" (218).

The bulk of Strauss's essay is devoted to showing that Locke questions or rejects each and every one of these elements of the traditional natural law. A particularly important element of traditional natural law that Locke rejects is the role of the natural inclinations. According to Thomas Aquinas, "reason naturally grasps as goods all those things to which man has a natural inclination, and consequently to be pursued in action, and the contrary of these are grasped as evils to be avoided. Therefore, there is an order of the precepts of the law of nature that follows the order of the natural inclinations" (S.T. 1–2, Q.94, A2). Locke, however, denies that "the law of nature can be known from man's natural inclination" (198, cf. 215; Locke 1954, 158). The significance of Locke's denial is often over-looked for two reasons. First, the scholars, like von Leyden, are often not aware of how important the claim about the natural inclinations is to the traditional natural law and therefore are not prepared to appreciate the reach of Locke's denial. Second, Locke's denial occurs in one of the three "essays" for which Locke supplied a title in the form of a question, and a one-word answer to the question, but no adumbration of the answer. Von Leyden seems to believe that these three are not properly part of the work, but, apparently not sharing the editor's view, Locke included them in the consecutive numbering he gave to the entire series of "essays." Not believing that this "essay" is truly part of the work, von Leyden consigns it to a footnote in very fine print, placed so that the English-language reader is not likely even to see it.

The second aspect of traditional law is the assumption "that each man is by nature ordered toward virtue." But, Strauss reveals, Locke rejects this also, for he affirms that "those who have no other guide than nature itself, those in whom the dictates of nature are in no way corrupted by positive customs, live in such ignorance of every law as if no attention had to be paid to the right and honorable" (221; Locke 1954, 141). Nature, Locke avers, guides not to virtue but to the reverse.

Strauss also brings out Locke's reservations about providence by call-ing attention to one very subtle theme in *ELN* regarding divine power, and a less subtle point regarding divine care for man. Divine providence can rule if God is all-powerful, i.e., capable of overriding any and all poten-tially resisting forces in the world. Otherwise, we cannot be certain that it is providence rather than chance or nature or some other power that rules. But Locke is very careful, Strauss points out, not to affirm divine omnipo-tence in his proofs for the existence of God (and thus in the place where he speaks most precisely of God's nature). He speaks rather of "an artificer" who is "powerful" and "wise" but noticeably is not affirmed to be omnipo-tent or omniscient in this important context (207; Locke 1954, 182).

Moreover, even if God were omnipotent and therefore capable of prov-ident care for mankind, Locke sets a landmine under the notion of divine providential care. As Strauss restates Locke's point: "After having proved the existence of God from the perfect order of the world . . . Locke shows parenthetically that man could not have been made . . . by man himself: if man were his own maker, he would give himself, i.e., every human individual, everlasting existence, for man cannot be conceived to be so full of hate and enmity against himself as to deprive himself of all the charms of life" (213; Locke 1954, 152). Strauss concludes, therefore, that according to Locke, "it would appear to follow that the creation of man as a mortal being which knows of its mortality cannot be due to a being which loves man" (214).

Strauss brings home the thought that God does not show loving care toward man in his discussion of the problem of the promulgation of the law of nature. "Nature—and, it would seem necessary to add, the author of nature—has not been so kind to man as to provide him with innate knowledge of natural law . . . but rather withholds knowledge of the natural law like a secret. . . . Therefore if nature is supposed to demand obedience to the natural law from man as man, nature would be a most cruel tyrant and not at all the kind mother of all" (214; citing Locke 1954, 124, 126, 114, 228, 190, 192).

Of the five aspects of traditional law, Strauss pays most attention to the fourth, the requirement that rational proof of immortality of souls be given. It is Locke not Strauss who calls attention to the key place of immortality of souls in Locke's list of rationally accessible knowledge necessary to establish natural law (210; Locke 1954, 172, 174). Since Locke mentions immortality only a few times, von Leyden and other orthodox scholars tend to pass it over and take little notice of the fact on which Strauss dwells: "in the essays Locke does not even attempt to demonstrate the immortality of the souls although that immortality is a necessary presupposition of the natural law" (210). No immortality, no natural law. Strauss teases out of some Lockean hints an answer to the question why Locke does not offer a proof of immortality; the soul, Locke believes, is not a separate immaterial substance but is itself matter (211–12).

The traditional view held that natural law was sufficiently promulgated though the conscience, or in Aquinas's technical language, synderesis. If the law is not directly implanted or innate, then promulgation in this way seems necessary, for the law is obligatory for all and must be known (somehow) by all in order for all to be capable of acting on it and for all to be justly held to account for not obeying it. But Locke denies that the law is known through conscience (204, 205). Instead he says that the law is secret and hidden, but knowable by those who put in the necessary effort to discover it. Those who do not are guilty for not doing so. Ignorance is no excuse—ignorance is itself guilty. This proves not to be a satisfactory substitute, for, to say nothing of all the nations that Locke identifies as entirely ignorant of the law of nature, there is the further problem that men need some direct knowledge of their obligation to hunt for the hidden and difficult knowledge of the natural law, if they are to be held guilty for not doing so and for not obeying the law of nature. In order to escape an infinite regress, that knowledge must be available either innately or via conscience. But Locke affirms no such thing. The inescapable conclusion, therefore, is that the law of nature is insufficiently promulgated and thus cannot be known to or binding on men, and thus cannot exist as law (212–13).

In measuring Locke's discussion of the law of nature against the "traditional" notion, Strauss at the same time displays Locke's doubts about his own particular or idiosyncratic version of natural law, for he picked out three of those traditional features as necessary presuppositions for his theory: the lawgiver, his will, and immortality. Since the historicist-inspired scholars are not interested in pressing the philosophic question of the adequacy of what Locke says, they are not driven to press the question of whether Locke's version of the "traditional" doctrine can hold up without the elements of the traditional doctrine that he jettisons.

Locke says that he has rationally established the existence and content of the law of nature; in fact he has failed to do so according to his own standards, and he has failed in a way that must be evident to him and indeed part of his intent. Watch what he says, not what he says he says. Strauss can see all this in Locke because he takes seriously the historian's task of probing the philosophic claims of the subject thinker as part of the mere effort to understand the thinker historically. The historicist-inspired historians fail to do that and are indifferent to whether Locke's argument succeeds or fails, even according to Locke's own stated criteria for success or failure. The historians thus not only fail to achieve a philosophical understanding of the topic at hand but fail even at their self-appointed task of historical understanding.

III. Political Philosophy

If Strauss's aim was to validate his general understanding of Locke as an adherent of modern natural right and not of traditional natural right or law, then his essay must be judged a success. Contrary to what many of the critics have said, Strauss more than adequately shows that *ELN* does not make a case for Locke as a traditionalist. This is a good historical conclusion. But is it enough? The essay on Locke appears in a collection entitled *What Is Political Philosophy? And Other Studies*, in the title essay of which political philosophy is said to be "the attempt to replace opinion about the nature of political things by knowledge of the nature of political things" (11–12, 73). Political philosophy thus understood is "fundamentally different from the history of political philosophy itself" (56, 76–77). "The question of the nature of political things and the answer to it cannot possibly be mistaken for the question of how this or that philosopher . . . approached, discussed, or answered the philosophic question mentioned" (56). The transformation of the one (history of political philosophy) into the other (political philosophy) is achieved via subjecting "the doctrines concerned to a philosophic critique concerned exclusively with their truth or falsehood" (66, 286). To make this inquiry, political philosophy would require a "critique concerned exclusively with . . . [the] truth or falsehood" of the traditional natural law or of the Lockean critique of the traditional law. Does Strauss's essay achieve that critique?

What exactly does Strauss believe he has achieved in this essay? He has a final paragraph beginning "In conclusion." But that paragraph is devoted to "some peculiarities of the edition and translation for which we have not found a convenient place" (219). These are almost entirely issues of translation. The final item in the final paragraph does not appear to fit the description given, however, for it does not concern a "peculiarity of the edition and translation." Rather it concerns a "slip" Locke "apparently made" in quoting from Aristotle on natural right. Locke *apparently* made a slip, but, Strauss concludes, "he *certainly* understood the passage in exactly the same way in which it been understood by Averroes"—the last words of the essay (220).

Without further adumbration one would have to say that the conclusion of Strauss's conclusion, however, is still opaque. The Aristotelian passage that Locke "certainly" understands in the Averroistic manner is the very passage to which Strauss devoted the concluding pages of his essay "Classic Natural Right" in *NRH*. Among other things, Strauss there explains what the Averroistic way of understanding that passage is. The Averroistic way is there contrasted with the Thomistic way and Strauss's own conjecture of the authentic Aristotelian way of understanding the doctrine of the changeability of all natural right.

The reference to the Averroistic understanding of natural right leads us to revisit *NRH*. Strauss's characterization of his intentions in *NRH* helps make the significance of this return to *NRH* in *WIPP* clearer. Strauss presents *NRH* as a response to the present "need of historical studies in order to familiarize ourselves with the whole complexity of the issue" of natural right. We must, Strauss continues, "for some time . . . become students of what is called the 'history of ideas'" (Strauss 1953, 7). That is to say, according to the distinctions drawn in *WIPP*, *NRH* is history of political philosophy, not political philosophy itself.

Strauss nowhere else so clearly demarcates the difference between these two pursuits as he does in *WIPP*. He, moreover, gives the collection of essays in the 1959 book a title that contains *the* Socratic "what is" question, the question of philosophy. The conclusion to which these various observations are tending is that, contrary to their worldly reputations, *WIPP* is the more fundamental and far-reaching book, the book in which Strauss transcends history of political philosophy and engages in political philosophy itself. However, the essay on Locke, to say nothing of many other parts of *WIPP*, still looks much like history of political philosophy; it explicates Locke's thought with subtlety and care, but the "critique concerned exclusively with . . . truth or falsehood" is nowhere evident. Perhaps we must look harder for it.

The Aristotelian passage misquoted by Locke in *ELN* is the subject of Strauss's comments at the end of his chapter on "classic natural right" in *NRH*. Strauss has presented to that point a composite account of the classic position, as though the premodern philosophers all understood natural right in the same way. The last forty percent (or so) of the chapter is devoted to disaggregating the classic position by distinguishing "three types of classic natural rights teachings"—the Socratic-Platonic-Stoic, the Aristotelian, and the Thomistic. The Socratic-Platonic-Stoic view affirms that "civil life requires the dilution of natural right by merely conventional right" (Strauss 1953, 152–53). The Aristotelian view denies that natural right must be diluted, for "man is by nature a political animal" and therefore what is required by civil life must be in accordance with nature. However, Aristotle also affirms that "all natural right is changeable" (Strauss 1953, 156–57). Finally, the Thomistic view, the perspective of the traditional natural law that Locke appears to endorse but in fact critiques, is, as Strauss puts it, "free from the hesitations and ambiguities" of the other two versions of classic natural right. Thomistic natural law rejects the Platonic-Stoic claim that natural right must be diluted to find a place in civil society: the dictates of natural law are binding in society without need for "diluting" or admixture. Moreover, Thomas interprets Aristotle's dictum on the changeability of natural right in a way that blunts the force of Aristotle's puzzling claim. Thomas makes a distinction between the principles and the specific precepts or rules of natural law. The latter are derived from the former and change somewhat according to circumstance, but the principles remain always the same. Thus Thomistic natural right to a great extent rejects those aspects of the Platonic and Aristotelian doctrines where there is "hesitation" or "ambiguity" in identifying right as it exists at any time in even the best regime with natural right per se.

The specific part of the discussion of the "types of classic natural right" to which Strauss implicitly refers the reader at the end of the Locke essay in *WIPP* is the central part of that discussion, the consideration of the Aristotelian version of natural right. In Aristotle the doctrine is presented so briefly and so abstractly that there has been a fair amount of disagreement over what it means in the course of Western philosophy since Aristotle. Strauss considers three interpretations of the Aristotelian doctrine: the Thomistic, the Averroistic, and his own conjecture of Aristotle's meaning. The discussion of the Averroists is thus the center of the center. We have already noted the Thomistic interpretation, which Strauss rejects as an interpretation of Aristotle, because Aristotle says "all natural right is changeable," whereas Aquinas makes only part of it changeable (Strauss 1953, 157). The Thomistic interpretation is geared to making Aristotle's dictum compatible with natural right understood in the Thomistic manner as natural law, for it allows changeable natural right to retain sufficient fixedness to have meaning as a binding mandate for all men and all times, i.e., to be conceivable as law. Granting that Strauss is correct in rejecting Aquinas's reading as a reading of Aristotle, in itself that implies at most that on this point Aquinas disagrees with Aristotle more than he usually lets on. However, there are many other places where he deviates from "the philosopher," in some cases arguably improving on Aristotle's position.[5] But if Strauss is correct it also means that Aristotle cannot be enlisted as a support for Aquinas's interpretation of natural right as natural law.

At the opposite pole from Aquinas's interpretation is the Averroistic position, apparently the one of most importance for Strauss's Locke essay. The Averroists, including Marsilius (and Locke) among the Christians, notice, like Aquinas, a certain universality, or at least "the same broad rules of what constitutes justice . . . in all civil societies" (Strauss 1953, 158). These rules "specify the minimum requirements of society." Despite their universality, the Averroists see them as "conventional," because "civil society is incompatible with any immutable rules." But these rules, to be effective, must be presented by society "as universally valid," even though they are not. To be true and truly valid, the universal rules would have to come with many "qualifications," but because the rules do hold in their pure or unqualified form most of the time and because the citizens cannot be encouraged to find or believe in exceptions to the rules as a matter of course, the rules do not contain the exceptions in their public expression. "The unqualified rules are not natural right but conventional right" (Strauss 1953, 158; cf. 146, 147). Thus Strauss says in one place that "Marsilius lives as it were in another world than Thomas" (Strauss 1963, 276). Strauss sees the Averroistic interpretation of Aristotle's text to be no more valid than the Thomistic interpretation, however, "in so far as it implies the denial of natural right proper" (Strauss 1953, 159). Just as Aquinas loses one part of Aristotle's two-part doctrine on natural right, so the Averroists lose the other part. But the political philosophic question is, of course, not who or what position agrees with Aristotle, but which (if any) is true. In the context of the topic of the Locke essay, what is at stake is the truth or falsehood of the traditional natural law doctrine that Locke apparently affirms but actually doubts.

In connecting Locke to Averroes, Strauss attributes to Locke a much more negative stance toward the law of nature than he explicitly stated in the essay itself. Strauss claims to have brought out "how doubtful [Locke] was, from the beginning of his career, of the traditional natural law teaching" (218). The Averroists, explicitly called by Strauss "philosophers," who stand at the opposite pole from Thomism, can be expected to subject the traditional natural law doctrine to the "critique concerned exclusively with truth or falsehood" characteristic of political philosophy proper. Strauss implies that Locke is thus a stand-in for, or even a representative of, the premodern Averroistic philosophic critique of traditional natural law. This conclusion coheres with Strauss's observation at the end of his *NRH* chapter "Classic Natural Right" that the moderns reacted against traditional natural law on the basis of a "premise, which would have been acceptable to the classics" (Strauss 1953, 164).

In *NRH* Strauss discussed the traditional natural law in a very brief two pages. The main point of that short discussion is to account for the Thomistic deviations from the Platonic and Aristotelian versions of natural right. Unlike the Platonists, the natural law doctrine has no doubts or reservations "regarding the basic harmony between natural right and civil society." Unlike the Aristotelian doctrine, Thomas has no doubts or reservations "regarding the immutable character of the fundamental propositions of natural laws" (Strauss 1953, 165). Strauss comments that "it is reasonable to assume that these profound changes were due to the influence of the belief in biblical revelation." The implications of that hypothesized dependence on revelation are far-reaching. "If this assumption should prove to be correct, one would be forced to wonder . . . whether the natural law as Thomas Aquinas understands it, is natural law strictly speaking, i.e., a law knowable to the unassisted human mind" (Strauss 1953, 163). What is at stake is nothing less than the existence of the natural law as natural, and therefore as discernible by philosophy as opposed to theology (Strauss 1953, 164). In other words, Strauss makes an assumption, a "reasonable assumption," about the natural law that explodes the natural law. But a "reasonable assumption," however reasonable, nonetheless remains an assumption and cannot be the basis for "a philosophic critique concerned exclusively with [the] . . . truth or falsehood" of philosophic doctrines. *NRH*, as we have noted earlier, remains a historical and not a fully philosophic book:[6] As Strauss wrote of *NRH* in a private letter, "I agree then with your judgment that the value of my book consists rather in its historical than its philosophic aspects. . . . I myself regard the book as a preparation to an adequate philosophic discussion" (Strauss 1978, 23).

Let us then hypothesize that the Locke essay completes, in effect, the discussion of natural law in *NRH* by fleshing out and providing support for the hypothesis in the earlier book that the natural law doctrine was illicitly dependent on revelation. That suggestion is at least supported if not confirmed by a comment Strauss made about the Averroists in a writing of a later date than the Locke essay. The Averroists were, according to Strauss, "those medieval Aristotelians, who as philosophers refused to make any concessions to revealed religion" (Strauss 1983, 226). The Averroists rejected natural law; they made no concessions to revealed religions. Is the one the result of the other? So far as that is so, the essay on Locke, who is said to be an Averroist on the decisive issue, looks to be the place where the philosophic critique of traditional natural law as dependent on biblical revelation is presented.

On the surface, at least, neither Locke himself in *ELN,* nor Strauss in explicating Locke in *WIPP*, explicitly forwards the claim that traditional natural law depends on acceptance of revelation. But Strauss comes very close. Indeed, he acts like the pious ascetic of whom he speaks in the essay on Farabi in *WIPP*. The lesson he extracts from the story of that pious man is "that one can safely tell a very dangerous truth provided one tells it in the proper surroundings, for the public will interpret the absolutely unexpected speech in term of the customary and expected meaning of the surroundings rather than it will interpret the surroundings in terms of the dangerous character of the speech" (136). That lesson bears in particular on the practice of Plato, who "established for himself the character of a man who never explicitly and unambiguously says what he thinks about the highest themes" (137). With that reputation secure, Plato can then "sometimes . . . say explicitly and unambiguously what he thought about the highest themes: his explicit and unambiguous utterances are not taken seriously" (137). However well the reputation imputed to Plato fits the Greek thinker, it surely fits Strauss well.

That tactic is on display when Strauss mentions, almost in passing, that Locke "follows," perhaps without knowing it, a claim made by Thomas Aquinas, "who says that it is not reason simply but reason informed by faith which dictates that God is to be loved and to be worshipped" (208). The connection of this bold claim to our question becomes clear if one notes that "love and worship" of God are dictates, indeed, "the first, the highest and the most weighty duties prescribed by natural law" according to Locke and, in slightly modified form, according to Aquinas as well (see *ST* I–II Q94 A2, resp.; Q99). Aquinas's admission is damning, for it concedes that the most important content of the natural law is not in fact accessible without "faith," i.e., without a nonrational source of belief. So far as Strauss has set up the question of the truth or falsehood of the traditional natural law doctrine to rest on whether it necessarily depends on an appeal to revelation, then Strauss has found an extremely authoritative witness in support of his "reasonable assumption."[7] Strauss explains Aquinas's problematic recourse to faith as a response to a "difficulty" to which Locke calls attention but which "was as well known in the middle ages as it is in modern times" (209). The difficulty to which Strauss adverts is the great variety of religious beliefs in the world, including much polytheism and atheism (208). That empirical fact implies that knowledge of the natural law and of propositions on which knowledge of natural law depends is insufficiently promulgated. Aquinas and Locke both admit that, like all binding law, the natural law must be sufficiently known or at least knowable by those (all humans) to whom it applies. That difficulty leads to alternative possibilities, either of which is fatal to natural law as such. Locke, Strauss suggests, saw the problem very clearly and used it in his critique, while Aquinas saw it and responded in a way that undermined his larger enterprise.

Strauss has Aquinas's own admission to validate his assumption, but in order to understand in greater depth Strauss's critique of Thomistic natural law one must return to the three "presuppositions" Locke identified as essential to the natural law. These correspond to three of the five elements of traditional natural law as identified by Strauss. The three are a natural demonstration of the existence of God, of his will for man (the content of the law), and of immortality of soul (the precondition for sanctions attached to the law of nature).

As should be clear already, Strauss approaches his critique in a very indirect manner—through the keyhole rather than through the front door as he once put it (Strauss 2000, 236). He is especially indirect in his approach to the first "speculative doctrine" required to establish natural law. The key to Strauss's thinking on this important topic is his identification of two kinds of natural law in Locke's text—a natural law that cannot be transgressed, and a natural law that can be transgressed. Only the latter is natural law of the moral type that is relevant to his discussion of natural right in *NRH*. Locke plays on the ambiguity between these different types of natural law; he devotes his central proof for the existence of natural law to an argument that establishes the nontransgressible kind of law on the basis of observations and reasoning that Christians like Aquinas and pagan naturalists like Hippocrates share (203–4). This is the law Locke claims is recognized and obeyed by all (204). This law, which "governs all things," is responsible for "the orderly character of all natural things and actions . . . [and] may be said to have its source in nature rather than God" (202). Strauss extracts from Locke the view that "in order to believe that man is subject to a law like all other beings, it is not necessary to reflect on God" (202). So the nontransgressible law of nature neither depends on nor contributes to a proof for the existence of God.

What about the moral law of nature? We have already seen that it does depend on the existence of God. Can reason establish the existence of a legislative God who could be the source of this law? Locke explicitly says yes, but Strauss shows him to have serious reservations about that, reservations that Strauss shares. In the central paragraph of the essay Strauss "note[s] that in demonstrating these two presuppositions of the knowledge of natural law [i.e., the 'existence of some wise and powerful artificer of all sensibly perceived things including man' and 'that God has a will as regards what one ought to do'], Locke presupposes the existence of natural law" (207). As part of the interpretation of Locke this observation brings out the circular or question-begging character of Locke's explicit argument. He seeks to prove the existence and content of natural law by proving the existence of God and God's will, assuming in doing so the very thing he is ultimately attempting to prove. Strauss cites two places in Locke where he does something like what Strauss says he does: Locke claims to have proved that there is a law of nature knowable by the light of nature before he has proved the propositions needed to establish God the legislator and his legislative will (Locke 1954, 136, 146).

And Strauss gives us another angle on this problem when we recall an observation he made earlier: in the fifth paragraph of his essay Strauss reports on Locke's subtle claim "that the existence of a God is [not] evident to all men . . . but only that it is evident to all morally concerned men" (202). Locke had connected the recognition of "virtue or vice" as the presupposition for those who find the existence of God to be "evident." Not only is Locke's argument viciously circular, as outlined above, but more significantly, it points toward the core of Strauss's "reasonable assumption" in *NRH*. The premise of the authoritativeness of moral "virtue or vice," understood in the authentically moral sense, i.e., not as instrumental to some nonmoral good, leads to the positing (or "proving") of God—as the source and support of morality thus understood. This argument will not do as a proof, for it takes as given that which cannot be taken as given and which requires the proof of God's existence as support, i.e., the unconditional or absolute validity of morality. But moral claims—from a philosophic perspective—can raise no such claims to a priori validity. Moral claims are not self-evident truths, as the variety of moral claims raised by human beings indicates. It is thus not possible for reason to establish the moral law as legislated by God, i.e., to establish that moral claims exist as natural law. Reason is not able to establish God as an intelligent, willing, morally concerned person, but only perhaps as the source of the order of necessary laws that constitute nature. Man does not have the capacity to reach or to know the existence of that morally concerned God who stands as the purported source of natural law. Man's knowledge, if it is truly knowledge, of that morally concerned God must thus come from God—reaching down, so to speak, and revealing himself to man. That is to say, knowledge of the natural law as natural law must depend on belief that God has so revealed himself; i.e., it must be "due to the influence of the belief in biblical revelation" (Strauss 1953, 163). And to repeat an earlier point: so far as the natural law depends on the God revealed in biblical revelation, it is not natural but supernatural. That in itself does not, of course, invalidate the law as divine law. Strauss's argument says nothing about the status of revelation and the revealing God. It merely reveals natural law to be an impossible synthesis of rational and revealed. It points once again to the "either-or" character of Strauss's thinking about the theological-political problem.

The Locke essay in effect completes or renders assertoric what was only a hypothetical argument against natural law in *NRH*. It thus validates my hypothesis that this essay, and perhaps the whole of *WIPP*, advances beyond the history of political philosophy of *NRH* into political philosophy itself. The same point might be made by following out what Strauss says about the two other "speculative principles" needed to establish the natural law: knowledge of God's will, knowledge of immortality, and ultimately knowledge of divine reward and punishment. Locke does not normally speak for Strauss, but the Averroistic Locke whom Strauss uncovers in *WIPP* does speak for him, at least so far as he is a critic of the traditional doctrine of natural law.

Notes

1. See, e.g., also John Yolton (2005, 281).

2. Unspecified page numbers refer to Leo Strauss, *What Is Political Philosophy? and Other Studies* (Strauss 1959).

3. Strauss (1958b, 104 [20 January]).

4. Translation here from Locke (1990, 235). All other translations of *ELN* are from Locke (1954).

5. See Mary Keys (2008).

6. Cf. Strauss's comments on *NRH* in an undated letter to Helmut Kuhn (Strauss 1978, 23).

7. One aspect of Strauss's discussion of Farabi might seem to ill fit Strauss's own deployment of the "Platonic" tactic of unobtrusively speaking on matters of a "dangerous character." "Danger" of course is contextual, and it may describe situations other than physical threat. The "danger" in Strauss's presenting an open refutation of Thomistic natural law derives from the fact that he (Strauss) regularly identifies Catholics and Catholic "social science" as a key ally in his opposition to positivism (Strauss 1953, 2). Of course Strauss does not see opposing Catholic philosophy as dangerous in the sense of personally threatening, nor does he go to very great lengths to conceal his real reservations about it, as is visible in the *NRH* discussion of Aquinas.

Works Cited

Keys, Mary. 2008. *Aquinas, Aristotle, and the Promise of the Common Good*. Cambridge: Cambridge University Press.

Locke, John. 1954. *Essays on the Law of Nature*. Ed. W. von Leyden. Oxford: Clarendon Press.

———. 1990. *Questions concerning the Law of Nature.* Ed. and trans. Robert Horwitz, Jenny Strauss Clay, and Diskin Clay. Ithaca: Cornell University Press.

Sigmund, Paul. 2005. Introduction to *The Selected Political Writings of John Locke.* New York: W. W. Norton.

Strauss, Leo. 1953. *Natural Right and History.* Chicago: University of Chicago Press.

———. 1958a. "Locke's Doctrine of Natural Law." *American Political Science Review* 52 (2): 490–501.

———. 1958b. Unpublished transcript of seminar on Locke.

———. 1959. *What Is Political Philosophy? And Other Studies.* New York: Free Press.

———. 1963. *History of Political Philosophy.* New York: Rand McNally.

———. 1978. "Letter to Helmut Kuhn." *Independent Journal of Philosophy* 2: 23–26.

———. 1983. *Studies in Platonic Political Philosophy.* Chicago: University of Chicago Press.

———. 2000. *On Tyranny.* Chicago: University of Chicago Press.

Yolton, John. 2005. "Strauss on Locke's Law of Nature." In *The Selected Political Writings of John Locke,* ed. Paul Sigmund. New York: Norton.

CHAPTER NINE

Fishing For Philosophers

Strauss's "Restatement" on the Art of Writing

David Janssens

> Es ist unendlich schwer, zu wissen, wenn und wo man bleiben soll, und Tausenden für einen
> ist das Ziel ihres Nachdenkens die Stelle, wo sie des Nachdenkens müde geworden.
> — G. E. Lessing to Moses Mendelssohn, January 9, 1771

The presence of "On a Forgotten Kind of Writing" within the whole of *What Is Political Philosophy?* is somewhat puzzling. Why did Strauss include it in the volume in the first place? After all, its central themes are somehow touched upon in every other chapter, either right under the surface or on it: the art of writing, the fundamental tension between philosophy and society, and the obstacles to genuine understanding posed by positivism and historicism.[1] Furthermore, besides being the shortest chapter in the volume, it is the only one that did not originate as a regular scholarly or academic article. As Strauss indicates, the article was initially written and published in 1954 as a note for the *Chicago Review*, a literary magazine, at the request of a student (7, 221). Yet, perhaps this very fact may contain the beginning of an explanation. Founded in 1946 and run by graduate students, the *Review* quickly acquired a reputation for publishing experimental and subversive writers such as Kenneth Patchen, Arthur Miller, the Beat poets, and William S. Burroughs.[2] Strauss was probably aware of this when he decided to honor his student's request, just as he must have been alive to the unique opportunity to address the *Review's* relatively young readership and to point some of them away from the newest and toward some of the oldest subversive writers.

A similar concern may be the reason why it was republished in *What Is Political Philosophy?* This becomes apparent when we compare "On a Forgotten Kind of Writing" with another chapter in *What Is Political Philosophy?* that closely resembles it in structure and general approach: the "Restatement on Xenophon's *Hiero*."[3] The similarities are conspicuous. In each chapter, Strauss responds to objections proffered by two contemporaries against views he expressed in one of his books (*On Tyranny* and *Persecution and the Art of Writing*, respectively). In each case, a brief introduction—pointedly critical of contemporary social science—is followed by a restatement or summary of the controversial view, and subsequently by rejoinders to each critic. Moreover, in each case it is clear that Strauss takes one critic more seriously than the other. Thus, he addresses them in a markedly different manner—as "Professor" in the case of Eric Voegelin and George H. Sabine, and as "M[onsieur]" in the case of Alexandre Kojève and Yvon Belaval—leaving no doubt that the absence of an academic title is hardly discrediting. Finally, the interrelatedness between the two chapters is underscored by the fact that Strauss's most esteemed philosophic interlocutor—"M. Kojève"—makes a brief but important reappearance at the end of "On a Forgotten Kind of Writing."[4]

The substantial connection between the two chapters can be brought to light as follows. Strauss concludes the "Restatement" with a particularly forceful warning against "the coming of the universal and homogeneous state" ruled by a "Universal and Final Tyrant," as propagated by Kojève. This, he contends, "will be the end of philosophy on earth" (133). Earlier in the chapter, however, he presented with equal force a possible way of averting this dire prospect, by harking back to the classical alternative: the philosophic community of friends constituted by the common pursuit of wisdom. The philosopher, he explained, "is highly sensitive to the promise of good or ill order, or of happiness or misery, which is held out by the souls of the young. Hence he cannot help desiring, without any regard to his own needs or benefits, that those among the young whose souls are by nature fitted for it, acquire good order of their souls. But the good order of the soul is philosophizing. The philosopher therefore has the urge to educate potential philosophers simply because he cannot help loving well-ordered souls" (121). Hence "[t]he philosopher must go to the market place in order to fish there for potential philosophers" (125).

However, the philosopher's venture into the marketplace also has an intrinsic motive that points beyond friendship: "The philosopher cannot lead an absolutely solitary life because legitimate 'subjective certainty' and the 'subjective certainty' of the lunatic are indistinguishable. Genuine certainty must be inter-subjective" (114).[5] This intersubjective certainty cannot be acquired merely in and through friendship, since "[f]riendship is bound to lead to, or to consist in, the cultivation and perpetuation of common prejudices by a closely knit group of kindred spirits" (114). In order to remedy the deficiency of his subjective certainty, then, the philosopher must also go to the marketplace to confront nonkindred spirits and their opinions. This amounts to a confrontation with the *political* men, whose opinions contain the theological-political problem that triggers the philosopher's quest for subjective certainty: "the conflict with the political men cannot be avoided. And this conflict by itself, to say nothing of its cause or its effect, is a political action" (114). The philosopher's appearance in the marketplace thus leads to a combination of fishing and fighting, or fishing while fighting: "His attempts to convert the young men to the philosophic life will necessarily be regarded by the city as an attempt to corrupt the young. The philosopher is therefore forced to defend the cause of philosophy. He must therefore act upon the city or upon the ruler" (125). This "philosophic politics" (126) consists in a defense of philosophy that reassures the political men while drawing the attention of thoughtful youngsters.

In the opening paragraph of "On a Forgotten Kind of Writing," Strauss makes it clear that the text has been written for the sake of the young: a student asked him to clarify his suggestions on the art of writing, on behalf of some of his friends who did not understand those suggestions. Apparently, Strauss takes the request, as well as the issue itself, very personally and feels compelled to speak in his own name: the first paragraph—as well as the rest of the essay—displays a frequency of "I" unmatched by any other chapter. Moreover, he is willing to go to the marketplace without any regard to his own needs or benefits: having presented his suggestions "both in the classroom and in print" (221), he now prepares to venture into the unfamiliar territory of the avant-garde periodical in order to fish for potential philosophers.[6] In doing so, he tailors his modus operandi to the audience: as he explains, rather than simply to reiterate what has already been written, he prefers to focus on the objections made publicly to his suggestion. In other words, Strauss also enters the marketplace ready to engage in the inevitable conflict with the political men of his time, those who champion the reigning opinions. In this respect, "On a Forgotten Kind of Writing" is at once a political action and an installment of philosophic politics.

As becomes quickly apparent, this means Strauss will engage with critics of *Persecution and the Art of Writing*, the book in which he presents these suggestions. But this may seem strange at first: how would the young reader be able to accurately estimate the weight and significance of the objections without a firm grasp of what is objected to? Admittedly, Strauss goes on to restate and summarize the core contention, but it is doubtful whether this suffices to adequately follow the ensuing debate. In this respect, Strauss's approach seems designed to direct curious readers toward the book itself. But this is not all: as Strauss explains, his ulterior aim is to address the difficulties from which the objections arose, because they are "similar to those that various students have felt" (221). Here again, the focus is on the young addressees of the essay.

Strauss's initial restatement of his basic suggestion concerning the art of writing is presented in syllogistic form. However, he inverts the usual order of the syllogism, starting with the minor premise, according to which philosophy is "the attempt to replace opinion of 'all things' by knowledge of 'all things'" (222).[7] The major premise or, as he calls it, "the crucial premise," is presented later: "the proposition that opinion is the element of society" (222). In fact, Strauss is required to further specify the major premise in order to bring out its point: opinion is the element of society by dint of the necessity of "unqualified commitment of the many to the opinions on which society rests," or of "wholehearted acceptance of the principles of society" (222).[8] Without such commitment and acceptance on the part of the majority of its members, he implies, no society can endure. Only after this specification does the fundamental problem, the *crux*, appear: in its attempt to replace opinion by knowledge, philosophy compromises this wholehearted acceptance, and in this way it endangers society. This primary conclusion explains the corollaries that Strauss then adds: since philosophy's attempt cannot be generalized and disseminated without destroying the foundations of society, it must remain limited to a small minority; and this small minority must respect opinions, albeit without accepting them as true. What they regard as true, finally, can be communicated only by using a specific manner of writing, based on the distinction between an exoteric, socially useful teaching and an esoteric, true teaching.[9]

The importance of the major premise is further underscored by the fact that Strauss immediately connects his discussion to a critique of modern social science and contemporary social scientists. The main thrust of this critique is that modern social science is oblivious of the tension between its own requirements of objectivity and impartiality and the requirements of society, which demand subjectivity and partiality. However, it is worth scrutinizing in some detail the implicit considerations that lead up to this objection. Although many social scientists accept the major premise that opinion is the element of society, they transform it and fail to understand its ramifications. To begin with, they replace the notion of "opinions" by that of "myths" or "values" (222). In both cases, this already means an estrangement from and demotion of the perspective of the members of society, who generally perceive their commitment as being based neither on myths nor on values, but rather on more or less considered views and more or less deeply cherished principles, that is, on opinions. Like its Greek counterpart *doxa*, which denotes the way in which our knowledge of the world is based on the cognition of appearances, the Latin *opinio* implies thinking as well as judging, and hence an act of cognition. As distinguished from "opinions," speaking in terms of "myths" and "values" fails to do justice to the emotional, cognitive, and intellectual dimensions of social and political commitment.[10]

As a result, contemporary social scientists quickly lapse into a facile relativism. Reducing opinions to myths and values amounts to treating them as "assumptions which are not evidently superior or preferable to any alternative assumptions" and which ultimately have an "arbitrary character" (222). In this way, however, the social scientists rashly pass over the fact that to those who hold them, opinions are anything but arbitrary assumptions but, indeed, often evidently superior and preferable to other opinions. Why this is so is a question social science does not even begin to raise. Likewise, it is unable to consider that instead of being arbitrary, the assumptions underlying opinions may be—admittedly inadequate and inarticulate—attempts to grasp the truth. As Strauss explains elsewhere, opinions may also be seen as "fragments of the truth, soiled fragments of the pure truth. In other words, the opinions prove to be solicited by the self-subsisting truth, and the ascent to the truth proves to be guided by the self-subsistent truth which all men always divine" (Strauss 1953, 124).[11]

As such, opinions command a respect of which the social scientists, as distinguished from the philosophers, are incapable. In this respect, social science's desire to be "objective" and "undogmatic" is in fact neither: it fails to grasp the full complexity of human social and political commitment because it is based on unwarranted assumptions regarding this commitment. By the same token, it is not just incapable of serious reflection on its own societal role and impact, but it even stifles such reflection. For this reason, Strauss eventually goes so far as to call it an "absurd dogmatism" (223), whose adherents are as dangerous to intellectual freedom as

Senator McCarthy. Undoubtedly, both the criticism and the comparison are also intended as a word of caution to the young readers of the *Chicago Review*, who, under the sway of social science, are perhaps more likely to perceive the latter danger than the former. This, at least, can be inferred from their unwarranted expectation that the suggestion concerning the art of writing would be received with considerable scholarly interest. However, Strauss apparently shares the hope that future generations will be more perceptive and open-minded than his own: he refers to them as "my young friends" (222).

In marked contrast to social science's dogmatism, Strauss explicitly avows that his own suggestion concerning the art of writing and the underlying view on the relation between philosophy and society ultimately consists of nothing more—and nothing less—than two *questions* elicited by his research on earlier thinkers.[12] The first of these questions is the historical question whether any great thinkers ever held the view and put it into the practice of an art of writing. The second is the philosophical question of whether the view itself is true, false, or only qualifiedly true. In the remainder of the chapter, the first question is largely addressed in Strauss's response to Sabine's objections, while the second question is more prominent in the exchange with Belaval. It is not clear whether this implies that Strauss holds the philosophic question to be more important than the historical. At the close of the article, he invites the reader "to begin to wonder whether the historical truth is not as difficult of access as the philosophic truth" (232).

Strauss's engagement with the first set of objections, those raised by George H. Sabine, focuses on a single question: what and who is an artful writer?[13] This question is then addressed in two subsidiary points: first, the qualitative difference between artful readers and writers on the one hand, and artless readers and writers on the other; second, the connection (or rather opposition) between esotericism and historicism. In his discussion of the first point, Strauss—not without a twist—exposes Sabine as a not particularly artful reader of *Persecution and the Art of Writing*. Largely impervious to its nuances, Sabine proves to be unwilling or unable to do what, according to Strauss, is required of the careful reader: to "adapt the rules of certainty which guide his research to the nature of the subject" (Strauss 1952, 30).[14] Instead, he seems to suspect Strauss of doing the opposite, as becomes apparent from his remark that "Spinoza's essay is well adapted to the use of Professor Strauss's method" (Sabine 1953, 221).[15] Throughout, he seems inclined to take the cautious and conditional rules of thumb offered by Strauss as hard methodological principles, to which the nature of the subject is then adapted. When Strauss turns to Sabine's critique of the Spinoza chapter in *Persecution and the Art of Writing*, the initial impression is confirmed: Sabine emerges as a less than careful reader, both of Strauss and of Spinoza, who systematically underestimates the ability and perspicacity of the latter (not to mention those of the vulgar of the seventeenth century). Underlying this heedlessness is a refusal or incapacity to take seriously "the theological problem" (226) with which Spinoza and his contemporaries grappled.[16] Here again, Strauss points to the sway that modern science, or rather "the belief that enthusiasm for science and progress constitutes a form of religion" (226), has over modern readers' minds.

More pointedly, Sabine proves to be unwilling to entertain the possibility that certain "great minds" (225) are writers "of another caliber" (224) with an exceptional command of their writings. It is important to note Strauss's nuance on this point: all he asks for in the careful reader is a willingness to reckon with this possibility, as only this will impel her to read with full attentiveness.[17] In fact, such attentiveness is no less called for in reading Strauss's further response to Sabine. When the latter attempts to trivialize Strauss's suggestion, asserting that every conceivable society somehow restricts the conditions under which an author may write, Strauss bluntly counters this unwarranted generalization with an assertion that attends scrupulously to particulars: "I assert that societies in which men can attack in writings accessible to all both the established social or political order and the beliefs on which it is based can not only be imagined but have existed, e.g., the Third Republic in France and post-Bismarckian Wilhelminian Germany" (224). However, he immediately goes on to call "the wisdom of such extreme liberalism" (224) into question. Very likely, he is thinking of the fateful end of both societies, both of which became increasingly polarized and eventually veered to authoritarianism, with the Vichy regime in France and National Socialism in Germany. When freedom of expression becomes extreme, he seems to suggest, it may lead to the suppression of freedom as such.

To the young reader of the *Chicago Review*, however, Strauss's examples as well as the question he raises must pose a puzzle: is not the United States a country where "men can attack in writings accessible to all both the established social or political order and the beliefs on which it is founded" (224)? Doesn't criticism of government even "find sanctuary" in the First Amendment, as Justice Black put it? Are we given to surmise, then, that the American regime is based on an extreme liberalism of questionable wisdom, and as such is in grave danger? If so, what constitutes the danger? And if not, is the implication that the American regime too imposes restrictions on writers, perhaps such that they may criticize the political order but not the beliefs on which it is founded? Would this constitute a "moderate liberalism" that is able to avert the danger? Or is Strauss's charge of "extreme liberalism" rather aimed at those writers who lack the wisdom or the prudence to compose their writings in such a way that they are not accessible to all? Be this as it may, his terse assertion against Sabine is sure to provide food for thought.

In Strauss's discussion of the second subsidiary point, the opposition between esotericism and historicism, the importance of the major premise is highlighted again. And, once more, Strauss hastens to emphasize that the premise is moot: only "*if* it is assumed" (227, emphasis added) that opinion is indeed the element of society does philosophy in its original sense—the attempt to replace opinion by knowledge—require an art of writing. Nonetheless, even the disagreement with Sabine about historicism turns on their different estimation of the possibilities and capabilities of the philosopher. For as Strauss explains, according to historicism "even the greatest minds cannot liberate themselves from the specific opinions which rule their society" (227). By the same token, historicism must reject the notion of philosophy in its original sense because historicism holds that "it is simply impossible to know the truth about the whole" (227). This, however, is a dogmatic assumption, Strauss points out. As he explains elsewhere, it is based on a non sequitur derived from historical experience that because philosophy so far has failed to find the truth, it is necessarily fated to fail. As we can learn from Plato's allegory of the cave, the attempt to find the truth is immensely difficult, but this does not warrant the conclusion that it is also impossible.[18]

At the same time, Strauss firmly rejects Sabine's imputation that his antihistoricism necessarily requires the opposite dogmatism of simply positing the availability of "a single true account of the whole" (228) and assuming total control on the part of the artful writer. Here again, Sabine misconstrues and misrepresents the position he is reviewing. As Strauss explains, he merely wants the historian to be open to the possibility that "the great thinkers" are pursuing the truth and that "they understood better what they thought than the historian who is not likely to be a great thinker" (228). In short, Strauss's argument is a plea for modesty and humility on the part of the historian, an invitation to recognize her ignorance in order to be able to learn from the great thinker. As he argues in *Persecution and the Art of Writing*, beyond the mutual protection of the philosopher and society, the ultimate purpose of the art of writing is *education*.[19]

Both the dogma "that the very notion of a final and true account of the whole is absurd" (228) and the opposite dogma that such an account is necessarily and readily available prevent the reader from ever developing such an attitude of modesty, and thus from being educated.

Such an attitude, at least, is more characteristic of the second critic, Yvon Belaval, whom Strauss praises for his open-mindedness.[20] Belaval indeed proves to be a more attentive and more generous reviewer who recognizes that historical exactness precisely requires reckoning with the possibility of an art of writing in interpreting the works of great thinkers. By the same token, Belaval is more sensitive to the philosophical stakes involved in Strauss's critique of historicism and positivism. Thus, it is interesting to note that Strauss (228) does not contradict Belaval when the latter attributes to him an antipositivist, "classical and rationalist conception of truth" as "untemporal." [21] However, Strauss immediately specifies what his understanding of the classic and rationalist conception of truth means, as well as the proper incentive for studying the history of philosophy, in a crucial statement that is at once categorical and conditional: "History of philosophy presupposes the persistence of the same fundamental problems. This, *and this alone*, is the trans-temporal truth which *must* be admitted, *if* there is to be history of philosophy" (229, emphasis added). Clearly, this assertion obviates any attempt—and many have been undertaken— to present Strauss as a partisan of an outdated metaphysical absolutism or essentialism.[22] Its importance is further borne out by the fact that it finds a resounding echo in the "Restatement on Xenophon's *Hiero*," which thus emerges even more pointedly as the companion piece to "On a Forgotten Kind of Writing." In his rejoinder to Kojève, Strauss provides a summation of his understanding of philosophy that is strongly reminiscent of his later assertion:

> What Pascal said with antiphilosophic intent about the impotence of both dogmatism and scepticism, is the *only* possible justification of philosophy which as such is neither dogmatic nor sceptic, and still less "decisionist," but zetetic (or skeptic [sic] in the original sense of the term). Philosophy as such is *nothing but* genuine awareness of the problems, i.e., of the fundamental and comprehensive problems. (116, emphasis added)

This passage reveals the full extent and implications of Strauss's appeal to interpretive modesty and openness on the part of the historian-reader: it is part and parcel of the zetetic attitude that attempts to steer a middle course between dogmatism and skepticism, both of which evade the problem of human knowledge, which is that "we know too little to be dogmatists and too much to be skeptics" (Strauss 2001b, 4).[23] Moreover, it is interesting to note that Strauss seems to consider a "decisionist" philosophy as even less acceptable, insofar as it simply short-circuits the problem through an arbitrary decision. Probably this is a critical thrust against Carl Schmitt, a historicist thinker and powerful proponent of decisionism whom Strauss debated in the 1930s (Strauss 1965, 331–51).[24]

But this is not all: the phrasing of the passage is wont to direct the attentive reader of *What Is Political Philosophy?* even further back, straight to the opening chapter. In "What Is Political Philosophy?," Strauss dismisses the objection that classical political philosophy is obsolete because it is "bound up with an antiquated cosmology" (38). Far from propounding any doctrine of the truth or of the whole, "it is knowledge of the elusive character of the truth, of the whole" (38) or knowledge of ignorance. The zetetic attitude avoids any commitment to ontology, cosmology, or physiology and instead pursues the truth by means of dialectic, as is exemplified by *Socrates*. Here again, the wording merits our attention as much as the substance:

> Socrates, then, viewed man in the light of the mysterious character of the whole. He held therefore that we are more familiar with the situation of man as man than with the ultimate causes of the situation. We may also say he viewed man in the light of the unchangeable ideas, i.e., of the fundamental and permanent problems. (39)[25]

In this way, the connection between the three chapters points us toward what Heinrich Meier has termed "the movement from the history of philosophy to the intention of the philosopher," in which "the hermeneutic effort turns smoothly into philosophical activity in the proper sense of the word" (Meier 2006, 64–65). By practicing the art of reading with a genuine concern for historical exactness, in full recognition of one's ignorance and with full attention to the problems inherent in the surface of the text that point toward the intention of the writer, the historian gradually develops a philosophic awareness of the fundamental problems. For the puzzling complexity and variety of the artfully written text are a reflection, through a glass darkly, of what Strauss elsewhere calls the "heterogeneity of being": its "cosmology" consists in "mysteriously [imitating] the mysterious *kosmos*," "[imitating] its model in order to awaken us to the mystery of the model and to assist us in articulating that mystery" (Strauss 1964, 61–62).[26]

Positivism, on the other hand, insofar as it "is blind to the fundamental problems" (229), prevents the historian from discerning the mystery of both the imitation and the model.

Still, all this should not make us forget the fact that Strauss's assertion in "On a Forgotten Kind of Writing" remains conditional. In his response to Belaval, he shows himself acutely aware of this. To Belaval's query whether there is a *necessary* conflict between philosophy and society, he answers by repeating that this is so only *if* one accepts the major premise of his argument, to wit that "opinion, i.e. assent to opinion" (229) is the element of society. However, he rejects Belaval's suggestion that accepting this premise and its consequences amounts to adopting a partial and incomplete view on the relation between philosophy and politics, which Belaval dubs "Averroism." Conspicuously, Strauss again doesn't quarrel with this designation. In fact, in the same context he brings up a consideration that sounds strikingly "Averroistic," not to say "Farabian." To Belaval's observation that persecution of philosophers more often came from religious than from political quarters, he responds, only to dismiss it immediately in such an offhand manner as to draw attention: "We do not have to consider whether every authority proper is not in the last analysis political" (229).[27] Once again, the young reader of the *Chicago Review* cannot but be tempted to ignore Strauss's dismissal and consider the question, especially in the light of what has been said earlier about Spinoza, revealed religion, and "the theological problem" (226).

Be this as it may, against Belaval Strauss insists—rather sharply—that "the 'Averroistic' view is no more partial than its contrary: both are *total* views about the relation of philosophy and politics" (229, emphasis added). At the same time, he acknowledges that the contrary view is equally a total view and as such a worthy alternative, from the perspective of which his own view remains fundamentally questionable. Oddly enough, however, he does not explicitly identify the contrary total view, which, we are left to infer, at least denies a necessary tension between philosophy and politics. Only at the end of the paragraph are we given a clue, when Strauss agrees with Belaval "that one cannot accept the 'Averroistic' view if one believes that M. Kojève teaches the truth" (230). Since Strauss declines to clarify what truth "M. Kojève" teaches, the curious reader of the *Chicago Review* has no choice but to turn to Belaval's review, which, however, is only marginally helpful, insofar as it merely states that "the Politician *ends up* by obeying the Philosopher" (Belaval 1953, 864).[28] If she remains unfazed and undaunted by yet another cryptic assertion, she may be led to consult the writings of Kojève, which is likely what Strauss envisages. By contrast, the reader of *What Is Political Philosophy?* has the advantage of being able to turn to the "Restatement," in which Strauss presents and criticizes "M. Kojève's" endorsement of the Hegelian alliance between philosophy and politics toward the universal homogeneous state.[29] However, in this case as well, it is no less clear that Strauss points the reader to Kojève's work as the most serious alternative to his own.

In spite of his esteem, Strauss nevertheless takes his second critic to task for reasons similar to those animating his rejoinder to Sabine. Like the latter, Belaval tends to misunderstand Strauss's hermeneutical rules of thumb as "axioms" of a "method" that can be applied without due regard for the nature of the subject. As a result, he likewise overestimates the abilities of most readers while underestimating those of an artful writer. Thus, like Sabine, he fails to appreciate that the guise of the philosopher may serve to hide his heterodoxy from his *allies* no less than from his attackers. More importantly, he doesn't reckon with the possibility that the philosopher could pose as a scholar or commentator and thus "[avail] himself of the specific immunity of the commentator or of the historian in order to speak his mind concerning grave matters in his 'historical' works, rather than in the works in which he speaks in his own name" (Strauss 1952, 14). By the same token, Belaval is seen to fall prey to the characteristically modern concern with originality as a necessary characteristic of a great thinker. On this point, it is worth quoting the crucial observation that Strauss makes elsewhere in similar terms:

> that by transmitting the most precious knowledge, not in "systematic" works, but in the guise of a historical account, [the philosopher] indicates his view concerning "originality" and "individuality" in philosophy: what comes into sight as the "original" or "personal" "contribution" of a philosopher is infinitely less significant than his private, and truly original and individual, understanding of the necessarily anonymous truth. (Strauss 1945, 377)

With the question of truth resurfacing in the background, no wonder the question of certitude reemerges in the foreground. In the final paragraph, Strauss addresses Belaval's complaint that artful reading "can never lead to absolute certainty" (231). As in the case of Sabine, Strauss rejoins by questioning whether other ways of reading are or have ever been truly successful in this way. At the same time, he calls the very concern with certainty into question and cautions against the dogmatism that may underlie it. This becomes apparent in his final response, which turns away from Belaval to address "M. Kojève's" objection that the artful reader's detective work can never yield a confession of the criminal, that is, the artful writer. A concluding exhortation to the undogmatic, zetetic attitude, Strauss's words are as much a demonstration of that same attitude: "I would be happy if there were suspicion of crime where up to now there has only been implicit faith in perfect innocence" (232). This suspicion may set a historical investigation on the path toward philosophical activity, since it impels us "to admit that the thought of the past is much more enigmatic than it is generally held to be, and to begin to wonder whether the historical truth is not as difficult of access as the philosophic truth" (232). These final words, a stab at the complacency of present-day historians, also bait the young reader of the *Chicago Review*. Wonder, after all, marks the beginning of both history and philosophy in their original sense.[30] Moreover, as Strauss came to surmise early in the process of rediscovering the forgotten kind of writing, the distinction between history and philosophy (and poetry, for that matter) in their original sense may not be as clear-cut as is presently assumed.[31]

The one question that lingers at the end of "On a Forgotten Kind of Writing" concerns the crucial premise of Strauss's suggestion: is opinion, or assent to opinion, the element of society? It is interesting to note, in passing, that Strauss sees fit to discuss it in what is generally perceived as a minor and unremarkable writing. This would seem to reflect the modus operandi of Plato, who frequently raises the most important questions in his shorter and more inconspicuous dialogues, which by that same token may be more attractive bait for young readers.[32] However this may be, although Strauss seems to subscribe to the affirmative answer given by classical political philosophy, he remains keenly aware of the alternative, which appears to find its most powerful representative in Kojève. At the same time, this may be just what a genuinely Socratic and zetetic attitude requires. For to embrace the affirmative answer too wholeheartedly would mean to abandon the question that for Strauss is concomitant with the Socratic question: is political philosophy possible and necessary?[33] In the "Restatement," immediately after having given his powerful characterization of philosophy as awareness of the fundamental problems, he states:

> It is impossible to think about these problems without becoming inclined toward a solution, toward one or the other of the very few typical solutions. Yet as long as there is no wisdom but only quest for wisdom, the evidence of all solutions

is necessarily smaller than the evidence of the problems. Therefore the philosopher ceases to be a philosopher at the moment at which the "subjective certainty" of a solution becomes stronger than his awareness of the problematic nature of that solution. At that moment the sectarian is born. (116)

Perhaps this awareness provides an additional clue to Strauss's selection of the chapters that make up *What Is Political Philosophy?* Besides bearing the most Socratic title of all his works, the book is arguably also the most dialogic or, to be more exact, the most dialectical, both in style and in content, with Strauss continually testing his own opinions as well as those of others. In fact, the book interweaves two dialectics: one with the dead, and one with the living. In the first two chapters (1–2), the former predominates, with only scant references to living contemporary authors. In the following six chapters, the two dialectics are intermingled: going from ancient (3–4) to medieval (5–6) to modern (7–8) writers, in each of these chapters Strauss also engages in a critical—and in some cases caustic—discussion with contemporary interpreters, translators, or editors.[34] In the ninth chapter, "On a Forgotten Kind of Writing," the emphasis suddenly shifts toward the latter dialectic, focusing almost entirely on the debate with living contemporaries (Sabine and Belaval), and with only a few references to dead writers. But this shift paves the way for the tenth chapter, in which the back-and-forth between dead and living finally comes to a head. There, Strauss retraces and subtly radicalizes the trajectory of Kurt Riezler: away from the "incipient *mythoi*" (246) of the contemporary figure of Martin Heidegger and toward "the hidden and serious meaning" (251) of the poem written by the pre-Socratic Parmenides. To grasp that hidden and serious meaning, Strauss suggests, would reveal "the true relation between truth and opinion" (251).

Notes

1. Leo Strauss, *What Is Political Philosophy? And Other Studies* (Strauss 1959). All unspecified references between parentheses are to this text. Compare 31, 32, 63, 67, 73, 93, 104, 109, 126–127, as concerns the first four essays. In the consecutive essays on Farabi, Maimonides, Hobbes, and Locke, the two themes can easily be identified. And even in the concluding essay on Kurt Riezler, Strauss makes a number of intriguing observations on the art of writing of Parmenides (250–51).

2. Cf. O'Neill (2006).

3. Strauss (1959, 95–133). Moreover, both essays were published in the same year, 1954.

4. Cf. 104. "M." could stand for "Mister" as well as for "Monsieur." Like Strauss, Kojève had never obtained either the German *Habilitation* or the French *agrégation* necessary to carry the title of "Professor." Perhaps it also shows Strauss's preference for the civil over the academic form of address, based on his criticism of intellectuals as distinguished from philosophers. See also his letter to Gershom Scholem of July 7, 1973 (Strauss 2001a, 770).

5. With the expression "subjective certainty," Strauss refers to Kojève's discussion of philosophic dialectic in the latter's *Introduction to the Reading of Hegel*: "Like all opinion, the Myth arises spontaneously and is accepted (or rejected) in the same way. Man creates it in and by his ('poetical') imagination, content if he avoids contradictions when he develops his initial idea or 'intuition.' But when the confrontation with a different opinion or myth engenders the desire for a *proof*, which cannot as yet be satisfied by a *demonstration through discussion*, one feels the need to found one's opinion or the myth that one is proposing (both being supposed to be unverifiable empirically—i.e., by an appeal to common sense experience) on something more than simple personal *conviction* or 'subjective certainty' (*Gewissheit*)—which is visibly of the same type and weight as the adversary's. A foundation of superior or 'divine' value is sought and found: the myth is presented as having been 'revealed' by a god, who is supposed to be the guarantee for its truth—that is, for its universal and eternal validity" (Kojève 1980, 182; see also 10–20, 151, 256–57).

6. Ferrari (1997, 36–37).

7. Cf. 73: "Political philosophy is the attempt to replace our opinions about political fundamentals by knowledge about them."

8. See also 229, where Strauss reiterates the major premise: "if the element of society necessarily is opinion, i.e., *assent to opinion*" (emphasis added).

9. It is important to note that the two teachings are part of one and the same text. In *Persecution and the Art of Writing* (Strauss 1952), observing that writings are accessible to all, Strauss asserts of an esoteric writer, both that "all of his writings would have to be, strictly speaking, exoteric" and that "no written exposition can be, strictly speaking, esoteric." Compare Strauss (1952, 35 and 187).

10. Cf. 21–25. In the background, it is easy to recognize Strauss's critique of Max Weber's value-free social science in *Natural Right and History* (Strauss 1953, 49–55, 77–80).

11. See also Strauss (1953, 12): "The public dogma is originally an inadequate attempt to answer the question of the all-comprehensive truth or of the eternal order."; Strauss (1959, 10): "The awareness of the good which guides all our actions has the character of opinion: it is no longer questioned, but on reflection, it proves to be questionable."

12. For a compelling account of the first and decisive steps in Strauss's rediscovery of the art of writing, the reader may fruitfully consult his correspondence with Jacob Klein, published in Strauss (2001a, 455–605); see also Janssens (2008).

13. George H. Sabine (1880–1961) was professor of philosophy at Cornell University and the author of *A History of Political Theory* (1937).

14. In the same book, Strauss quotes Sabine's assertion that Montesquieu's *Spirit of the Laws* has no design, contrasting it with statements to the contrary by Montesquieu himself as well as by certain contemporaries. In his review, Sabine nowhere addresses this issue (Strauss 1952, 29).

15. When Strauss quotes this remark in his own essay, he tellingly omits "Professor." In his correspondence with Hans-Georg Gadamer, Strauss emphatically denies that he has a method. See Strauss (1978, 6–7, 9, 11).

16. Although Strauss speaks of "the theological problem" of the seventeenth century, it is clear that this problem has a marked political dimension. Hence, the designation "theological-political problem" would have been equally apt.

17. In one of his earliest books, Strauss quotes approvingly the words of the nineteenth-century French theologian Alphonse Gratry: "L'essence de la critique, c'est l'attention" (Strauss 1997a, 137–38 n. 13).

18. Cf. Strauss (1997b, 2: 284, 373); Strauss (1953, 21–34).

19. Strauss (1952, 37); cf. Melzer (2007, 1015–31); Major (2005, 484).

20. Yvon Belaval (1908–88) was professor of philosophy at the University of Lille and at the Sorbonne. A specialist in early modern philosophy, he also wrote on the problem of expression. Belaval's lengthy (almost fifteen pages) review is composed of two parts: the first part (twelve pages) concisely and clearly renders the main points of *Persecution and the Art of Writing*, while the second part (two and a half pages) focuses critically on the book's philosophical premises (Belaval 1967). In "On a Forgotten Kind of Writing," Strauss responds only to the second part.

21. Belaval (1953, 864).

22. See also Strauss (1953, 23–24).

23. Strauss paraphrases Pascal; cf. Blaise Pascal, *Pensées* 6.395: "Instinct, raison. Nous avons une impuissance de prouver, invincible à tout le dogmatisme. Nous avons une idée de la vérité invincible à tout le pyrrhonisme." (Instinct, reason. We have an incapacity of proof, insurmountable by all dogmatism. We have an idea of truth, invincible to all skepticism.)

24. Cf. Meier (1995); Janssens (2008, 133–47). Incidentally, Strauss's suggestion in the "Restatement" that "perhaps it is not war nor work but thinking that constitutes the humanity of man" (131) envisages Schmitt no less than Kojève.

25. Strauss (1936, 145).

26. Cf. Strauss (1959, 39).

27. Cf. 146, 150, 163; Strauss (1952, 15).

28. "[L]e Politique *finit* par obéir le Philosophe."

29. Cf. 105 110–12,127–33.

30. Cf. Aristotle, *Metaphysics* 983a12–15; Herodotus *Histories*, I.7–13.

31. See Strauss (2001a, 556–59); cf. Benardete (1999, 12); Janssens (2010).

32. Cf. Alfarabi (2001, 53–54); Davis (2006, 563). I am grateful to Chris Nadon for drawing my attention to this point.

33. Strauss (1936, 136).

34. Kojève and Voegelin (4), Gabrieli (5), Wolfson (6), Polin (7), and von Leyden (8).

Works Cited

Alfarabi. 2001. *Philosophy of Plato and Aristotle*. Ithaca: Cornell University Press.

Belaval, Yvon. 1953. "Pour un sociologie de la philosophie." *Critique* 9 (77): 853–66.

———. 1967. *Philosophers and Their Language*. Athens: Ohio University Press.

Davis, Michael. 2011. *The Soul of the Greeks: An Inquiry*. Chicago: University of Chicago Press.

Ferrari, G. R. F. 1997. "Strauss's Plato." *Arion* 5 (2): 36–65.

Janssens, David. 2008. *Between Athens and Jerusalem: Philosophy, Prophecy, and Politics in Leo Strauss's Early Thought*. New York: SUNY Press.

———. 2010. "The Philosopher's Ancient Clothes: Leo Strauss on Philosophy and Poetry." In *Modernity and What Has Been Lost: Considerations on the Legacy of Leo Strauss*, ed. Paweł Armada and Arkadiusz Gornisiewicz, 53–71. South Bend, IN: St. Augustine's Press.

Kojève, Alexandre. 1980. *Introduction to the Reading of Hegel*. Ithaca: Cornell University Press.

Major, Rafael. 2005. "The Cambridge School and Leo Strauss: Texts and Context of American Political Science." *Political Research Quarterly*, 58 (3): 477–85.

Meier, Heinrich. 1995. *Carl Schmitt and Leo Strauss: The Hidden Dialogue*. Chicago: University of Chicago Press.

———. 2006. *Leo Strauss and the Theologico-Political Problem*. Cambridge: Cambridge University Press.

Melzer, Arthur. 2007. "On the Pedagogical Motive for Esoteric Writing." *Journal of Politics* 69 (4): 1015–31.

O'Neill, Brooke E. 2006. "60-Year Review." *University of Chicago Magazine* 99 (1). http://magazine.uchicago.edu/0610/chicagojournal/review.shtml.

Sabine, George H. 1937. *A History of Political Theory*. New York: Holt, Rinehart and Winston.

———. 1953. "Review of *Persecution and the Art of Writing*." *Ethics* 63 (3): 220.

Strauss, Leo. 1936. *The Political Philosophy of Hobbes: Its Basis and Its Genesis*. Oxford: Clarendon Press.

———. 1945. "Farabi's Plato." In *Louis Ginzberg Jubilee Volume*, ed. Saul Lieberman, Shalom Spiegel, Solomon Zeitlin, and Alexander Marx, 357–93. New York: American Academy for Jewish Research.

———. 1952. *Persecution and the Art of Writing*. New York: Free Press.

———. 1953. *Natural Right and History*. Chicago: University of Chicago Press.

———. 1959. *What Is Political Philosophy? And Other Studies*. New York: Free Press.

———. 1964. *The City and Man*. Chicago: Rand McNally.

———. 1965. "Comments on *Der Begriff des Politischen* by Carl Schmitt." In *Spinoza's Critique of Religion*, by Leo Strauss, 331–51. New York: Schocken Books.

———. 1978. "Correspondence with Hans-Georg Gadamer concerning *Wahrheit und Methode*." *Independent Journal of Philosophy* 2: 5–12.

———. 1997a. *Philosophy and Law: Contributions to the Understanding of Maimonides and His Predecessors*. New York: SUNY Press.

———. 1997b. *Gesammelte Schriften*. Ed. Heinrich Meier and Wiebke Meier. Vol. 2. Stuttgart: J. B. Metzler.

———. 2001a. *Gesammelte Schriften*. Ed. Heinrich Meier and Wiebke Meier. Vol. 3. Stuttgart: J. B. Metzler.

———. 2001b. *On Plato's Symposium*. Chicago: University of Chicago Press.

CHAPTER TEN

"Kurt Riezler: 1882–1955" and the "Problem" of Political Philosophy

Susan Meld Shell

What Is Political Philosophy? And Other Studies consists of ten formal chapters, followed by sixteen briefer critical appraisals. The book begins with the eponymous essay "What Is Political Philosophy?," which Strauss delivered in Jerusalem, and ends with a chapter on Kurt Riezler, based on a talk Strauss presented to the General Seminar of the New School following Riezler's death in 1955.[1] The intervening chapters include studies, in roughly chronological order, of classical political philosophy and aspects of the thought of Xenophon, Farabi, Maimonides, Hobbes, and Locke, with a penultimate chapter on "a forgotten kind of writing." An immediate question thus presents itself: why end a book devoted to the explication and recovery of political philosophy with what could be deemed a personal eulogy? That this is the only eulogy (or eulogy-like work in honor of a friend) that Strauss ever published makes its placement in *What Is Political Philosophy?* all the more striking. In what way or ways is Strauss's eulogy of his late friend directed toward enhancing our understanding of political philosophy? The task of answering that question is rendered especially difficult by the peculiar density of Strauss's essay, which not only touches upon the thought of Kant, Goethe, Heidegger, and others, but also contains perhaps the most extended treatment of a pre-Socratic philosopher (Parmenides) in any of Strauss's writings. It is also complicated by the unusually personal character of Strauss's essay, with its oblique references to the "meaning" of 1933 (27, 260). Still, even on a provisional reading, his essay sheds instructive light, as I will try to show, not only on the ongoing possibility of political prudence but also on the nature of political philosophy itself.

Some preliminary biographical details are here in order. Riezler was born in 1882 to a prosperous Bavarian banking family. He earned a doctorate in classics with highest honors in 1906. Riezler worked as a political journalist and then as a high-ranking cabinet advisor under both the Imperial and the Weimar governments; he served as an important conduit between the Kaiser and the Bolsheviks and was later involved both in the drafting of the Weimar Constitution and in its subsequent defense from militant attacks from both the right and the left. At the age of thirty he married the daughter of the distinguished German (Jewish) painter Max Liebermann, whose substantial art collection he and she later inherited. In 1927 Riezler was appointed Kurator of the University of Frankfurt, to which he attracted a diverse community of talented scholars, including Max Horkheimer, Theodor Adorno, Ernst Kantorowicz, and others. In 1933 Riezler was forced to resign from the university. He emigrated to the United States with the help of the aristocratic anti-Nazi Kreslau Circle and served on the faculty of the New School until his retirement in 1953; he died in Europe in 1955. His published writings ran the gamut from an early study of ancient Greek economics (based upon his dissertation) to late writings on the political dangers facing a mass society.[2]

In sum: Riezler was a man of action, as Strauss puts it, as well as thought (234). Indeed, his political judgment was in some ways superior to Strauss's own. (On the few occasions they disagreed about the war, Riezler later proved correct [235].) He was less a "professor" in the ordinary sense than a "gentleman" employed in the "noble and serious occupation of leisure"—one whose Bavarian "sturdiness" had transformed itself into "an unpretentious strength and greatness of soul" (234). And yet despite these classical qualities of mind and soul, Riezler's attempted retrieval of the ancient understanding of human things fell short: Riezler remained a "social," not a "political" philosopher, for reasons that Strauss gradually makes clear. Riezler, as interpreted by Strauss, emerges as a kind of test case for the history of political philosophy as mapped out in the book's preceding chapters.

I

Strauss's acquaintance with Riezler, as Strauss immediately informs us, began in 1938 at the New School of Social Research, i.e., when both were recently arrived refugees from Nazi Germany. Riezler, who was seventeen years older, had already had a distinguished career, whereas Strauss's most important writings still lay before him. During the ensuing decade "complex" collegial relations developed into a "simple and firm friendship" that was attenuated but not broken off by Strauss's departure for the University of Chicago in 1949. Withal, Strauss confesses to his inadequacy to the task at hand: to speak to the New School's General Seminar "on the thought of [their recently deceased] friend." The difficulty lies not only in the fact that Strauss has not read Riezler's work with sufficient care. It also arises, Strauss says, from Riezler's "rare human depth and breadth." To honor him adequately would require gifts of narrative and characterization that would bring his late friend to life, gifts whose absence Strauss has never, as he here puts it, more deplored.

Strauss's expression of regret not only is in keeping with ancient formulas;[3] it also calls to mind an earlier expression of regret as to his own narrative inadequacy, presented in the course of another lecture to the General Seminar. During that other speech, delivered just prior to U.S. entry into the Second World War (and at which his friend Riezler is likely to have been present), Strauss confessed that he lacked the journalistic gifts necessary to convey, to those who had not directly shared their experience, the *emotions* of those who had been attracted to German nihilism.[4] What he could and did do in that lecture was to describe certain factors that encouraged the emergence of German nihilism and the Nazi movement with which it was associated. One factor was the extreme youth of those so attracted; the other the collapse of "the great and noble educational system founded by great liberals of the early 19th century."[5] On both fronts, a reader of both lectures might incidentally observe, Riezler was protected: both by his relative maturity at the time of greatest German "fermentation" and by his earlier exposure to an educational system that had not yet succumbed to its fatal weakening under the government of Kaiser Wilhelm.[6] Here is one reason, perhaps, why, as Strauss later puts it, Riezler "could not been mistaken or misled by the events of 1933" (259–60). But there is surely more to Riezler's achievement than the good luck of not being born later.

In the present lecture Strauss's regret partly arises from his inability to honor Riezler adequately by "narrat[ing his] actions" in a manner that would "bring to light and life the man himself." Riezler's actions are as impressive as his words; he represents more than does anyone else with whom Strauss has been acquainted the "virtue of humanity" (234). Riezler seems to have been formed especially by Goethe, and was thus exposed, if only indirectly, to the "great German liberals" whose lack of pedagogical influence upon a younger German generation Strauss's earlier lecture before the General Seminar specifically deplored. Riezler, one is almost tempted to say, was the last of the great German liberals who represented and reflected Weimar at its best.[7]

II

Strauss begins his examination of Riezler's writings with a book composed on the eve of the First World War (but published only after the war ended): *Grundzüge der Weltpolitik in der Gegenwart* (Outlines of Current World Politics),[8] a work that Strauss compares to Burke's 1791 *Thoughts on French Affairs*.[9] The young Riezler is a nationalist, both because the conflict among nations is the "most massive political fact" of his time, and owing to a deeper conflict between nationalism and "politically relevant" cosmopolitanism as ideas rooted in antagonistic "living forces." Nationalism moves Riezler, in other words, not only because nationalism is the more powerful of the two contemporary forces, but also because it is guided by a nobler ideal.

Strauss endorses Riezler's analysis of the sources of the new cosmopolitanism—an analysis that anticipated his own later treatment of Hobbes's "new morality."[10] Modern (or "politically relevant") cosmopolitanism is based on a valuation of life without regard to how it is lived and as such leaves no room for reverence, the "matrix of human nobility" (236). It thus distracts man from "concentration on the few things on which man's wholeness entirely depends" (236). For the first and last time in the essay, Strauss's and Riezler's approach to "wholes" and "wholeness" nearly coincide: both share an understanding of the practical connection between reverence and tradition, and of the moral challenge posed by an ideal that deprives life of its seriousness and with it an essential condition of human "wholeness" (236). At the same time, Strauss indicates almost immediately a major point of divergence: Riezler does not do justice either to an earlier cosmopolitanism (that may not be "politically relevant") or to the idealistic promise of cosmopolitanism of the contemporary sort, a failure all the more remarkable given his understanding of the nation as open-ended as to its future—indeed, as essentially eternal (237).[11] Riezler's understanding of wholeness, both individual and national or collective, takes its fundamental bearings, not from the "ends" to which individuals and communities aspire but from a notion of organic form that has its origins, as we will shortly see, in the thought of Kant and Goethe. Even where Strauss finds Riezler to be "historically correct" –i.e., in the latter's insight into the shortcomings of an outlook that would provoke immoderate indignation in the young "German nihilists" who were to follow[12]—he also takes Riezler gently to task both for his failure to appreciate the power of cosmopolitanism's "promise" and for a misplaced idealism vis-à-vis the nation as the pretended bearer of the hope for eternal life. Unable or unwilling to account for the "wholeness" of the political community in the classical manner (i.e., in terms of its own highest aspiration), Riezler looks to "life as such" independent of the "kind of life one leads" (236)—that is to say, to a principle that he himself identified as the ultimate root of the ideal that he rejects. What is more, he adopts the (Raskolnikovian) view that "there is no universally valid concept of good and evil" (237). Strauss interrupts his summary at this point to declare Riezler's position "unsatisfactory" if "for no other reason" that there may be an essential necessity to the death of nations as "beings" that "have come into being,"[13] an argument that in its general form Riezler already grants. His embrace of a view associated with the literary figure of Raskolnikov is in tension with an insight into the nature of politics that already points beyond his youthful nationalism. At the same time, Riezler does not try to dignify the nation by emphasizing the connection between thought and language (following Herder and/or in anticipation of Heidegger). That route seems to have been blocked by his actual familiarity with world politics: as the examples of Switzerland on the one hand and Great Britain and the United States on the other show, there is no necessary link between political community and community of language. Still, his rejection of this route may also indicate a premature dismissal of language as the "matrix of the truth" (237) to which Strauss will later return (258).[14]

In sum: Riezler's youthful nationalism is neither theoretically satisfactory (even from his own point of view) nor fully expressive of his own attraction to the individual quest for truth as an alternative route to "eternity" (240). Still, it provides a framework for contemporary political analysis superior to the available alternatives (238). His early nationalism, moreover, is concerned not only with "the power of force" but also with "culture" and "and the power of ideas." His conception of national vitality is neither crude nor militaristic. He took as his model—far earlier than did Strauss, who evidently needed the example of Churchill[15]—empire of the British sort, "patient, prudent, and farsighted" and tending toward the "soberly democratic" (239). On the eve of the Great War he still harbored a restrained confidence that the "system of slowly shifting alliances" that had kept the peace for fifty years might yet be maintained—an attitude of subdued hopefulness, "if sanity will but assert itself," that persisted into Riezler's final years (241).

What is perhaps most striking in Strauss's treatment of Riezler's political analyses is the scope and maturity of Riezler's early achievement: between 1913 and 1953 his approach hardly changes (239), except in grasping more clearly the source of the weakness of modern nontyrannical governments in the face of demagogues—a veiled reference, perhaps, to Riezler's own fateful decision, undertaken in the heat of war, to facilitate Lenin's return to Czarist Russia.[16] Almost equally striking is the contrast between the relatively unchanging character of Riezler's political approach and the significant changes in his "metaphysics." From the start, he adopts the view that "political life cannot be understood with the means of . . . natural science" (241). This assumption, which is not altogether foreign to the spirit of the classics,[17] rests, however, on a methodological distinction between the ways of "science" and those of "historical understanding" that is distinctly modern, as Strauss sees it, and that reflects the influence of Kant, Nietzsche, and, above all, Goethe (234).[18]

Caught up, in the aftermath of the First World War, in a time of intellectual "fermentation," Riezler was moved by the then-current neo-Kantian school, owing to the "force and passion" of its leader, and despite its having less in common with his own "aspirations" than its phenomenological and "Diltheyan" rivals (242). In *Gestalt und Gesetz* (1924) Riezler attempts to comprehend the dualism of nature and mind from a single "human" point of view. At the same time, his "critical metaphysics" also insists upon the Kantian insight that "the whole conceived as a totality of things cannot exist" (243).[19] In so assuming, Riezler implicitly rejects the goal of ancient philosophy or science as Strauss earlier described it: knowledge of "the whole" understood as "the natures of all things" in "their totality" (11). The key to understanding the "whole," for Riezler, lies not with "man" (and/or "God") but with the "subject" or "monad" (243).[20] At the same time, in thus privileging the (Leibnizian) concept of the "monad," Riezler strays from Kantian assumptions as to the specifically moral dignity of man in comparison with other forms of life. Necessity becomes the mutual limitation of man and other forms of life as free, creative powers. Riezler's understanding of "form" (as a combination of "law" and "will") bears instructive comparison with the classical idea of "form" that is its distant ancestor (243): unlike the latter, however, Riezler's form has no end beyond the production of new and higher forms. Life, or reality, is an "eternal antinomy" of Is and Ought, an eternal striving of infinitely many monads, in which all things are both ends and means: an infinity, in short, where there is no hierarchic order that might give substantive meaning to the term "higher."

As Riezler's own text makes clear, his conception of form is partly based on Kant's concept of a "natural product" as a whole in which every part is both end and means.[21] In contrast with Kant, however, Riezler dispenses with the "political" analogy that alone, according to Kant, makes form divorced from any concrete end intelligible, if only from a practical or moral point of view.[22] Riezler's "critical metaphysics" is "no longer theoretical" (245), in other words, without paying homage (in the Kantian manner) to the moral law, which has been replaced by a principle of eternal becoming reminiscent of the thought of Nietzsche. Philosophy for Riezler proceeds neither by attempting to grasp "any suchness" (in the manner of Plato) nor by turning to the moral law but through awareness of its own tragic limitation. Though philosophy cannot grasp the whole conceptually, "it represents the whole" by its "fate"—an "eternal antinomy" that is also the fate of "every other manifestation of life." This antinomy cannot be understood theoretically or "in detachment" but only through an experience of "anguish" by the individual in radical isolation. Only through the latter's "obstinate refus[al of] the delusion of redemption" does it "appear that not everything is permitted" (244–45).

Strauss's depiction of the pre-Heideggerian Riezler calls to mind Strauss's description elsewhere of the "new kind of fortitude which forbids itself every flight from the horror of life into comforting delusion" (by which he may once himself have been attracted).[23] It is distinguished, however, by Riezler's continuing attachment to "History" understood as an arena for the creation of ever new and higher (natural and artistic) forms. Indeed, Riezler's early metaphysics is, as Strauss puts it, ultimately an attempt to understand nature on the analogy of history so construed (245). One is struck, indeed, by the similarity between Riezler's "critical[ly] metaphysical" view of history and his understanding of the vital struggle of nations as earlier described. His political analysis is indeed, as Strauss has earlier averred, the not insignificant "foreground" (241) of a "critical metaphysics," into which certain modern theoretical assumptions (e.g., as to "homogeneity" as a mode of access to "the whole") are implicitly inscribed.[24]

III

The thought of Martin Heidegger decisively affects not Riezler's "deepest tendency," according to Strauss, but the way in which he did or did not "express it" (245). For reasons that Strauss does not here pause to explain, Heidegger's "overwhelming power and clarity" about the necessary "first decisive steps" did not afflict Riezler with the same paralyzing "reverence" that Heidegger aroused in many others (246).[25] Still, his power and clarity had their effect. Already, in *Gestalt und Gesetz*, Riezler had sought the world's unity, not in any "suchness" accessible to theory, but in the "fate" or "specific finiteness" of its parts, and was to this extent prepared for Heidegger's identification of "substance" with *Existence*. What Riezler learned from Heidegger "in the first instance," according to Strauss, was the need to clarify the fate or existence of man, an understanding of which he had previously drawn upon without "go[ing] to the root." What he learned "above all" was that "philosophy is ontology" (247). Heidegger's famous ontological distinction between Being and beings enabled Riezler to express more adequately than before the difference between "fate" and "things" that informed his earlier work: the "critical metaphysics" that explored historically changing forms gives way to an "ontology" devoted to examining the "existence" of man (247).

Riezler's *Parmenides* (1934), the first work he wrote in the wake of Heidegger's impact, gives further indication as to what Strauss regards as Riezler's "deepest tendency." Riezler follows Heidegger in his destructive recovery of the grounds of (Western) metaphysics; unlike Heidegger, however, he endeavors to remain there by accepting the Greek identification of "to be present" with "to be truly" (248). At the same time, Strauss indicates the peculiarity of what Riezler takes early Greek ontology to be. In place of the modern identification of "to be" with "to be observable by anyone" and hence with objectification by an "anonymous observer," he links "to be" with "to be concretely" (249). As Strauss here puts it, "we divine somehow that 'to be' means above all 'to be in itself' and not merely 'to be relative' "; and "we divine somehow that 'to be' means primarily 'to be concrete.' " But to be concrete means, in Riezler's view, "to belong to a dynamic context." Hence, "the fundamental question cannot concern this or that concrete someone or something, nor the totality of concrete someones and somethings in their concrete contexts, but concreteness as such" or (more cautiously) "beingness" (249).

But does it follow from the aforementioned "divination" as to the primacy of the concrete that "concreteness as such" *is* the fundamental question? Certainly, Strauss's treatment of what he earlier calls the "fundamental and eternal problems" (39) would lead one to think otherwise. And even here Strauss indicates his doubtfulness as to whether beingness can depend upon human beings in the manner Riezler implies (cf. 38).[26] Furthermore, Riezler's insistence on the inseparability of things from their "dynamic context" seems to make a "science" of politics in the classical sense impossible. Nor, apparently, does he consider the possibility that something may be both concrete and observable by everyone.[27] Perhaps most tellingly, the concrete is not Riezler's starting point (as with classical political philosophy as Strauss earlier described it [28–29]) but his goal.[28]

Strauss wonders, indeed, whether Riezler's implicit identification of "to be concrete" with "to be seen," and hence with man, does not suggest the need to start with beings of a particular sort, and hence with the questions with which classical political philosophy begins, rather than with the issues that he brings to Parmenides's poem. Still, it suffices for Strauss's present purposes to underscore those issues: namely, arrival at the concrete through an appreciation of the "absent present" that that poem makes visible. Riezler is particularly at pains to undercut the conventional or vulgar reading of the poem, according to which part 1 stands for "the way of truth" and part 2 for "the way of opinion." In opposition to this simple dichotomy, he holds part 2 to be as much related to the truth as is part 1, indeed, as furnishing part 1 with a decisive corrective in its identification (nowhere furnished in part 1) of being and thinking. According to Riezler's own and—in his view—improved and deepened reading, the dichotomy of truth and opinion is itself related to the way of opinion in a manner that closes itself off to the poem's underlying unity.

While praising Riezler's approach as a "high point" in the "modern study" of the work, Strauss also wonders whether it does not lose sight of something that the conventional view retains: an awareness of the gulf separating truth and opinion, and, with that awareness, access to the importance of the "surface" as the "indispensable condition of progress toward the center" (251).

No section of the essay is more elusive than Strauss's guarded indications as to his own preferred reading of the Parmenides fragments. On the one hand, one can "hardly go further" than Riezler, so long, as Strauss puts it, "as one remains concerned with what Parmenides himself taught, as distinguished from what his poem may convey without his necessarily being aware of it." Riezler's reading, on such a (Heideggerian) view, might understand Parmenides's intended teaching while failing to grasp its deeper, and not altogether consciously intended, significance.[29] On the other hand, Parmenides may not have wished to fulfill "in an obvious manner" the expectation he arouses of a setting forth of pure truth and pure opinion. On this alternative view, Riezler fails to fully grasp Parmenides's own deeper intention, owing to inadequate attention to a "surface" that Strauss here links to what is first for us as readers of the poem (251). Does Parmenides, as Strauss sees it, mean to represent the "world" (rather than "concreteness") by reproducing in poetic form the philosopher's "erotic" ascent from opinion about the whole to knowledge?[30]

IV

What is crucial for our present purposes is not Parmenides's ultimate intention (assuming that the extant fragments of his poem permit it to be known), or Strauss's views thereon, but what Riezler's reading of the poem reveals about his own deepest concerns. In turning from "critical metaphysics" to "ontology," Riezler continues to seek structural support in "History" (251). This gives rise to two related problems, according to Strauss: a tension between the temporal and the a-temporal; and a tension between the "relativism" of every standpoint and "ontology's" claim to be "simply true" (252). "Art" furnishes Riezler with a provisional, and in Strauss's view inadequate, resolution of these conflicts, as brought out in the *Traktat vom Schoenen. Zur Ontologie der Kunst* (Treatise of the Beautiful: Toward an Ontology of Art) (1935). It is impossible to reproduce Strauss's sweeping summary of the work, which he himself describes as merely a "rough outline" (253). Strauss's intention is less to reproduce Riezler's argument in any detail than to indicate the general movement of his thought: toward Plato (via art) without quite arriving there (238, 255). Art is the proper introduction to a "doctrine of History" and the "comprehensive ontology" that would be based on it, because art, in its kinship with "beingness," brings one into the proper "mood" for such a task (252). Great art, for Riezler, embodies the dynamic complexity of "beingness" as described in his earlier book on the Parmenides poem. More specifically, art reconciles the eternal and the occasional, inasmuch as different eras and civilizations can exhibit artistic greatness or "classicism" in their own way. (Art, one might say, takes the place previously occupied in Riezler's thought by anguished resignation to fate in fending off the nihilistic implications of his own "structural" reliance upon History.) As "man's self-affirmation," or "religiousness without the gods," it also serves him as "supreme remedy" for that "Christianity without God, which, as Riezler suspected [and Strauss here implicitly affirms], limits Heidegger's perspective" (252).

The "essence" of art lies in its capacity to make the absent (that every "thing" encountered in the abstract isolation of opinion actually presupposes) present. In Strauss's words, great art "brings out possible states of the soul as co-present with their absent opposites" and in this way bears "living" witness to the inseparability of being and awareness of being, an inseparability on which Riezler's interpretation of the Parmenides fragment earlier insisted. This understanding of the inseparability of being and its being manifest makes possible a rank ordering among ways of human being: a "soul is to a higher or lower degree to the extent that it is more or less aware of its own beingness and with it being as such." But such manifestation of being is itself only an "occurrence," without its own inherent "necessity." Beingness thus comes to sight in every case "in a different matter" (253). Riezler's fixed principle as to degrees of being contrasts with the ever-changing flux of styles and shapes in which great art presents itself.

To be sure, Riezler's account would seem to harbor the possibility of a privileged moment among the flux. Healthy societies regard their own understanding of beauty as the only understanding. Only in a time of decay like our own can the art of Greece, Japan, and medieval Europe appear as equally "classical": only in a time like our own, in which all values are open to question, can the "eternal" problem of art as such emerge (254).

Strauss draws specific attention to the tension between these two positions—the eternity of the problem of art on the one hand and the historicity of its becoming manifest on the other. One way to resolve this tension might be to absolutize the moment of the present, making possible the assertion of a final Yes and No beyond the relativity of history (254–55). Riezler rejects the possibility of such a final Yes and No and instead identifies philosophy with the "formal" understanding of man's historicity: "the immutable form of man's mutability." But if this is the "eternal problem" to which philosophy seeks a solution, then there would seem to be a final Yes after all: namely, that "knowledge of being" which Riezler comes to call "the good itself."[31] His description of this ultimate "end" is taken, however, not from Plato but from an Aristotle of his own devising, who defines it as "Being's pure activity" and its "Whither" (255).[32]

According to Strauss's final, incisive summary of Riezler's intellectual career: "If historicism is the view according to which . . . all concrete . . . thought essentially belongs to a concrete dynamic context" and "Platonism is the view . . . [that] pure thought, being 'anonymous,' transcends every dynamic context," then Riezler "felt too strongly the difficulties of historicism not to be attracted by Platonism, but was too deeply impressed by both art and historical change resolutely to follow Plato" (255).

Riezler, it seems, was too quick to identify concrete thought with a "dynamic context" in the manner of historicism, and too quick to identify knowledge of "suchness" with the pose of an "anonymous observer" (in the manner of "Platonism").[33] He failed, in other words, to find his way back to the concrete starting point of Plato himself.

V

Riezler's American writings bear out Strauss's "general impression" of Riezler's achievement and its limitations (256). As in his earlier post-Heideggerian writings, Riezler's professed return to ancient thought is modified by a continuing attachment to certain modern assumptions that bear especially on his understanding of the "world" and its relation to the "concrete." To summarize Strauss's findings: On the one hand, these assumptions block Riezler's full recovery of the prephilosophic horizon from which classical political philosophy takes its initial bearings: that of civic life as understood by ordinary citizens and statesmen. On the other hand, his own intelligence and human awareness carry him within what seems to be hailing distance of that vital starting point.

The two main works of this period—*Physics and Reality* (1940) and *Man: Mutable and Immutable: The Fundamental Structure of Social Life* (1950)—attempt to articulate the physical and social implications of man's experience as a "a being that moves or changes in time." In partial contrast with his earlier work, Riezler now presents human life as "radically social" (257). Especially striking to Strauss, however, is the altogether secondary status, in Riezler's account of human sociality, of politics, including the interests and institutions with which political life is typically associated. His focus is not "virtue and justice" but "attitudes and moods." For Riezler, "the core of society," as Strauss puts it, "is not institutions, interests, or even ideas" (as it was in his earliest work on international politics) but "passions and the striving after happiness." In the "language of the schools," as Strauss adds with unmistakable emphasis, Riezler's doctrine is "social philosophy as distinguished from political philosophy."[34] His guiding "idea of society" is not the "ideal" or comprehensive aim that the members of the community themselves take seriously or deem authoritative; it is instead "the scheme of a relational structure," a scheme that specifically "abstracts" from "the purposes of society" (257).[35]

As in his earliest work on the organic form of nations, his understanding of the social "whole" takes its primary bearings not from its highest aspirations or its ruling element but from a reciprocity of means and ends in which no concrete end predominates. Riezler's opposition to the notion "that there can be a single purpose to which everything else is a mere means" is continuous with his earliest "Kantian" reflections on the nature of organic form, in which wholeness consists in a reciprocal community of means and ends.[36] From here, as Strauss concludes, "we can understand why Riezler's social philosophy, as distinguished from the political philosophy of the past, does not contain an ethics proper." For "his central subject is not virtue and justice" but abstractions (like the "I," "thou," and "they") that are foreign to the thinking of actual political actors (257–58). In sum: in his effort to articulate the meaning of the social "whole," Riezler abstracts from the moral understanding of its members—an understanding that, on Strauss's view, furnishes our primary mode of access to the nature and meaning of the whole (i.e., "the totality of beings") as such (27, 28, 34, 79–80).

Although Riezler acknowledges that one must not look at social phenomena in the light of questions and doctrines "to which no society pays any attention," he does not conclude that social phenomena must be understood, in the first instance, from the perspective of the citizen and statesman. In short: he does not begin "at the true beginning of analysis, with the surface" (257).

Hence, in the end, Riezler's insistence on man's radical sociality only modifies without fundamentally challenging an underlying "Cartesianism"—Cartesianism that prevails even when he is defending Aristotle's physics against the criticisms of modern science (256). Proceeding from the "physical" to the "social," his starting point is "man's understanding of himself as a being that changes or moves in time," not man as the member of a community that makes comprehensive claims to his admiration and allegiance. Proceeding (like Descartes) from the abstract, in other words, Riezler attempts but fails "to arrive at the concrete" for "he does not ascend" (in the manner of classical political philosophy) "from the phenomena as primarily given to their principles" (258; cf. 28).

In sum: Riezler's putative return to ancient thought is hampered throughout by an underlying "Cartesianism," accompanied by an obscuring of the "world" as it immediately or naturally comes to sight in ordinary civic life. From the start, Riezler takes his bearings from life understood from the standpoint of the "monad," or the Cartesian ego endowed with "spontaneity." Unlike Leibniz, however, Riezler rejects "cosmology," owing to the seeming impossibility of speculative metaphysics—a move that is not fundamentally altered, as Strauss insists, by Riezler's later turn from "I" to "We" (258; cf. 28, 79–80). As a result, the world for Riezler becomes a mere "x": it is no longer the "visible whole limited by the 'starred heaven above me' and the visible firm earth" (258).

Strauss's allusion here to Kant's famous phrase—"the starred heaven above me and the moral law within me"[37]—is as remarkable for what it omits as for what it says. The apparent impossibility of speculative metaphysics did not block Kant's interest in cosmology, and with it, some remaining access to claims of height, even if the natural and moral worlds for him no longer coincide. Kant still in some way "looked up," if only by "looking to the moral law." For Riezler, for whom art has supplanted ethics proper as an area of inquiry, the onslaught of modern science has also been more thorough. (Hence the telling "correction," on the part of Riezler's "Aristotle," of the classical distinction between heavenly and earthly bodies [Riezler 1924, 6, 51, 90].)[38] "Heaven and earth and what lies between them have lost [the visible] contours," as Strauss puts it, that were still evident to Kant. Such contours are instead sought by Riezler in the multiplicity of historical worlds, whose unfolding "fabric" alone has the dignity for him of the "immutable." In sum: despite his attempted return to ancient thought, "modern physics and its twin sister, 'the historical consciousness,' remain "the fundamental presuppositions of his ontology" (259).

Strauss's terse summary of the basic inadequacies of Riezler's philosophic approach calls to mind Strauss's earlier description, in his lecture "German Nihilism," of a certain tendency characteristic of nineteenth-century Germany: namely, the elevation of art above ethics or religion, as the epitome of a "civilization." No less than the German liberals preceding him, Riezler, it seems, is tempted to replace ethics (or religion) with aesthetics. For related reasons, he does not begin his analysis with the whole that is most immediately or naturally accessible to us. We can know the whole, as Strauss elsewhere put it:

> Only by starting from what we may call the phenomenal world, . . . the whole which is permanently given, as permanently as there are human beings, the

whole which is held together and constituted by the vault of heaven and comprising heaven and earth.[39]

All human thought, as Strauss goes on to insist, "begins with this whole." But the whole first comes to sight from the standpoint of a given political community, with its own comprehensive view about what is highest or most admirable. There is thus a fundamental kinship or similarity between the world and the city:

> The "highest" is that through which a society is "a whole," a distinct whole with a character of its own, just as for common sense "the world" is a whole by being overarched by heaven of which one cannot be aware except by "looking up."[40]

In sum: by virtue of its comprehensive claim to rule men's lives in light of what is "best," the city is the only "whole within the whole," or the only "part of the whole" whose "essence can be fully known."[41] For Riezler, by way of contrast, there cannot be "a single purpose to which everything else . . . is merely a means" (257).

In drawing attention both here and elsewhere to this singular cosmological blind spot on Riezler's part, Strauss returns the reader to the central theme of chapter 1, which characterized classical political philosophy as follows:

> Life is activity which is directed toward some goal; social life is an activity which is directed toward such a goal as can be pursued only by society; but in order to pursue a specific goal, as its comprehensive goal, society must be organized . . . in a manner which is in accordance with that goal; this, however, means that the authoritative human beings must be akin to that goal. There is a variety of regimes. Each regime raises a claim . . . which extends beyond the boundaries of a given society. These claims conflict, therefore, with one another. . . . Thus the regimes themselves . . . force us to wonder which of the given conflicting regimes is better, and ultimately, which regime is the best regime. Classical political philosophy is guided by the question of the best regime. (34)[42]

Led by assumptions about the character of human "life" that are fundamentally aesthetic, rather than ethical or moral, Riezler pays insufficient attention to differences in *ways* of life (and the ideas or ends that guide them). "Riezler the analyst" diverges from the outset "from the perspective of the citizen and statesman" (257).

VI

It is almost equally telling that these limitations fade, as soon as Strauss turns from Riezler's framework to his actual analyses of the human passions, analyses whose "breath, earnestness and delicacy," in Strauss's words, "surpass by far everything now attempted within psychology or any other discipline" (259). That framework, though still rooted in a "modified Cartesianism,"[43] proves superior to that of most "contemporary social science" (258), not least by allowing Riezler to progress with "perfect legitima[cy]" to "non-arbitrary assertions about the nature of the good life," just as his earlier treatment of "the beautiful" enabled him, despite his historical relativism, to distinguish art from trash (256). In "speaking humanly" about the passions, he inevitably grasps the "fact" of laughter and of "love," "hate," and "friendship" in a manner that exposes the "narrow," factually impoverished character of the so-called distinction between facts and values (259). He thereby not only shows in passing "why he could not have been mistaken about the meaning of 1933"; he also criticizes the "narrow humanity" that informs Heidegger's existential analysis, while pointing to the riddle of the latter's "obstinate silence" about "love and charity" on the one hand and "laughter and the things that deserve to be laughed at" on the other (260).

Like Churchill, Riezler proves that human excellence (in the specific shape of "magnanimity") remains a living possibility.[44] He also shows that the unchanging human phenomena remain accessible to those who approach them in a "human" manner, even when they labor under constricting theoretical assumptions. Strauss draws particular attention to Riezler's emphasis on shame and awe, an emphasis that suggests a deeper kinship with the "thought of ancient Greece than the thought of his own time." Not anguish (as with Heidegger) but awe is, for Riezler, "the fundamental mood" (260).

In the end, indeed, it is Thucydides of whom his late friend's "highest aspiration" reminds Strauss—Thucydides who similarly contemplated "the opposites whose unity is hidden," and for whom "the higher of the opposites" was not, as it was for Socrates, the stronger but instead the weaker and more vulnerable (260). This concluding thought is developed in a roughly contemporaneous lecture, "Thucydides and the Meaning of Political History."[45] In this lecture, Strauss traces Plato's and Thucydides's opposing assessments of the relative strength of "low" and "high" to their differing understandings of "the whole."[46] For Thucydides, the whole consists of motion and rest of which motion is primary and rest derivative. Thucydides, as Strauss here suggests, takes his fundamental bearings from the thought of Heraclitus, i.e., from a "natural philosophy" in which knowledge of the whole does not entail knowledge of the parts, and that has no specific place for the study of human things. Political history of a Thucydidean sort is, as Strauss concludes, the resort of political wisdom against the "backdrop" of philosophy prior to the Socratic revolution. Thucydides, in short, as Strauss here ventures to say, was a "pre-Socratic":

> Pre-Socratic philosophy was a quest for an understanding of the whole which was not identical with an understanding of the parts of the whole. It is for this reason that pre-Socratic philosophy did not know of a relatively independent study of the human things as such. Pre-Socratic philosophy needed, therefore, something like Thucydides' history as its supplement: a quest for the truth that was primarily a quest for the truth about the human things.[47]

Socratic philosophy, by way of contrast, begins with knowledge of the "parts," among which the human occupies a privileged place. Plato's starting point is the everyday speech about "better" and "worse" to which political life constantly gives rise.[48]

In sum, for Plato, in contrast to the pre-Socratic philosophers, man's highest aspiration matters, not only (as with Thucydides) to human beings themselves, but also as a mode of access to the "highest" as such. Human aspiration and the principle governing the whole are fundamentally "akin": "the low exists by virtue of the high." For Thucydides, by way of contrast, the highest in man—man's "humanity"—is "too remote from the elements" to claim such support; the high (for man) depends upon the low.[49]

Such considerations shed supplementary light on the comparison of Riezler and Thucydides with which Strauss concludes his own funeral speech. Like his "gentle and manly" predecessor, Riezler sought to comprehend the "opposites whose unity is hidden," as Strauss puts it, without reducing the higher to the lower, and this despite the relative weakness, as each saw it, of the higher (260).

To be sure, unlike that of his great political-historical predecessor, Riezler's understanding of human "wholeness" was limited by modern "constructivism." No less than for Descartes, the "abstract" was his

starting point.[50] Given that orientation, his attempted philosophic overcoming of the modern problem of relativism was bound to fall short, not
least, perhaps, because "art" for him trumped ethics (and religion) as a
major subject of interest.[51]

That neither the acuteness of Riezler's "political judgment" (which was
not misled by "passion," "system," or "prejudice" [235]) nor the force of
his psychological insight was appreciably diminished by those "analytic"
shortcomings may be even more revealing: for it suggests both the relative autonomy of practical wisdom in the classical sense, and the power
of Riezler's own "highest aspiration," which enabled him, despite those
shortcomings, to "divine" something to be "treasure[d]" (260). Riezler's
"deepest tendency," one is tempted to conclude, was guided by the same
aspiration toward the eternal that moved Thucydides.[52]

Strauss's comparison of Riezler to Thucydides is of interest for a further reason, one that is brought out in the lecture on Thucydides. If, as
that lecture suggests, Thucydides's "political history" throws the emergence of political philosophy into defining relief, Riezler's writings cast
reflective light on a more personal path of discovery. Strauss's reading of
Thucydides leads us to wonder to what extent Riezler's failure "resolutely
to follow Plato" might somehow be linked with his debt to a German liberal educational system that had not yet completely collapsed. It leads us
to reflect, in other words, on the conditions that enabled Strauss's own
recovery of political philosophy in the classic sense. For this reason as well,
"Kurt Riezler (1882–1955)" is a fitting (near) conclusion to a book that
makes the "problem" of political philosophy (9) its opening theme.

Notes

I wish to thank Christopher Kelly for his insightful remarks on Rousseau, and
Nasser Behnegar and Robert K. Faulkner for their many helpful comments on an
earlier version of this chapter.

1. The essay "Kurt Riezler (1882–1955)" is an enlarged version of a lecture originally delivered before the General Seminar of the New School of Social Research
on an occasion in honor of his memory. An earlier version was published in *Social
Research* 23 (1956): 3–34. All unspecified page numbers that appear hereafter are
to Leo Strauss, *What is Political Philosophy? and Other Studies* (Strauss 1959).

2. In addition to his journalism, Riezler's published works include (among others) *On Finance and Monopoly in Ancient Greece* (1907); *The Indispensability of
the Impossible: Toward a Theory of Politics and Other Theories* (1913); *Form and
Law: Project of a Metaphysics of Freedom* (1926); *Parmenides* (1934); *Treatise on*

the Beautiful: Toward an Ontology of Art (1935); *Physics and Reality. Lectures of Aristotle on Modern Physics at an International Conference of Scientists* (1940); *Man: Mutable and Immutable—The Fundamental Structure of Social Life* (1950); *Political Decisions in the Modern Mass Society of the Industrial Age* (Walgreen Lectures)(1953).

3. According to the *Encyclopedia Helios*, the traditional Athenian funeral oration typically opened with an expression of the speaker's inability to adequately convey the virtues of the deceased, and closed with an exhortation to the audience to imitate the virtues of the deceased, as Strauss proceeds, indeed, to do (260). (See *The Encyclopedia Helios* [1952], s.v. "Funeral Oration"). In other respects, including its elevated praise of the deceased individual (as distinguished from his "city"), Strauss's speech resembles a traditional Jewish funeral eulogy (*hesped*). According to that tradition, a slight exaggeration of the virtues of the deceased is permitted on the assumption that his good qualities may not be fully known. The ascription to him of good qualities he did not possess, or other outright falsehood, however, is forbidden as an instance of "mocking the dead." On Plato's famous "satire" of Pericles's "Funeral Speech" as recounted by Thucydides, see Strauss (1959, 82 n. 3). Strauss's only other well-known eulogy of this kind (combining, as it were, the conventions of Athens and Jerusalem) was delivered in 1961 on the occasion of the death of Jason Aronson.

4. Strauss (2009, 359–60; see also Shell (2009).

5. On the specific weakness of liberal democracy in Germany, see Strauss (1965, 2). For an incisive discussion of the various meanings of "liberal" for Strauss, see Nathan Tarcov, "Leo Strauss: Critique and Defense of Liberalism," unpublished essay.

6. Compare Strauss's earlier reference to that period as one of "extreme liberalism," in which one could "attack in writings accessible to all both the established social or political order and the beliefs on which it is based" (224).

7. See also 260 and Strauss (1965, 1, 17; 1999, 361); cf. Riezler (1954, 57).

8. Published under the pseudonym "J. J. Ruedorffer" (1914).

9. See also Strauss (1953, 308 and note). Like Burke (and Churchill), Riezler displays an extraordinary degree of astuteness about practical political affairs. And like that of Burke, his theoretical insight is, as we shall see, ultimately limited, in Strauss's view, by the uncritical acceptance of certain modern philosophic or scientific premises. Strauss specifically contrasts Riezler with Thomas Mann, whose *Reflections of an Unpolitical Man* appeared around the same time as Riezler's *Outlines*. Riezler cites both Thucydides and Burke approvingly and at length in "Political Decisions in Modern Society."

10. Strauss (1952, 108–28).

11. Compare Riezler (1914, 35).

12. See Strauss (1999, 356–59).

13. The passage as originally published in *Social Research* ends with "beings"

(7). The later version would seem to admit the possibility of being that does not come into being – an ambiguity reflected in Riezler's later theoretical position, as Strauss will go on to stress. On this point, see also *Parmenides* (Riezler 1970, 59); *Physics and Reality* (Riezler 1940, 111–15).

14. Evidently, the "matrix" of truth and the "matrix" of nobility (236) for him are not the same.

15. On Riezler's "greatness of soul," see 234; compare "German Nihilism" (Strauss 1999, 366) and Strauss's letter to Karl Löwith, 20 August 1946 (Strauss 2008, 667).

16. On this issue, see also Riezler (1954, 18–22, 50–55).

17. On the relation between "political science" and political practice as classically understood, see Strauss (1959, 14, 28). See also Behnegar, chap. 1 above.

18. For Strauss's views on the peculiar strengths (and limits) of Goethe's thought, compare "On the Intention of Rousseau" (Strauss 1947, 479n) and *What Is Political Philosophy?* (Strauss 1959, 269) with Strauss, letter to Eric Voegelin, December 17, 1949 (Strauss and Voegelin 1993, 63). Goethe represents a "Rousseauian" possibility not followed up by Rousseau's other great German interpreters. That he does not seem to represent a genuine alternative for Strauss appears to be connected to the absence (or diminution) in Goethe of what Strauss calls the "mania" for truth, a mania he sets "in opposition" to Goethe's own "painstaking researches."

19. Cf. Strauss (1959, 39).

20. Riezler (1924, 253ff.).

21. See Riezler (1914, 40; 1924, 101, 115, 167, 301, 319). Compare Kant, *Critique of Judgment* (1968, 5: 373–74). Riezler's idea of form in *Gestalt und Gesetz* would seem to be a compromise, partly inspired by Goethe, between the Kantian notion of artistic "purposiveness without purpose" and Kant's notion of an organic whole.

22. Kant, *Critique of Judgment* (Kant 1968, 5: 375n).

23. Strauss (1965, 30).

24. On the peculiar temptations of modern philosophy in this regard, see 39–40.

25. Heidegger may still the ferment but is hardly the "man of great virtue and long service" who, in the line of Virgil that Strauss here ironically quotes, calms the raging crowd (*Aeneid* 1. 155–56).

26. Strauss leaves open, however, the issue of whether "if there are no human beings," there can be "concreteness" (249). He makes a related suggestion in *Natural Right and History* (1953, 32).

27. Compare 16: A scientific or philosophic approach to politics "can emerge" only when "the Here and Now ceases to be the center of reference."

28. On Riezler's specific understanding of the "concrete" and the "abstract," see also his "Political Decisions in Modern Society" (1954, 54n), and *Man: Mutable and Immutable*, (1951, 319–26).

29. I am indebted to Nasser Behnegar for drawing my attention to this aspect of the argument.

30. See Strauss, *On Plato's Symposium* (2001, 47); on the "exoteric" Parmenides, see Strauss to Kojève, 28 May 1957 (1991, 277); Strauss (1959, 39–40).

31. Riezler (1951, 346).

32. See also Riezler (1940, 108).

33. "Platonism," it would seem, isn't the same as "Plato." If "Platonism" is the view "according to which pure thought, being 'anonymous,' transcends every dynamic context," political philosophy in the original "Platonic" sense does not presuppose the standpoint of a "mere bystander" (34); its "purity" in other words is crucially qualified by what Strauss earlier in the volume calls "the dual nature of man" (35). On "Platonism" and "history" as nonexhaustive alternatives, see also 26.

34. On political as distinguished from social philosophy, see also chap. 1: political philosophy "rests on the premise that the political association . . . is the most comprehensive or the most authoritative . . . whereas social philosophy conceives of the political association as a part of a larger whole" (13).

35. Compare Strauss's roughly contemporaneous letter to Kojève, 28 May 1957 (Strauss 1991, 279). "Regime is the order . . . which gives society its character. . . . Regime means the whole. . . . We may try to articulate the simple and unitary thought, that expresses itself in the *politeia*, as follows: life is activity which is directed toward some goal; social life is an activity which is directed toward such a [comprehensive] goal as can be pursued only by society" (1959, 34).

36. Riezler (1914, 7, 40).

37. Kant (1968, 5: 161–62); cf. Riezler (1924, 176).

38. See also Riezler (1940, 91). Riezler's Aristotle, for whom nature is both *natura naturans* and *natura naturata*, would seem to have more in common with Spinoza on this score than with the historical Aristotle.

39. Strauss (1997, 361).

40. Strauss (1968, 214).

41. Strauss (1964, 29).

42. See also *Natural Right and History* (1953, 123–25): "All knowledge . . . presupposes a horizon, a comprehensive view within which knowledge is possible. All understanding presupposes a fundamental awareness of the whole. . . . However much the comprehensive visions which animate the various societies may differ, they are all visions of the same—the whole."

43. On Riezler's "I-Thou-We" framework, see also chap. 1 (1959, 28–29): "Adequate 'speaking about' in analytic . . . speech must be grounded in and continue the manner of 'speaking about' which is inherent in human life. . . . [otherwise] I am untrue to the phenomena; I miss the concrete." The artificial character of Riezler's terms, which do not arise in ordinary speech, furnishes additional evidence that, as Strauss earlier suggests, language, for Riezler, "is not the matrix of the truth toward which thought is directed" (237). His relative immunity to the enchantments

of Heidegger goes hand in hand, it seems, with a certain indifference to the truth harbored by ordinary speech as understood by Strauss. To be sure, Riezler's inclusion of the "They" (along with "I," "Thou," and "We") adds an unmistakable "political" dimension to his framework not fully captured by the word "society."

44. See Strauss (1999, 363); Strauss to Karl Löwith, 20 August 1946 (Strauss 2008, 667).

45. The lecture, which was apparently delivered at the University of Chicago, was published under that title in *The Rebirth of Classical Political Rationalism: Essays and Lectures by Leo Strauss* (1989, 72–102). I have not been able to ascertain the exact year of its composition, but similarities of emphasis strongly suggest that it was written at roughly the same time as Strauss's Riezler essay. Strauss's other major treatments of Thucydides (Strauss 1964) and "Preliminary Observations on the Treatment of the Gods in Thucydides' Work" (Strauss 1974), pursue rather different themes.

46. Strauss (1989, 100).

47. Strauss (1989, 101).

48. Strauss (1989, 100). The complexity of this issue and its implications for an understanding of "our situation as human beings, i.e., the whole situation" (17) is a prominent theme of the first chapter, "What Is Political Philosophy?," which also contains what is perhaps Strauss's clearest, or most forthcoming, discussion of the "problem of cosmology" (39–40). On this score especially, Riezler's in its own way admirable attempt to understand "*la condition humaine* as occurrence" (256) (or what Riezler himself calls, citing Montaigne, "*l'entière condition humaine*") falls short. Cf. Riezler (1954, 2); and Strauss (1959, 17): "The ambiguity of the political goal is due to its comprehensive character. Thus the temptation arises to deny, or evade, the comprehensive character of politics. . . . This temptation must be avoided if it is necessary to face our situation as human beings, i.e., the whole situation." Evidently, on Strauss's view "*la condition humaine* as occurrence" differs from what he himself here pointedly calls "the *whole* situation" (emphasis added).

49. Strauss (1989, 101).

50. See also Strauss (1959, 28).

51. Strauss (1989, 102). If further hints as to the latter point were needed, Strauss repeats, in closing, the same criticism, developed at greater length in his Riezler essay, of appealing to differences in "artistic style" to distinguish one civilization from another.

52. Strauss (1989, 100–101).

Works Cited

Kant, Immanuel. 1968. *Werke* [Akademie Text-Ausgabe]. Berlin: Walter de Gruyter.

Riezler, Kurt. 1914. *Grundzüge der Weltpolitik in der Gegenwart* (published under the pseudonym "J. J. Ruedorffer"). Stuttgart: Deutsche Verlags-Anstalt.

———. 1924. *Gestalt und Gesetz: Entwurf einer Metaphysik der Freiheit.* Munich: Musarion Verlag.

———. 1935. *Traktat vom Schoenen. Zur Ontologie der Kunst.* Frankfurt am Main: Klostermann.

———. 1940. *Physics and Reality.* New Haven: Yale University Press.

———. 1951. *Man Mutable and Immutable: The Fundamental Structure of Social Life.* Chicago: Regnery.

———. 1954. "Political Decisions in Modern Society" (The Walgreen Lectures). *Ethics* 64 (2): 1–55.

———. 1970. *Parmenides: Text* [with a new afterward by Hans-Georg Gadamer]. Frankfurt am Main: Klostermann. Originally published, 1934.

Shell, Susan Meld. 2009. "Strauss on 'German Nihilism.'" In *The Cambridge Companion to Leo Strauss*, ed. Steven B. Smith, 171–92 Cambridge: Cambridge University Press.

Strauss, Leo. 1947. "On the Intention of Rousseau." *Social Research* 14: 455–87.

———. 1952. *The Political Philosophy of Thomas Hobbes: Its Basis and Its Genesis.* Trans. Elsa M. Sinclair. Chicago: University of Chicago Press. Originally published, 1936.

———. 1953. *Natural Right and History.* Chicago: University of Chicago Press.

———. 1959. *What Is Political Philosophy? and Other Studies.* New York: Free Press.

———. 1964. *The City and Man.* Chicago: Rand McNally.

———. 1965. *On Spinoza's Critique of Religion.* Trans. Elsa Sinclair. New York: Schocken.

———. 1968. *Liberalism: Ancient and Modern.* New York: Basic Books.

———. 1974. "Preliminary Observations on the Treatment of the Gods in Thucydides' Work." *Interpretation: A Journal of Political Philosophy* 4: 1–16.

———. 1989. "Thucydides: The Meaning of Political History." In *The Rebirth of Classical Political Rationalism: Essays and Lectures by Leo Strauss*, ed. Thomas L. Pangle, 72–102. Chicago: University of Chicago Press.

———. 1991. *On Tyranny.* Ed. Victor Gourevitch and Michael S. Roth. Revised and expanded edition, New York: Free Press.

———. 1997. "On the Interpretation of Genesis." In *Jewish Philosophy and the Crisis of Modernity: Essays and Lectures in Modern Jewish Thought*, ed. Kenneth Hart Green, 32–53. New York: SUNY Press.

———. 1999. "German Nihilism." Ed. David Janssens and Daniel Tanguay. *Interpretation* 26: 359–60. Based on manuscript version of a lecture originally delivered at the New School in 1941.

———. 2001. *On Plato's Symposium.* Ed. with an introduction by Seth Benardete. Chicago: University of Chicago Press.

————. 2008. *Gesammelte Schriften: Hobbes' politische Wissenschaft und zuge-hörige Schriften—Briefe*. Ed. Heinrich Meier and Wiebke Meier. 2nd ed. Stuttgart: J. B. Metzler.

Strauss, Leo, and Eric Voegelin. 1993. *Faith and Political Philosophy: The Correspondence between Leo Strauss and Eric Voegelin, 1934–1964*. Trans. and ed. Peter Emberley and Barry Cooper. University Park: Pennsylvania State University Press.

List of Contributors

NASSER BEHNEGAR is Associate Professor of Political Science at Boston College University. He is the author of *Leo Strauss, Max Weber, and the Scientific Study of Politics* (Chicago: University of Chicago Press, 2003). Behnegar also contributed to *The Cambridge Companion to Leo Strauss*, ed. Steven B. Smith (Cambridge: Cambridge University Press, 2009) and is currently completing a monograph titled *Tough Liberals* that explores the epistemological foundations of secularism.

DAVID JANSSENS is Assistant Professor of Philosophy at Tilburg University, The Netherlands. He is the author of *Between Athens and Jerusalem: Philosophy, Prophecy, and Politics in Leo Strauss's Early Thought* (New York: SUNY Press, 2008) and numerous articles on ancient law, philosophy and poetry, and Leo Strauss. His current research focuses on the quarrel between philosophy and poetry.

RAFAEL MAJOR is the Director of Faculty Development at the Jack Miller Center (Philadelphia) and teaches at Ursinus College. He is the author of articles on Leo Strauss, Quentin Skinner, Machiavelli, Abraham Lincoln, and William Shakespeare. His current research is a book-length study of political and philosophic issues in Shakespeare's comedies.

CHRISTOPHER NADON is Associate Professor of Government at Claremont McKenna College. He is the author of *Xenophon's Prince: Republic and Empire in the Cyropaedia* (Berkeley: University of California Press, 2001). Nadon has written articles on Xenophon, Machiavelli, Aristotle, and issues of church and state. His current research explores the secular basis of the separation of church and state in early modern European thought.

JOSHUA PARENS is Professor and Graduate Director of Philosophy at the University of Dallas. He is the author of *An Islamic Philosophy of*

Virtuous Religions: Introducing Alfarabi (Albany: SUNY Press, 2006) and *Metaphysics as Rhetoric: Alfarabi's "Summary of Plato's 'Laws'"* (Albany: SUNY Press, 1995) and co-editor (with Joseph Macfarland) of *Medieval Political Philosophy: A Sourcebook* (Ithaca: Cornell University Press, 2011). A book-length study entitled *Maimonides and Spinoza: Their Conflicting Views of Human Nature* is forthcoming from the University of Chicago Press.

SUSAN MELD SHELL is Professor of Political Science at Boston College University. Her most recent publications include *Kant and the Limits of Autonomy* (Cambridge: Harvard University Press, 2009) and "Strauss on 'German Nihilism,'" in *The Cambridge Companion to Leo Strauss*, ed. Steven B. Smith (Cambridge: Cambridge University Press, 2009). She is also the author of *The Embodiment of Reason: Kant on Spirit, Generation and Community* (Chicago: University of Chicago Press, 1996) and numerous articles and monographs focusing on the character of liberalism and its roots in Enlightenment thought.

DEVIN STAUFFER is Associate Professor of Government at the University of Texas at Austin. He is the author of *The Unity of Plato's Gorgias: Rhetoric, Justice, and the Philosophic Life* (Cambridge: Cambridge University Press, 2006) and *Plato's Introduction to the Question of Justice* (Albany: SUNY Press, 2001). Stauffer's current research explores Thomas Hobbes's break with the classical tradition of political philosophy and his role in laying the foundations of modern thought. He recently published an article in the *American Political Science Review* on Strauss's first published work on Hobbes, *The Political Philosophy of Hobbes*.

DANIEL TANGUAY is Associate Professor of Philosophy at the University of Ottawa. He is the author of *Leo Strauss: Une biographie intellectuelle* (Paris: Grasset, 2003), recently published in English translation as *Leo Strauss. An Intellectual Biography* (New Haven: Yale University Press, 2007). Tanguay still works on Strauss but his main field of research is currently the contemporary return to political philosophy in France.

NATHAN TARCOV is Professor in the Committee on Social Thought, the Department of Political Science, and the College at the University of Chicago. He has published several books, including *Locke's Education for Liberty* (Chicago: University of Chicago Press, 1989), *Machiavelli's Discourses on Livy* (Chicago: University of Chicago Press, 1998), and *The Legacy of Rousseau* (Chicago: University of Chicago Press, 1997). Tarcov's scholarly interests include the history of political philosophy, education and the family, and U.S. foreign policy. He is also Director of the Leo Strauss Center at the University of Chicago.

CATHERINE ZUCKERT is Nancy Reeves Dreux Professor of Political Science at the University of Notre Dame and currently serves as Editor-in-Chief of the *Review of Politics*. Most recently she is the author of *Plato's Philosophers: The Coherence of the Dialogues* (Chicago: University of Chicago Press, 2009). Zuckert specializes in the history of political philosophy and the relation between literature and politics. She is also author of *The Truth about Leo Strauss*, with Michael Zuckert (Chicago: University of Chicago Press, 2006), and *Postmodern Platos* (Chicago: University of Chicago Press, 1996).

MICHAEL ZUCKERT is Nancy Reeves Dreux Professor at the University of Notre Dame. Zuckert is the author of *Natural Rights and the New Republicanism* (Princeton: Princeton University Press, 1998), *The Natural Rights Republic* (Notre Dame: University of Notre Dame Press, 1996), and *Launching Liberalism* (Lawrence: University Press of Kansas, 2002) and co-author (with Catherine Zuckert) of *The Truth about Leo Strauss* (Chicago: University of Chicago Press, 2006). He is currently finishing a book called *Natural Rights and American Constitutionalism* and is co-authoring another monograph on Machiavelli and Shakespeare.

Index